THE
NEW
RIGHT
PAPERS

THE
NEW
RIGHT
PAPERS

Edited
by
Robert W. Whitaker

ST. MARTIN'S PRESS
NEW YORK

Design by Deborah Daly

Library of Congress Cataloging in Publication Data

Main entry under title:

The New Right papers.

   1. Conservatism—United States—Addresses, essays,
lectures. 2. Libertarianism—United States—
Addresses, essays, lectures. I. Whitaker, Robert M.,
1941–
JA84.U5N39   320.5′2′0973   81–18229
ISBN 0–312–56927–0   AACR2

10 9 8 7 6 5 4 3 2 1

First Edition

The New Right Papers could not have been completed
without the help and literary skills of Brigitte Whitaker,
my dedicated ally and friend.

TABLE
OF
CONTENTS

FOREWORD

THE DANGERS OF DISESTABLISHMENT

The combination of voters which elected President Reagan was not a new one, nor did it spring forth abruptly in late 1980. It consisted of two major elements. The first was the basic Republican presidential vote, about forty percent, which has suffered little defection even in Democratic landslides. The second element, which turned the election into a rout, was made up of voters who, in earlier days, were overwhelmingly Democrats. These former Democrats are largely white Southerners and blue-collar Northerners, who, when the focus of debate between the parties was economic, voted for Roosevelt, Harry Truman, and John Kennedy. But the focus of political debate shifted in the 1960s, when the Democrats became the party of social engineering. Thereafter, these voters began to vote for third parties or for Republicans, or to stay home on election day. Social engineering is a massive manipulation of a society's structure and values, aimed at bringing about desired "social change" in the direction considered best by a small elite. It is carried out through programs to achieve racial balance, "progressive" education, the discrediting of traditional values and parental authority, and imposition of a new ideology and morality. The opponents of social engineering are fittingly referred to here as social conservatives.

From Andrew Jackson to John Kennedy, for over a century and a quarter, the bedrock base of the Democratic Party was made up of white Southerners and Irish-Americans. The latter group was joined in its firm party loyalty by later immigrants from southern and eastern Europe, who also make up a major portion of the social conservative exodus from the party.*

In 1980, when this former bedrock of the Democratic Party pulled out at every electoral level, the party collapsed with a crash heard in that citadel of deafness, Washington, D.C. But, though the sound was louder this time, it was not new. As far back as 1968, social conservatives abandoned the ticket led by Hubert Humphrey to vote for the third party bid of Governor George Wallace of Alabama. Governor Wallace received almost ten million votes, 13.8 percent of the total, while the winner, Richard Nixon, received the basic Republican support of 43.1 percent of votes cast. Added together, these two groups constituted almost 57 percent of the total, more than the percentage obtained by Mr. Reagan when social conservatives joined with traditional Republicans to vote for him in 1980.

Democrats showed their obliviousness to the lesson of 1968 by nominating the all-time champion of social engineering, George McGovern, to head their ticket in 1972. He was crushed in a landslide victory for President Nixon, as social conservatives unanimously rejected McGovern. In 1976, Jimmy Carter, using the rhetoric of social conservatism, drew a sufficient number of social conservative votes to defeat President Ford. But his performance showed President Carter to be a captive of the social liberal elite.

The lesson of 1980 was the fourth successive repetition of a

---

*They are usually referred to as "ethnics," but I prefer my own term, "identity groups," which includes non-"ethnic" groups, like mountaineers, who are seeking to preserve their own identity against the educational establishment. The considerable number of so-called ethnics with whom I have marched and worked also prefer this term.

rule which should have been obvious to anyone outside the confines of deepest, deafest Washington: When Democrats lose the social conservative vote, they lose the election. In 1980, social conservatives voted Republican, not only at the presidential level, but for Congress as well. As a result, Democrats lost their Senate majority and over thirty House seats. The balance of power in the House is now held by the Conservative Democratic Caucus, made up of Southern social conservatives.

Mr. Reagan's electoral strategy was successful, but the process it should represent is dangerously incomplete. Social conservatives have left their old party, but they have not found a new home. They have left a party ruled by liberals to vote for one ruled by fiscal conservatives. Republican policy at this point remains a matter of fiscal conservatives on the inside using the votes generated by an appeal to social issues to pursue tax cuts and military expansion. The primary objective of the New Right, then, is the formation of a true alliance of social and fiscal conservatives as equal partners, preferably within the Republican Party.

Obvious as this combination may seem for the success of a permanent conservative ruling party, there are substantial barriers to it in practice. The Republican Party has developed as the party of less government and balanced budgets, and many within it who are fiscal conservatives are not so on social matters. They hold powerful positions within the party, and use their power to prevent the natural alliance from being formed.

Until 1980, as William A. Rusher explains in more detail in his essay, Republicans did not so much attract social conservatives as Democrats, in their obsession with social engineering, drove them out. Mr. Reagan's open campaign for social conservative votes is a major step toward a new majority coalition, but only a step. A permanent coalition cannot consist of a party of fiscal conservatives electing its candidates by handing out crumbs to social conservatives who are left outside. For the new majority to be built, social conservatives must become an integral part of the Republican Party.

As an electoral strategy, this is an important matter. The social issues themselves, an end to the imposition of the crackpot schemes of liberal elitists, are even more important. But, possibly most important of all, this may be our last chance to prevent a major portion of the American electorate from abandoning present political approaches and turning to desperate and dangerous alternatives.

My own field time in the political struggle has been spent among people who previously voted Democratic and who carry union cards, but who are angrier at the liberal establishment than any Washington conservative. These are the West Virginian textbook protestors, wildcat coal strikers, Boston and Louisville anti-busing people, and other working people who are in revolt both against those who set the liberal direction and against those who claim to oppose it.

Through its control of working people's traditional means of expression—unions, local governments, even most churches—America's establishment of the left has been able to smother protests against its social and moral policies. The traditional result of suppressing anti-establishment protest, whatever that establishment has called itself, has been to make the final overthrow more violent and more dangerous.

Above all, liberals still control the media, so that anti-liberal working class protest has been left without an open conduit of public expression. The present drive to represent the 1980 election as a sudden show of dissatisfaction with the economy, rather than as a result of twelve years of clear electoral history, is a fairly blatant example of a last-ditch attempt to prevent any serious airing of popular complaints about liberal social policy. The only accepted critic of liberalism remains the fiscally obsessed Republican Old Right, which has no tradition of sympathy with working people's problems.

There is no way of knowing how dangerous such frustration now is, for the same reason which makes it dangerous: Our system presently provides means for neither its expression nor its measurement. I have been a part of the social issues protest from its earliest days, and have worked in Washington politics for over four years. As a result of my observations, one of the major messages contained in *The New Right Papers* is something of a warning.

My thesis is based on two general propositions. First, the liberal establishment is on its way out. It is now a small, powerful elite which is in retreat, protecting itself behind unelected judges and bureaucrats, and able to impose its will to the exact extent that it can avoid subjecting its dictates to the consent of the governed.

One cannot expect our people to keep faith with a system under which the decisions which affect them most are made by judges and bureaucrats, and guided by an ideology they had no part in making. By definition, the people have no part in social engineering. If the new majority is not formed, social conservatives, a major portion of our population, will be faced with the choice of permanent submission or of going outside the political limits as we know them. They will not submit.

Several papers presented in this book deal, in one way or another, with the restoration of popular rule. Professor William A. Stanmeyer's discussion of the imperial judiciary explains, from the point of view of a legal scholar, the steady erosion of the power of elected officials, and the increasing use of the Constitution as an excuse for, rather than a source of, judicial decisions. Behind such decisions ranges the full power of the United States Government. A situation where one man's personal judgment is law has a name, and it is not democracy.

My second proposition is that rule by the elite through judges and bureaucrats has gone so far that its removal will constitute a revolution, political or otherwise. A major function of the New Right is to provide a means by which it can be kept political.

Five years ago, in *A Plague on Both Your Houses,* I described the decline of our liberal ruling powers, at a time when they still held control of both Houses of Congress, and were about to elect their last sympathetic president. The two houses I was attempting to plague were, philosophically, liberals and the old right, and, politically, Democrats and Republicans. The book had few friends in high places, and its thesis was certainly not one calculated to make any. But most of what was said about politics which was then most offensive to the ruling cliques of the old right is now an accepted part—or "common sense"—of today's daily political practice, so much so that everyone now claims he knew these things all along. But the danger signals I pointed to, which are also developing on schedule, are still ignored.

It is pretty clear today that the liberal establishment will be overthrown. The critical questions are how and by whom. President Reagan represents a rebellion, but not the final outcome.

From a historical point of view, the liberal establishment is just one more ruling group whose time has passed. The slaveholder aristocracy of the South elected eight of our first eleven presidents from its ranks, but by 1850 was in decline. It, too, used the courts to defend its remaining power, and exercised considerable control over the press to suppress real opposition, so that, by the time such a counterforce did arrive on the scene, the result was civil war and political revolution. The succeeding business establishment, which dominated politics from Grant through Hoover, also used the courts—lower court anti-strike injunctions and the Supreme Court against the New Deal—to defend its old power. But that establishment went relatively peacefully, and co-opted many liberal initiatives. For that reason, unlike the slavocracy, the business establishment kept many of its principles and privileges alive after its displacement at the head of affairs by the liberal establishment.

Both the slavocracy and the liberals put race into central focus. Lincoln, who was a radical in the context of regular politics, said in 1858 that neither he, nor anyone he knew, sought political or social equality for blacks. Ten years later, that same equality had been written into the Constitution by the revolution which overthrew the slavocracy. An upheaval of a similar sort today, against the busing and affirmative-action oriented liberal establishment, would put Klan- or Nazi-types into power, a prospect as unthinkable now as racial equality was to Lincoln.

It has been said that Theodore Roosevelt's trust-busting and Franklin Roosevelt's New Deal helped prevent communist and socialist influence from growing in America. Certainly it is not hard to imagine what would have happened if the business establishment had been able to discredit all genuine opposition until the 1930s.

Genuine opposition to the expansion of chattel slavery did not develop until the nation was hopelessly divided. Probably the group most responsible for the Civil War was the leadership of the Whig Party, which, while slavery expansionism burned and grew as an issue, used the votes it generated against the slaveholder-dominated Democratic Party to pursue the old Whig aim of raising tariffs.

Slavery was not seriously addressed until the Whig Party was swept out of the way, too late, by the Republican Party. This is the danger posed by a Republican Party today, which merely "appeals" to social conservatives for votes. They tend to use grassroots rejection of social engineering to serve their traditional causes of government reduction and military expansionism. The New Right seeks to give "social issues"—a term used by Republicans and liberals alike to describe any domestic issue not concerned with the size of government—more than lip service. Among the powers-that-be in Washington, only the New Right is capable of seeing busing and other social experiments as mere symptoms of a deeper malady, and being aware of the dangers that arise from treating only symptoms.

I emphasize busing and racial quotas as a part of the liberal program which has driven social conservatives from their ranks because they are illustrative of the broader implications of the division in our country, and of the dangers it entails. Both are results of bureaucratic and judicial tyranny in the teeth of solid popular opposition. They show the raw power of liberal ideologues over every community in this country. By putting racial minorities in an apparently superior position under the liberal establishment, they threaten, as pressure builds, to make white supremacy a part of what will be publicly perceived as a true opposition. Lastly, these issues illustrate the underlying class struggle building in America, as wealthy suburban liberal judges and liberal ideologues force the children of middle class Americans to be bused, while their own go to private schools or to public ones well outside busing jurisdictions.

The growing class division in America, of which busing is only a symptom, is examined by Dr. Samuel T. Francis in his discussion of the growing number of Middle American Radicals (MARs). These are middle class people who are also middle-of-the-road politically—in the sense that they are neither fiscal conservatives nor liberals. But whereas such a median position usually implies satisfaction, MARs are growing violently hostile to our present system.

This hostility is described from first-hand experience by Robert Hoy, my partner, along with Brigitte Whitaker, in the activities of The Populist Forum. Aiding working people in expressing their grievances against the liberal establishment, we witnessed the potentially revolutionary passion of which deaf Washington, whose information is received only after passing through the media strainer, could remain unaware until it was too late.

THE ALTERNATIVE TO REAGAN POLICY— OLD LEFT OR NEW RIGHT?

A continuing theme of writers of every shade of opinion is the similarity between the election of 1932 and that of 1980. At the same time, relative to 1980, they have insisted that, "Reagan had better deliver, or else." The few who have spelled out the "or else" have done so by saying that this is the "Republicans' golden opportunity": If Reagan doesn't cure our problems, the Democrats, and presumably liberal Democrats who dominate the party led by Kennedy, Mondale, and Glenn, will be brought back by the electorate. In other words, what happened in 1980 was a victory of conservatives over liberals, but Democrats remain the popular alternative. Experts reasoned similarly in 1932, and they were wrong.

What happened in 1932 was more profound than the obvious victory of liberal candidates over conservative ones. They didn't know it then, but that year conservative Republicans had ceased not only to govern, but to be the real alternative to those who had displaced them. One of the standard jokes in college political science courses has been the confident prediction by the *Literary Digest* that Alf Landon would trounce Roosevelt in 1936. But the logic which made this prediction believable to the *Digest* in 1936 is precisely that followed by commentators today in discussing the Reagan Administration.

Like Reagan, Roosevelt inherited a huge problem, the Depression. In 1936, the economy was not noticeably better off than it had been in 1932. Following the "FDR had better deliver, or else," line of reasoning, it seemed that voters would return the Republicans, the opposition party, to power.

As it turned out, the Republicans experienced one of the worst beatings in American electoral history in 1936, carrying only two states at the presidential level, and being reduced to 89 of 435 seats in the House of Representatives.

Two things were wrong with 1936 analysts' conclusions. First, while voters might have been upset with FDR's failure to end the Depression, they had no intention of bringing back to power those they blamed for causing it. Similarly, even the obvious difficulties President Reagan faces today are without exception known to have been caused by Democrats generally, and liberal Democrats in particular. If he fails to deal with them, will the electorate return liberal Democrats to power? Will they elect Walter Mondale, Edward Kennedy or John Glenn to reduce the size of government, end inflation, and strengthen defense, problems even the national media admit are serious problems created by liberal policies?

Today's pundits wrinkle their noses, finger their long beards, and speak of the "middle of the road," as if the positions taken by liberal Republicans like Charles Percy or moderate Democrats like Daniel Patrick Moynihan represented a midway between American political poles fixed eternally by some law of nature. Following this same line in 1936, one would have confidently predicted victory for the relatively liberal Republican, Alf Landon. But when the votes were counted, even Roosevelt was surprised to discover that the political center had shifted to his own left, represented by support for liberal Democrats and the popularity of the share-the-wealth schemes of Huey Long.

Today, there is an excellent chance for a similar trend in near-term politics. In such a case, 1984 will find Reagan victorious and pollsters again scrambling to cover their tracks. "Middle of the road" sermons are only meaningful if the poles have not shifted. If 1980 is indeed like 1932, nothing could be more absurd than the endless preachments that Reagan must move to the old center.

The New Right insists that, for the good of the country, Reagan begin co-opting potential radicals as soon as possible. This is a recommendation which pundits must see as unrealistic, since their expertise resides in discussing politics as it is and recently has been. Further, it rests on an assumption which is violently rejected by the still-powerful passing establishment, and by those who cater to it.

The idea that the American left has lost its status even as a primary opposition is not one that the media are likely to embrace with cries of joy. In 1936, the national press was as conservative as the big media today are liberal. Certainly, this as much as anything else was the reason they clung so single-mindedly to the idea that Roosevelt's failure would mean a return of the conservative establishment to Washington.

This brings up the second mistake made by those who thought the Republicans would win in 1936. They thought 1932 was a one-time revolt, whereas it was actually the beginning of a long-term revolution. Voters who had, out of a sense of hopelessness, accepted their frustrations with rule by the business establishment through the 1920s, suddenly found that it could, indeed, be beaten. Instead of being pacified by the 1932 results, they were encouraged to aim for more.

Those frustrations of the 1920s have their parallels today. In 1928, the average industrial worker in Cleveland was as helpless against his autocratic factory owner as his grandson is today against court-ordered busing or hiring quotas. Southerners and Westerners faced discriminatory rail rates which kept industry in New England, while their farms suffered a recession during what the East called the Roaring Twenties. Today, with regional prosperity reversed, liberals pour billions into eastern cities, while robbing the sunbelt of billions through oil and gas price controls. Also in the 1920s, the original attempt at social engineering, Prohibition, was in force throughout the decade. After 1932, when voters discovered City Hall could be beaten, all these issues became open political questions, and the revolt grew into a revolution.

Liberals cannot think of themselves as tyrants. Dictators, they feel, transport children in the name of Nazism or Communism, whereas liberals order busing in the name of Social Progress, a different thing altogether. Stalin and Hitler broke up communities for evil purposes, whereas liberal programs break them up to achieve racial balance. Down through the ages, rulers have used government power to train children in morals and values different from those of their parents. Liberals use public schools for the same purpose. But that is all right, because liberal values are the right values.

Few rulers have ever felt otherwise. But social engineering is pure tyranny, and it has been tolerated largely because those subjected to it had no hope that it could be stopped. As the awareness that it can be stopped grows, social conservatives will object violently to abuses they previously had no alternative but to accept.

Like the slavocracy of the 1850s, the liberal establishment still has many weapons, including the federal courts, at its disposal. It has the power of the national press to discredit the New Right and thereby retain the modern Whigs—moderate and fiscally-obsessed conservative Republicans—as the only "respectable" opposition. If it is successful in preventing the formation of a New Right alternative, a true coalition of social and fiscal conservatives, from being formed, it will have used the slavocrats' methods, and the results could be very similar as well.

Richard A. Viguerie and Paul M. Weyrich are engaged in the building of a New Right alternative in Washington. Their papers describe the development of the genuine combination of fiscal and social conservatism to which President Reagan and his successors will have to turn once the middle-of-the-road myth is discredited.

The Washington New Right has been described as unwilling to compromise with politics as usual. In a true coalition, where fiscal and social conservatives are equal partners, there is no room for a simultaneous catering by the Republican Party to moderates and liberals.

A New Right coalition will reject liberal policies, but it will not adopt the indifference to the needs of the poor which is part of libertarianism, or the monomaniacal pursuit of bigger defense budgets to which the old right has devoted itself. It will require new, non-liberal approaches and points of view. In the stagnation produced in Washington by over a generation of fixed, liberal versus conservative competition, it will be a much-needed breath of fresh air.

Papers presented here show the scope of such a new search for non-liberal alternatives. From Ronald Docksai's discussion of the potential for expanding the private nonprofit sector to replace and improve on government social programs, and Robert Moffit's plan for a modern policy to deal with the Soviet Union, to Jeffrey Hart's refreshing look at philosophy and politics, policy alternatives are offered. Clyde Wilson's discussion of the proper relation of citizen and government and Thomas Fleming's exposition of a Southern traditional criticism of present-day America represent points of view which are relevant, but do not fit into the two-dimensional context of today's liberal-conservative debate. The thrust of my own essay is that Americans have first call on the fruits of the society they have, by their political wisdom, made productive. They have a right, therefore, to restrict immigration. Today, as immigration from backward countries run by demagogues becomes an ever greater pressure on developed countries, such a stand must be taken or developed countries must resign themselves to being overrun.

As implied by the term "papers," this book is not meant to

cover all aspects of the New Right, or to indicate that the authors
are in full agreement with each other. The New Right is not an
ideological construct, but a growing and developing movement.
This is not a still life, but a mosaic, the only proper representation
of a many-faceted coalition.

—Robert W. Whitaker
Washington, D.C.

THE
POLITICAL
CONTEXT

William A. Rusher

THE NEW RIGHT: PAST AND PROSPECTS

As a recent law school graduate, William Rusher became publisher of National Review *in its earliest days. He has remained at the forefront of the conservative movement ever since, representing it nationally as a columnist and television commentator and debater.*

In 1975, Mr. Rusher declared the need for an alliance between traditionally conservative and socially conservative working people in The Making of the New Majority Party, *the blueprint which was successfully followed in 1980. No one could describe more knowledgeably the struggle against the liberal establishment at the centers of power, and the critical choices that must be made today.*

I.

Ronald Reagan's impressive victory in 1980, and the election of a pronouncedly conservative Senate, have generated a great deal of discussion about when the present conservative upsurge began. The history of the modern conservative movement in this country is not widely understood, primarily because our largely liberal media and academic analysts first ignored it as long as possible, then minimized it, and continue relentlessly to distort it.

Nevertheless, Ronald Reagan did not spring full-blown from the brow of Jove in 1980 or any other recent year, and the conservative movement whose triumph he symbolizes has been around for quite a while. Even those with short memories can recall that Richard Nixon defeated George McGovern 49 states to 1 in 1972. If that landslide is to be attributed solely to the extremism of McGovern or his followers, it should be remembered that Nixon had also defeated the much less extreme Hubert Humphrey four years earlier in an election in which George Wallace drained away nearly ten million votes, few of which would have gone to Humphrey if Wallace hadn't run.

Even the events of 1964, properly understood, and certainly in retrospect, gave clear warning that conservatism had come of age as a serious political movement. Attention is usually focused on Barry Goldwater's landslide defeat by Lyndon Johnson that November, a defeat which is often assumed to have signaled a powerful liberal tide in the public opinion of the day. But while Goldwater's defeat unquestionably indicated that the voters were not yet ready for Goldwater, it is much less clear that they were in a very liberal mood. Time and sentimentality have softened the image of the Kennedy years into Camelot; but in fact the John Kennedy of 1963 was undergoing powerful and increasing conservative criticism. The Draft Goldwater movement, which became a riptide that year, was staging "resignation rallies" in important states (Texas for one), at which Democratic county committees resigned en masse and joined the GOP to work for Goldwater. *Time* magazine, which was scarcely enthusiastic about Goldwater, conceded in 1963 that he might well present a formidable challenge to Kennedy.

But even rejecting any possibility that Goldwater could actually have defeated Kennedy in 1964, there can be little dispute that the assassination of Kennedy greatly strengthened the Democratic vote in the 1964 election. For one thing, it made the voters understandably reluctant to change presidents yet again, less than a year after Kennedy's death. For another, and probably far more important, it confronted Goldwater not with a Massachusetts liberal as his opponent, but with a Texan who was widely and rightly regarded as a relatively conservative Democrat. These were devastating blows to the Goldwater strategy, based as it was on mustering the social conservatives of the South and West against the liberal East. Add to these difficulties the inevitable disaffection of many Northern and Eastern Republicans, from whom the Goldwater forces had just wrested control of the party at its San Francisco convention, and one can understand Johnson's victory quite easily without positing a massive "liberal trend."

But the modern conservative movement goes back even further. Its origins are to be found in the early 1950s. There had of course been conservative tides—and powerful ones at that—much further back along the 200-year course of American history. But the great issues of those earlier decades—national banks, the extension of slavery, free silver, protectionism, prohibition—are difficult to place in any intelligible relation to the major structural principles of the modern conservative movement. The latter arose in response to two principal challenges: (1) the enormous expansion of the federal government in and after Franklin Roosevelt's administration, and (2) the emergence of world Communism as America's principal international enemy in the years following World War II.

It is instructive to note how a non-liberal critic of the movement perceived this development at the time. Murray Rothbard is and has been one of the leading spokesmen for "libertarianism," that often stimulating if spectactularly impractical half-brother of conservative thought that concentrates on the evils and misdeeds of government to the exclusion of all else (even, fortunately for its exponents' peace of mind, the existence, intentions and capabilities of the Soviet Union). The libertarians, who trace their honorable lineage back to Albert Jack Nock (1873–1945), Frank Chodorov (1887–1966) and others, apparently considered themselves in comfortable possession of the conservative movement up through World War II.[1] If Big Government was to be the issue, and it was certainly one of them, they felt well equipped to do battle with it at the intellectual level. Presumably mass support, perhaps solicited on their behalf by the Republican party, would follow in due course.

Unfortunately the onset of the Cold War in 1946, and the manifest threat to freedom everywhere presented by the Soviet Union, provided persuasive justification for a much bigger government, at least in some respects (defense, etc.), than Rothbard & Co. were willing to consent to. The stage was accordingly set for the emergence of a more broadly conceived conservatism, which would adopt much of the libertarian critique of Big Government while adding to it a determined opposition to world Communism.[2]

Making due allowances for his libertarian bias, and discounting his overemphasis on my own role in events, observe how Rothbard, writing in *Inquiry* (October 27, 1980), describes what happened to conservatism in the early 1950s:

> What happened was this. The political leaders of the Old Right began to die or retire. Taft's death in 1953 was an irreparable blow,

and one by one the other Taft Republicans disappeared from the scene. In fact, Taft's defeat in the bitterly fought 1952 convention was to signal the end of the Old Right as a political force . . . Goldwater was—and is—an all-out interventionist in foreign affairs; it is both symbolic and significant that Goldwater was an Eisenhower, not a Taft delegate to the 1952 Republican convention.

Meanwhile, the intellectual leaders of the Old Right too were fast disappearing. Nock and Mencken were dead or inactive, and Colonel Robert R. McCormick, publisher of the *Chicago Tribune,* died in 1955. *The Freeman,* although the leading right-wing journal in the late forties and early fifties, had never been a powerful force; by the mid-fifties it was weaker than ever. Since the thirties, the Right had suffered from a dearth of intellectuals; it had seemed that all intellectuals were on the left. A disjunction therefore existed between a tiny cadre of intellectuals and writers, and a large, relatively unenlightened mass base. In the mid-1950s, with a power vacuum in both the political and the intellectual areas, the Right had become ripe for a swift takeover. A well-edited, well-financed magazine could hope to capture the dazed right wing and totally transform its character. This is exactly what happened with the formation of *National Review* in 1955.

In a sense, Joe McCarthy heralded the shift when, after his censure by the Senate, he feebly changed his focus in early 1955 from domestic Communism to the championing of Chiang Kai-shek. For *National Review,* led by Bill Buckley and William Rusher, was a coalition of young Catholics[3]—McCarthyite and eager to lead an anti-Communist crusade in foreign affairs—and ex-Communists like Frank Meyer and William S. Schlamm dedicating their energies to extirpating the God that had failed them. *NR* filled the power vacuum, and . . . managed, in a scant few years, to transform the American right wing beyond recognition. By the early 1960s, the Rusher forces had captured the Young Republicans and College Young Republicans, established Young Americans for Freedom as their campus arm, and had taken over the Intercollegiate Society of Individualists as a more theoretical organ.

By the 1960 GOP convention, Barry Goldwater had become the political leader of the transformed New Right. By 1960, too, the embarrassing extremists like the John Birch Society had been purged from the ranks, and the modern conservative movement was in place. It combined a traditionalist and theocratic approach to "moral values," occasional lip service to free-market economics, and an imperialist and global interventionist foreign policy dedicated to the glorification of the American state and the extirpation of world Communism. Classical liberalism remained only as rhetoric, useful in attracting business support, and most of all as a fig leaf for the grotesque realities of the New Right. (This entity is not to be confused with the fundamentalist factions now on the warpath against abortion and ERA.)

In a few brief years the character of the right wing had been totally transformed: Once basically classical liberal, it had become a global theocratic crusade.

Actually, of course, the whole process was a great deal less conspiratorial than Rothbard alleges and certainly far less preoccupied with theology. The menace of world Communism, fueled and led by the Soviet Union, was quite obvious enough to suggest itself as a matter of concern to many conservative observers in the early 1950s, even if they lacked the theological baggage to which Rothbard objects. (Max Eastman was for several years listed on the masthead as a contributor to *National Review,* as have been other well-known atheists and agnostics.) And the fact that combatting Communism sometimes required a scope and level of government activity that made conservatives uncomfortable was simply one of those paradoxes in which politics abounds.

This updated conservative view of America and the world was probably not yet, in the early 1950s, the clear opinion of a majority of the American people. Dwight Eisenhower, though elected as the candidate of a Republican party that formally objected to ever-larger government, gave early indications that he intended simply to preside over, rather than attempt to reduce, the Leviathan state; and in foreign affairs, although on the whole a Cold Warrior, he was not beyond inviting a Soviet head of government to visit this country for the first time, during a brief flowering of "peaceful coexistence," which was *détente's* predecessor. In both cases, Eisenhower probably reflected the majority sentiment of the American public at the time.

But there were plenty of people who disagreed deeply with these amiable policies, and Rothbard is right in remarking how rapidly they mobilized in the mid-1950s. They did not always agree among themselves, by a long shot: The John Birch Society, founded by Robert Welch in 1958, subscribed to a conspiratorial theory of events not to be matched, on the American scene, until the rise of the New Left in the 1960s. Other organizations and individuals stressed other concerns: the practical interests of business, the pure theory of free enterprise, the victory-oriented strategies of the Republican party, the culture of the American South, the problems of military defense, the unfolding interpretation of the Constitution, the devolution of the Judaeo-Christian tradition, and much else. But gradually most of these various strands were evaluated, traced to their intellectual origins, and woven into a reasonably consistent and coherent pattern of thought. By 1960 the conservative movement was ready to play a part in not only the intellectual but the political history of the United States.

II.

Among the matters on which conservatives disagreed *inter sese* in 1960 was whether the Republican party was an appropriate political vehicle for their movement. In a sense, the very launching of the movement five years earlier had answered this key question in the negative; obviously, if the GOP had effectively reflected the conservative concerns already described there would have been no need for a separate conservative movement in the first place.

But, as the conservatives of the late 1950s ruefully realized, it is one thing to launch a movement—even a mass movement (and the number of those directly involved was still relatively small: probably less than half a million, nationwide)—and quite another to focus its influence effectively at the polls. For that purpose it still seemed to many conservatives essential to make use of one of the two traditional means of access to those polls: the two major parties —specifically, in the case of the conservative movement, the Republican party.

This proposition was made even more seductive to conservatives because the entire right wing of the GOP was naturally sympathetic to their views and eager to solicit their support. Their most enthusiastic spokesman in the party was, of course, Senator Barry Goldwater of Arizona. At the 1960 convention of the Republican party, which nominated Nixon on the first ballot, Goldwater allowed his name to be placed in nomination by conservative delegates, but withdrew it before the balloting and exhorted his fellow-conservatives to work within the party to move it to the right.

It is tempting to speculate how the conservative movement might have developed if Nixon had defeated Kennedy that year. Before the campaign was over, a group of militant young Goldwater enthusiasts, unsatisfied to remain simply part of a faction (albeit the dominant conservative faction) of the Young Republican organization, founded Young Americans for Freedom, which has been a prolific source of conservative cadres ever since. Older conservatives might soon have followed them into activity squarely outside the GOP.

But Nixon lost to Kennedy, and suddenly the whole Republican party seemed up for grabs. Its Eastern leadership, so vigorous and competent in the days of Thomas E. Dewey and Brownell, had passed into the eager but inexpert hands of New York Governor Nelson Rockefeller, who manifestly had no problem financing his ambitions but was light-years distant from several of the major concerns of the conservative movement. ("I'm hard on defense and fiscal policy but soft on welfare. You've got two-thirds of me; what more do you want?" he once argued plaintively to a group of YAF leaders.) Moreover, the 1959 convention of the Young Republican National Federation, whose state organizations roughly reflected the sentiments of their seniors, had been taken over by a conservative coalition of Southern, Western and East Central states, a little-noticed but highly suggestive demonstration of what was accomplished in the party as a whole just four years later—in many cases by those same Young Republicans, now active in the senior party.

The term "social conservative" was not yet in vogue in the early 1960s, but the voters to whom it was later applied were the ones on whom the Republican politicians allied with the conservative movement focused in those years.

An attempt to woo Southern Democrats from their ancestral allegiance had been an official aspect of GOP strategy, under the label "Operation Dixie," since the mid-1950s. Now, it was adopted as an integral part of the conservative victory plan (though "the Southern strategy" became a false label applied to the entire plan by liberal critics to suggest that it was little more than an appeal to racism).

But Republican conservatives had discovered that their social-conservative concerns—crime, pornography, Soviet imperialism, etc.—were anxiously shared by several other traditionally Democratic blocs: Northern blue-collar workers, Catholic urban ethnics, and small Western farmers, to name only three. The intuition was irresistible that the Republican party, with the right candidate, could make an enormously powerful appeal to these groups. And it seemed equally apparent that that candidate was Barry Goldwater.

Barry Goldwater didn't especially want to be the Republican nominee in 1964; he would have to surrender his Senate seat (which came up that year) to run, and he was under no illusions about his presidential prospects. But the Draft Goldwater movement of 1961–64 was an authentic draft—one of the very few in American political history.[4] Even after Kennedy's assassination, which made defeat certain, Goldwater could not refuse the pleas of his conservative admirers. As he has proudly written, "On the first ballot I received more votes than any candidate in either party had ever achieved on the first ballot of a contested convention . . . : 883 out of 1308."

I have already explained why it is wrong to regard Goldwater's defeat by Johnson that November, huge as it was, as in any serious sense evidence of a public groundswell in favor of liberal principles. As a matter of fact, just four years later that beau ideal of American liberalism, Hubert Humphrey, would lose the presidency to Richard Nixon. But the lengthening perspective of time increasingly suggests that the most important event of 1964 not only was not Johnson's landslide victory; it was not even the transfer (never since reversed) of control of the GOP from the North and East to the South and West; it was not the speech by Ronald Reagan that catapulted him into national politics. Rather, it was the fact that the Goldwater campaign introduced the conservatives of America to one another.

The growth of direct-mail promotion in general, and of direct-mail political promotion in particular, has attracted considerable attention in recent years, but it is not widely realized how absolutely critical this development was to the expansion of the conservative movement, or why it should (as it undoubtedly does) benefit the right far more than the left.

Communication is manifestly essential to all politics. Candidates and spokesmen for political causes must find, woo, and organize their constituencies; the constituencies must finance and vote for those causes and candidates. The process is by no means automatic, and can be extremely difficult, especially for conservatives. During the quarter-century under discussion here, the writers for the news departments of all three major television networks, as well as the reporters and editors of both *Time* and *Newsweek* and their opposite numbers on the two most influential national newspapers, *The New York Times* and *The Washington Post,* were almost unanimously liberal in their politics. Without suggesting any elaborate conspiracy among them, it is obvious that they tended to see events and individuals in much the same light. They came to oppose the Vietnam war at about the same time; most of them favored first Romney, then Rockefeller, for the 1968 Republican nomination; almost to a man they detested Richard Nixon and George Wallace. Inevitably, their product reflected these biases. The merits of liberal candidates for any important office, from the presidency to a seat in the House of Representatives, were reasonably sure to receive sympathetic attention; the merits of conservative candidates for the same positions were quite likely to be ignored, and their defects (if any) stressed.

This bias put heavy pressure on conservative candidates and spokesmen to find alternative ways of reaching the voters, and especially those voters disposed to be sympathetic. The mailing lists built up during the Goldwater campaign—and it must be remembered that Goldwater received, in overall terms, a larger number of contributions (most of them small) than any other presidential candidate up to that time—were therefore a priceless asset to the conservative organizations that subsequently acquired them. They could be and were used to promote conservative publications and action organizations such as *Human Events, National Review,* and the American Conservative Union; they were also used to solicit votes and financial support for conservative candidates in both primaries and general elections.

These various activities in turn generated still more and fresher names, which in turn were fed into the computers. By the mid-1970s it was possible for a major entrepreneur in the field of conservative mailing lists, such as Richard Viguerie, to address carefully tailored letters on behalf of, say, a Congressional candidate, to all of the members of half a dozen or more special interest groups whose addresses included zip codes in that particular Congressional district. And the same applied to statewide races or, for that matter, presidential elections. The devastating efficiency of this process received a dramatic demonstration when conservative Republicans toppled half a dozen of the Senate's leading liberals in November 1980. (The technique is of course available to liberals, too, but their constituencies were already largely mobilized, via the media.)

All this, to repeat, began for practical purposes with the Goldwater campaign of 1964, and it had the effect of solving brilliantly the communication problem of the conservative movement. Nowadays conservatives often complain bitterly of the blizzard of mail —most of it soliciting money—that they receive from various conservative candidates and organizations; but what they are really doing is testifying to the efficiency and articulation of the communications network that now serves them.

III.

In the immediate aftermath of Goldwater's defeat in November 1964, it was an open question whether the conservative movement would retain the control of the GOP that it had seized under the Goldwater banner in the 1964 convention. Ray Bliss, a "nuts and bolts" politician from the formidable Ohio Republican machine, became the party's national chairman, while first George Romney and then Nelson Rockefeller was hailed by the liberals in the media as the "odds-on front-runner" for the 1968 presidential nomination. But Richard Nixon, in fact a far more likely choice than either, had recruited Goldwater to his banner, and slowly during 1967 and the first half of 1968 a substantial part of the conservative movement, and especially those segments of it with the closest ties to the Republican party, swung behind Nixon. Another group of conservatives, almost equally large and probably including most of the movement's purer ideologues, preferred California Governor Ronald Reagan; but Nixon, occupying as he did the central ground between Reagan and Rockefeller, was able to win narrowly on the first ballot, thanks to a coalition of centrists plus those conservatives who calculated that Nixon was "conservative enough." In effect, the 1968 convention remained under conservative control, but the control was exercised gently; and the destiny of the conservative movement, at least in its Republican form, was confided, along with that of the country as a whole, to Nixon.

It is true, of course, that nobody in 1968 could foresee Watergate and the consequences that would flow therefrom, but it is still hard not to fault the pro-Nixon conservatives of that year for failing to support Ronald Reagan instead. He was already Governor of California, and only 57; and while he had not declared an all-out candidacy for the nomination, or (until the convention actually met) campaigned hard for it, he was most certainly eager to have it. What might have happened—and not happened—to America if he had received the nomination in 1968 are speculations at once fascinating and fruitless.

Independent conservatives, however, and especially social conservatives, did not all follow the lead of their more Republican brethren in uniting behind Nixon once he was nominated. Alabama Governor George Wallace astonished the experts by managing to put his third-party candidacy on the ballot in all 50 states, and received just under ten million votes in the general election. Wallace's votes were drawn heavily from the ranks of blue-collar workers, farm labor, and Southern whites of all classes, and consisted primarily of former Democrats. These were, of course, precisely the social conservatives on whose conversion to Republicanism the strategy of the Goldwater draft had been so largely based, and their defiant break with the Democratic party when it dumped Lyndon Johnson in 1968 was dramatic evidence of their volatility. As a matter of fact, it is debatable whether Wallace would have run if Reagan had declared his candidacy early on and the Republicans had nominated him—in which event the Republican victory that November would probably have resembled 1980, rather than being the near thing it actually was.

Nonetheless, the prospects following Nixon's narrow victory in 1968 undoubtedly favored consolidation of a coalition of economic and social conservatives, constituting a comfortable majority of the electorate, under Republican auspices. That was the theme of Kevin Phillips's magisterial demographic analysis, published in 1969 under the title *The Emerging Republican Majority*. And while it is always risky to accept uncritically what any politician, let alone Richard Nixon, tells us in retrospect about his intentions, it is certainly worth noting that Nixon, in his recently published memoirs, proclaims that it was his own intention, in his second term, "to revitalize the Republican Party along New Majority lines."

Apparently Phillips's 1969 book had failed to convince Nixon, but George McGovern's nomination by the Democrats in 1972 persuaded him that the time was at last ripe. Nixon writes: "McGovern's perverse treatment of the traditional Democratic power blocs that had been the basis of every Democratic presidential victory for the last 40 years had made possible the creation of a New Republican Majority as an electoral force in American politics." Pointing to the component parts of his landslide victory over McGovern, Nixon notes that "four of these groups—manual workers, Catholics, members of labor union families, and people with only grade-school educations—had never before been in the Republican camp." Accordingly, Nixon tells us, in his second term he "planned to give expression to the more conservative values and beliefs of the New Majority throughout the country."

Watergate, of course, thwarted that project, and much else besides. As Norman Podhoretz has recently pointed out, the liberals were able to use the Watergate scandal as the basis of an authentic coup d'état—a swift and successful rebellion against an established majority. In one Watergate-related development after another, Vice President Agnew was forced to resign under a cloud (an essential preliminary, in liberal eyes, to any move against Nixon); serious discussions in the House of Representatives, looking toward assumption of control of that body by a bipartisan conservative coalition, were aborted; and, as we have seen, Nixon's own decision to revamp the Republican party along New Majority lines was rendered nugatory. The Democrats swept the Congressional elections of 1974 despite Nixon's resignation and replacement by Ford.

IV.

In my 1975 book, *The Making of the New Majority Party,*[5] I pointed to the mounting evidence that there was now—and had been for some time—a conservative majority in the country, comprised of economic conservatives largely based in the GOP and social conservatives recently recruited from the Democratic party. I discussed the various difficulties in the path of domesticating this coalition more or less permanently in the Republican party: not only the contemporary aura of corruption stemming from the resignations of both Agnew and Nixon, but the more general problem presented by the determination of the Republican left to bar any effective alliance between the GOP and Democratic conservatives. I suggested that in the circumstances the best solution was the creation of a brand-new party expressly designed to house the coalition—ideally, in time for the 1976 presidential election.

My proposal was aimed, of course, straight at Ronald Reagan, whose participation and candidacy on the new party's line would be necessary to give it a serious chance of immediate victory. In February 1975, in Washington, I gave Governor Reagan one of the four manuscript copies of the book, and in May of that year we discussed its thesis over dinner at his home in Los Angeles.[6]

As Jesse Unruh has remarked, one of Ronald Reagan's greatest gifts is his ability to say "No" to his friends; and that was what he said to me. Aside from various statements in the text having to do with his own attitude toward the possibility of the presidential nomination in 1968, his only quarrel with the book involved its stress on the necessity, or desirability, of going outside the Republican party to achieve victory and consolidate the conservative majority that (he emphatically concurred) existed in the country. If only he could win the Republican nomination, he argued, he could lead that conservative majority to victory. And *then* he could and would consolidate it, for further victories over the longer term, under the aegis of the Republican party.

In response, I was deeply skeptical that he could wrest the Republican nomination from Gerald Ford in 1976, and said so. In the event, however, I was struck by how close he came—and perhaps he in turn, from time to time afterward, remembered my skepticism.

The presidential campaign of 1976, however, reflected and ultimately hinged upon the continued (and in this case separate) existence of major blocs of economic and social conservatives. The Ford-Dole ticket fielded by the Republicans possessed almost no attraction whatever for formerly Democratic social conservatives, consisting as it did of two men both splendidly representative of the sort of center-right sentiments, especially on economic issues, that have been typical of the GOP since the nineteenth century. The Democratic convention, on the other hand, nominated a candidate well calculated to win back those social conservatives who had strayed to Wallace in 1968 and who preferred Nixon to McGovern in 1972. Jimmy Carter—the first Southerner to be nominated by either party since the Civil War, an avowed "outsider," and in Democratic terms a relative conservative—narrowly defeated Ford. Once again circumstances had conspired to preclude an unmistakable conservative victory.

The shift of many social conservatives from Nixon in 1972 to Carter in 1976 was brilliantly pinpointed by Kevin Phillips in a study published in his *American Political Report* in 1977. In 20 key states, Phillips studied the decline in the Republican vote from 1972 to 1976 in that particular county in each state where the decline was heaviest. In every case they were rural or small-town

WASP counties, composed, as Phillips put it, of "the working-class
and lower-middle-class constituencies—perhaps 15 percent of the
national electorate—routinely ignored by Gerald Ford–type Establishment Republicanism." Here is the Phillips list:

State	Most-shifting County	1972 GOP %	1976 GOP %	Shift	Intrastate	Geographic-Demographic Description
N.J.	Cumberland	59%	42%	−17	South Jersey rural-smalltown*
Pa.	Greene	57	38	−19	SW Pa. Appalachian WASP*
Md.	Dorchester	76	51	−25	Chesapeake Bay smalltown-rural*
W. Va.	Wyoming	64	32	−32	Southern poor white coal area*
Va.	Franklin	67	35	−32	Rural Appalachian-Southside*
N.C.	Columbus	72	23	−49	SE coastal poor white*
Ky.	Marshall	60	27	−33	SW "Little Dixie"*
Tenn.	Lake	68	23	−45	West Tennessee rural white
Ala.	Lawrence	76	18	−58	Tennessee Valley rural white*
Miss.	Tippah	88	31	−57	Poor white NE foothills*
Fla.	Holmes	93	37	−56	NW Panhandle "Cracker" country*
Texas	Delta	62	21	−41	East Texas-Sulphur River delta
Okla.	Atoka	74	25	−49	SE farm-coal area (poor white)*
Mo.	Dunklin	68	32	−36	SE "Boot" rural area*
Ill.	Massac	70	45	−25	"Little Egypt" poor white*
Ind.	Owen	70	48	−22	Southern Indiana rural WASP*
Ohio	Meigs	71	48	−23	Ohio River-Appalachian*
Iowa	Ringgold	69	46	−23	South Iowa WASP (poor farms)*

*Asterisk indicates this was also states's general region of *worst* GOP decline.

Drawing the lesson for the GOP, Phillips put it this way: "In
contrast to Nixon-Agnew ability to woo low- and low-middle-
income white voters with a mix of social conservatism, economic
activism and cultural anti-establishment postures, Gerald Ford
had little rapport with these voters—and their heavy shift was the
key to his loss. From South Jersey and Appalachian Pennsylvania
west through the Ohio Valley to Kansas and down to New Mexico's
'Little Texas,' this Southern-tinged low-income and low-middle-
income white vote probably accounts for 15 percent of the U.S.
total. And our estimate is that among such voters, the GOP presidential vote slipped from 70 percent in 1972 to 30 percent in 1976.
Such slippage among a 15 percent-of-the-country voting group
would be enough to turn a 54 percent national victory into a 48
percent loss."

It may be debated whether the Democratic convention delegates who nominated Carter in 1976, or even Carter himself, were fully aware of the strategic implications of his selection (though for what it is worth I believe that many of the delegates were, and that Carter himself certainly was). But it is simply purblind not to recognize that the Democratic party's recapture of a substantial part of the social-conservative vote was what narrowly elected Carter. The blacks have claimed the honor, because the percentage of blacks who vote Democratic is traditionally high, and was higher than ever for Carter (no doubt thanks to his Baptist background). But as Phillips pointed out, "Ford's black percentage was only a few points lower than Nixon's. Overall, black ballots—either via slightly increased turnout or 1972–76 party shifting—were only a minor factor in the Republican presidential vote plummet from 61 percent in 1972 to 48 percent in 1976." The major factor, to repeat, was the return of many social conservatives to the Democratic fold.

V.

By now (i.e., 1976) all of the various subspecies of conservative thought and activity (save one) that were to receive such heavy attention after Reagan's victory in 1980 were on the scene, and it will be useful to pause here and engage in a little clarifying taxonomy.

Up until the mid-1960s, intellectuals and activists of a generally conservative persuasion were often called simply "conservatives." Students of the subject, however, could easily make out two quite different intellectual strains at work, sometimes in tandem but often in competition or even conflict: a "libertarian" element, derived from the works of Rothbard, Chodorov et al., and a Burkean, "traditionalist" school, associated in this country with the writings of Russell Kirk. Each viewpoint had its passionate exponents (for years the national conventions of Young Americans for Freedom were divided into "lib" and "trad" caucuses), and their constant quarrels led *National Review*'s house metaphysician, Frank Meyer, to propose a compromise called "fusionism"—which, of course, failed to satisfy the purists in either camp.

In the 1960s the rise of the New Left profoundly unsettled a number of liberals who had been among the leading spokesmen of that genre in the 1950s: Irving Kristol, Norman Podhoretz, Midge

Decter, Daniel Bell and their circle. Breaking with liberalism, and gradually adopting some (though not always all) of the views associated with standard conservatism, they had established by the mid-1970s a new and separate identity under the name "neo-conservatives." As apostates from liberalism, they had particularly high visibility in the eyes of their former colleagues. The latter, who still dominated the media, were soon giving many people the quite mistaken impression (which some of them probably shared themselves) that conservatism was born the day Irving Kristol defected from liberalism. To negate any such impression, those who preceded him in the conservative movement have sometimes offered to be called "paleo-conservatives"—a ghastly fate, but perhaps better than being forgotten altogether.

During the 1970s a certain difference, first in philosophical emphasis and then in operational style, began to appear between more orthodox conservatives and the group centered around Richard Viguerie, who by this time had established himself as perhaps the leading exponent of direct-mail political warfare. The latter group (which included such activist organizations as Howard Phillips's Conservative Caucus, Terry Dolan's National Citizens' Political Action Committee, Paul Weyrich's Committee for the Survival of a Free Congress, Woody Jenkins's American Legislative Exchange Council, and Viguerie's own *Conservative Digest*) was in favor of appealing far more explicitly to social conservative voters on the basis of social issues (right-to-life, anti-gun-control, anti-pornography, etc.) than some of their colleagues, who preferred to continue to stress such economic issues as balancing the budget. This philosophical preference rapidly produced operational differences as well: Viguerie and his allies, who now began to be called the New Right, were broadly sympathetic to my own 1975 call for a new party to institutionalize the majority coalition of economic and social conservatives, whereas most other conservative analysts and activists preferred to stick with the GOP.

Now that the Republican party's nomination of Reagan, and his election, have mooted (or at least temporarily muted) that controversy, the New Right and more orthodox conservatives have fewer open disagreements, but a certain difference in operational styles is still apparent. The New Right seems somewhat quicker to object when it thinks President Reagan has strayed from the path of conservative virtue, and it has already boldly listed various of the remaining liberal senators as its "targets" in 1982.

The so-called Religious Right was not yet on the scene in 1976, at least under that name or in anything like its present size and form, although Carter's appeal to unorganized evangelicals was an important feature of his campaign. Its mushroom growth between 1976 and 1980, and the part it appears to have played in Reagan's election and the conservative victories in the Senate, are probably the most important recent developments in American politics. Whether this proves true or not, however, there can be no doubt about its origins: It is a direct reaction to the blows the family and related values have suffered in American society in the past twenty years.

VI.

As we have already seen, Carter's nomination by the Democrats in 1976 was, at least in its effects, a successful attempt to win back many of the rebellious social conservatives and accommodate the Democratic party, to some degree, to the imperatives of the conservative national mood. In the following four years, however, Carter treated observers to a spectacular demonstration of how difficult it is to broaden such a mandate into a viable administration if one's party is still largely dominated by dedicated liberals. The attempt exhausted what little capacity for leadership Carter possessed, and though he managed to compel his own renomination by the Democrats in 1980 he suffered major liberal defections to Anderson in November.

For the Republicans, on the other hand, the years 1976–1980 saw the final collapse of the Republican liberals and centrists who had staved off the nomination of Ronald Reagan ever since 1968. The mood of the party is now so unrelentingly conservative that Republican National Committee Chairman Bill Brock, himself a centrist, and Republican Senatorial Campaign Committee Chairman Robert Packwood, a liberal, were both reduced to signing money-raising letters heavily laced with conservative rhetoric. Late in 1977 for example, the Republican National Committee and the Republican Congressional Campaign Committee obtained Reagan's permission to send out over his signature a letter announcing that the two groups "have joined together to establish an Emergency Panama Canal Fund and to launch an unprecedented campaign to defeat the treaty and elect more Republicans to Congress who will vote against any giveaway schemes." Opponents of the treaties contributed $700,000 in response to that letter—not realizing that other RNC funds were being sluiced into the campaigns (including the primary campaigns) of such treaty supporters as Edward Brooke, Clifford Case, Mark Hatfield and Howard Baker. Senator Paul Laxalt, Reagan's closest friend in the Senate and leader of the anti-treaty forces, failed in an attempt to obtain just $50,000 of that $700,000 to help pay for the chartered plane of an anti-treaty truth squad—a rejection that probably cost Brock his chairmanship of the party three years later.

Meanwhile the success of Proposition 13 on the California ballot in 1978 (a proposal to reduce state property taxes sharply) quickly gave rise to a whole series of constitutional amendments and referenda in other states, limiting taxes and/or expenditures in various ways. It became apparent that the job of converting social conservatives to the frugal prescriptions of economic conservatives in the matter of government spending—a task which even New Majority theorists in the early 1970s had considered formidable, and which many liberals had gratefully proclaimed impossible —was already rather more than half done.

To ease the pain, Congressman Jack Kemp and Senator William Roth proposed their famous 30 percent slash in tax rates—10 percent in each of three successive years. Arguing that the stimulus this would give the economy would soon actually raise government tax revenues despite the lower rates, Kemp persuaded Reagan, who added Kemp-Roth to his own set of campaign proposals. Republican rhetoric, which had traditionally insisted on lowering expenditures and raising taxes until the budget was in balance, now had a way to regale blue-collar audiences with promises of lower taxes rather than higher ones—while still increasing revenues to pay for popular government services.

The Reagan campaign picked up steam. By the end of 1979 it seemed that only the "age issue" could block his nomination, and the very first 1980 primary—in New Hampshire, on February 26 —proved conclusively that the voters, or at any rate the Republican voters of New Hampshire, were thoroughly unimpressed by that objection.

So, as November demonstrated, were the voters at large. The "new" majority coalition of economic and social conservatives (though no longer really new—remember 1972) was back together again, and under Republican auspices at that.

VII.

The great question now awaiting an answer is whether President Reagan will succeed in domesticating the social conservatives in the Republican party and thereby make that party the long-term vehicle of the conservative majority coalition that elected him.

We may, I think, assume that Mr. Reagan is aware of the question in roughly those terms and firmly intends that it shall be answered in the affirmative. Certainly his comments to me, in May 1975, were convincing enough on that score. But he would undoubtedly also be the first to agree that the job hasn't been done yet: that the mere fact that the coalition came together long enough to elect him does not guarantee that its components won't separate again —just as they came together in 1972 to elect Richard Nixon overwhelmingly, then separated again in the Ford-Carter race of 1976.

Obviously, nothing succeeds like success, and the strongest possible cement for the alliance would be the success of Mr. Reagan's own administration. If he can bring inflation under control, keep unemployment at endurable levels, strengthen our defenses, reduce tax rates (not necessarily tax revenues), and restore American prestige abroad, he will face little criticism from either economic or social conservatives. Liberals would undoubtedly continue to argue, on compassionate grounds, for greater concessions in the direction of redistributionism; but that plea necessarily faces rough going in a society dominated by a coalition dedicated to the virtues of productivity.

But Mr. Reagan will probably not be so fortunate as to have everything go his way, and it is here that real dangers threaten his coalition.

In the first place, it is by no means certain that future Republican conventions will understand what is necessary to further victories. Politicians as a class are not gifted with second sight, and the Republican conventions of 1968 and 1976 stoutly resisted, in the name of what they firmly (if wrongly) believed was shrewd opportunism, the chance to win spectacular victories through a coalition with social conservatives recruited from the Democratic party.

Prior to 1980, the only time the coalition actually came into existence was in 1972, and that year the Republican party had nothing to do with its formation, being involved in the routine renomination of an incumbent president. (It was, of course, the Democratic party's nomination of McGovern—a performance that demonstrated that stupidity is nonpartisan—that alienated the social conservatives and delivered them to Nixon.)

It is therefore by no means impossible that in four or eight years—whenever Mr. Reagan steps down—the GOP will revert to form and move somewhat to the left, in the hope of picking off centrist Democrats and/or simply to mollify the remaining centrist Republicans. It will, of course, by that ruinous tactic be reducing *pro tanto* its grip on the social conservatives; but whether that proves fatal will depend upon external circumstances—notably the response of the Democrats.

The Democratic party is a remarkably protean institution, capable of assuming a great variety of forms in its single-minded pursuit of public office. If it were to nominate a candidate capable of appealing to social conservatives (as Carter appealed to many of them in 1976) more powerfully than the man the GOP chooses to succeed Ronald Reagan, it is entirely possible that it could win the White House in a rough replay of the 1976 election. Mr. Carter's subsequent troubles with his party's left wing suggest that his spiritual heir might have as much difficulty as Carter did in actually governing; but electoral victory is at least a possibility.

It can thus be seen that retention by the liberals of firm control of the Democratic party is, paradoxically, of critical importance if social conservatives are to be slowly acclimatized to their new Republican home. More broadly, of course, it is also true that the principal relevant dividing-line in the society must continue to be the one that separates producers from nonproducers. (For the basic argument that this is presently the case, see *The Making of the New Majority Party.*) Any development that revives and inflames the old division between haves and have-nots in the producing segment of the society could quickly disrupt the coalition—as could some brand-new social division not presently foreseeable.

In the present state of affairs, however, it is the New Right that most accurately perceives the nature of the victorious conservative coalition and the steps, both policy-oriented and pragmatic, that must be taken—in many cases by President Reagan himself—if it is to persist and prevail.

First and foremost, due attention must be given to the issues that brought the social conservatives into the coalition and under the Republican tent in the first place. These are, of course, the so-called "social issues"—the entire spectrum of "pro-family" issues (right-to-life, opposition to the constant expansion of "gay rights," and general support for the institution of marriage), pornography, gun-control, street crime, busing, drug abuse, capital punishment, etc. It is undoubtedly true that the economy must have the Reagan administration's first attention, and defense matters its second; but we should know well before the Congressional elections of 1982 whether the social issues are on its agenda in a serious way. Not only by legislative recommendations, but by executive orders, and by the character of the individuals he appoints to key positions in the courts and the Department of Justice, President Reagan will have literally scores of opportunities to mark out a new direction for the development of American society on these important social fronts.

At the pragmatic political level, the New Right has already demonstrated its almost unique mastery of the art of political communication via direct mail. In a country where every pass in the political Alps save that one is controlled by liberals, the ability to reach and mobilize conservatives on behalf of candidates favorable to conservative views is plainly of vital importance. And there is no reason why the process of compiling and using conservative mailing lists ought not also to be deployed against those remaining liberals in the House and Senate who have made a career out of posing as one thing to their constituents and being, in fact, something very different on Capitol Hill. Finally, direct mail obviously has its uses in presidential elections, too, though of course it is less possible for liberals to freeze out or misrepresent their opponents *in toto* at that level.

At bottom, however, I suspect that the most important contribution of the New Right to the cause of conservatism is neither theoretical nor technical, but emotional. There is something in the sheer passion of the members of the New Right that is impossible to weigh, but which unquestionably has an impact on events. It is related to the adjective most often applied to them as a group—

"feisty"—and undoubtedly has its negative as well as its positive aspects. They can be quarrelsome, censorious, uncompromising, extreme, overly assertive, pugnacious, and (sometimes) just plain wrong; but they bring to mind Lincoln's reply when somebody complained about Grant's drinking: "I can't spare the man: He fights."

ENDNOTES

1. This view, however, does somewhat less than justice to the prewar anti-Communists, like Martin Dies and J.B. Matthews.
2. Interestingly enough, the Cold War forced a parallel modification on the non-Communist left, spawning the domestically liberal but internationally anti-Communist ADA.
3. Rothbard is in error, as far as my religious views were concerned. In the 1950s I was little more than a theist. It was not until 1978 that I was baptized and confirmed in the Anglican Catholic Church.
4. For the best full-length account of it, see *Suite 3505* by F. Clifton White (Arlington House, 1967). An article on the same subject by the present author appeared in the August 11, 1964 issue of *National Review.*
5. Published by Sheed and Ward.
6. That the idea was not wholly quixotic is suggested by the comment on it made by the notably non-quixotic John Connally in a television interview on January 8, 1976, after Reagan had officially declared his decision to seek the Republican presidential nomination that year: "If Governor Reagan had . . . said, 'I'm not going into the Republican party; I'm going to lead a third party movement in this country,' I think he could have had an enormous influence, not just this year but in the years to come."

Richard Viguerie

ENDS AND MEANS

The Congressional Quarterly, *in describing a liberal fund raiser, said that he "may become the Richard Viguerie of the left." But Mr. Viguerie is more than a raiser of funds. He has used his direct marketing and management skills to help the conservative cause try to become the dominant political force in America. As an author (he wrote* The New Right: We're Ready To Lead*), publisher, political strategist for New Right groups, and business executive, he gives advice about what must be done as one who knows how to act on it. In 1979,* Time *Magazine chose Mr. Viguerie as one of its "Fifty New Faces for America's Future."*

If there was a single moment you can point to as the beginning of the New Right, it came in August 1974.

Richard Nixon had just resigned the Presidency. Gerald Ford had succeeded him. And Ford now announced his own choice for Vice President, Nelson Rockefeller.

Conservatives—which usually meant conservative Republicans—couldn't have been more dismayed. We had been urged all along to tie our fortunes to those of the Republican Party, to go along with the "moderate" Nixon as opposed to a more natural preference like Ronald Reagan, to accept Ford as Nixon's successor. And who should Ford pick as his possible successor but the aging Rockefeller.

Rockefeller was the very symbol of old, Eastern, liberal establishment Republicanism. His non-support of the 1964 Republican presidential nominee, Barry Goldwater, had helped produce a liberal landslide. And now the party was rewarding him with the Vice

Presidency—and expecting conservatives to support their old be-
trayer for the sake of "party unity."

For many of us, it was the last straw. More than that, it was
a revelation. It taught us that our very loyalty to the Republican
Party had made us powerless—even within the Party. The only
way for conservatives to have influence, or to bring pressure on the
Republican Party in the future, was to declare our independence.

The night after Ford's announcement, I held a dinner for about
fifteen conservative friends in Washington to plan a strategy to
stop Rockefeller from winning confirmation. It was no use. We
couldn't do it; we didn't have the clout. The force of liberalism, in
both parties, already had victory locked up.

There was the problem. Conservatism was only a force within
the Republican Party, and Republicans knew conservatives had
nowhere to go. But liberalism was a force within *both* parties: it
owned the Democrats, and had made inroads among the Republicans.

The problem was how to make conservatism an independent
power, so that the Republicans couldn't take us for granted, lock
us up, and set off in quest of liberal votes. The so-called moderates
always "compromised" in one direction, and got almost nothing in
return.

A new strategy was called for. Conservatives had to have their
own base, their own institutions, their own agenda, and above all
their own leaders. We had never lacked talent. We had a great
symbol and spokesman in Barry Goldwater. We had a tremendous
debater and editor in Bill Buckley. We had marvelous philosophers
and analysts like Frank Meyer and James Burnham. And we knew
—despite 1964—that we could have the votes.

But we needed that leadership. Spokesmen are often mistaken
for leaders, and of course it is possible to be both. Their actual
functions, however, are distinct. Leaders do more than talk; they
organize, plan, raise money, call the shots. This doesn't mean they
have to be bosses or "godfathers," but at least they are focal points
for action.

An idea, however eloquently expressed, doesn't automatically
translate itself into votes. Unless there are leaders using real issues
to reach the voters, even the most brilliant ideas won't penetrate
into politics.

It isn't easy balancing party and principle. For a while, some conservatives, myself among them, considered launching a new political party, to be devoted to true conservative principles. But this idea faded for several reasons. Some of those reasons were practical, but there was one more basic reason: Any party would find itself facing the same dilemma—votes or principles?—the Republicans faced.

Maybe I was too hard on the Republicans. After all, a party's job is to win elections. That is the kind of institution a political party is. If it loses, some of its officers will lose their jobs. But if it wins by cutting corners on fundamental truths, their jobs will be safe. Nothing succeeds like success.

We soon realized there was a better way for conservatives to win power than by forming their own party. We didn't have to look far for models: The Democrats had known it all along.

The Democrats consist of many groups—ideological groups like the Americans for Democratic Action, pork barrel groups like big labor, single issue groups like the National Abortion Rights Action League. Together they form a coalition, but just as important, each can walk out if it is displeased. Consequently, the Democratic Party has to try to keep them all happy.

The party's main job is to win elections, pure and simple. The various coalition groups help them win it in exchange for promises as to how the resultant power will be used. This is exactly what conservatives, before the New Right, were in no position to do. So it was only natural that the Republicans would show us little respect and concentrate their efforts on appealing to others who might help them win elections.

Not that they were any good at it. They took the view that only "moderates," carbon-copy Democrats, had a chance of beating real Democrats. Gerald Ford was still saying this in early 1980, after he had become the first incumbent President since Hoover to lose to a challenger!

This dogma goes back to 1964, when many Republicans stabbed Barry Goldwater in the back and then used the size of his defeat to try and prove that conservatism was dead. Since then, until 1980, only moderate Republicans were allowed to run—and even when they won, they had no agenda, no strategy, and did little good to speak of.

In 1980 Ronald Reagan finally destroyed the Republican "law" according to which the fewer principles you have, the more votes you will get. In 1976 he had nearly toppled Ford when he violated the "Eleventh Commandment": Thou shalt not attack a fellow Republican. Despite his strong party loyalty, Reagan's strength has always been to put principle ahead of party. He has only faltered when he has tried to reverse this priority: The only reason he didn't overtake Ford in 1976 was that he delayed criticizing him until Ford's lead was too big to overcome.

There has been a lot of criticism of single-issue groups lately, and it is important to understand why. The single-issue groups have been mostly conservative. The critics have been mostly liberal. We heard very little of this kind of criticism in the 1960s, though the Vietnam and civil rights protests were certainly examples of single-issue politics.

What these critics were recognizing, whether they fully realized it or not, was that conservatism had broken loose and was spilling out over the old party boundaries. Conservatives, at long last, were building independent constituencies and pressure groups to match those of the liberal coalition. The Republican Party was no longer a "reservation" where conservative concerns could be conveniently segregated. Pro-lifers, gun owners, religious groups: each of these now developed its own base. No Republican "Uncle Tom" could quiet them down to suit the liberals who owned the plantation.

Contrary to the myth that single-issue groups were fanatical extremists, each group was able to come to terms rather easily with the others. The pro-life and anti-gun control groups had no conflict with each other that might prevent them from uniting behind one candidate. And by shunning old party channels and affiliations, the single-issue people could attract the bids of both parties.

So conservatives found what liberals had long known: that single-issue politics is only an aspect of coalition politics. We learned to organize, lobby, and bargain just as our opponents had been doing for so many years. In time we began beating them at their own game.

The New Right—a term coined by Kevin Phillips—is basically this new style of non-party conservatism. It speaks to and for disillusioned Republicans, as well as to people who never quite trusted the Republican Party in the first place. Many people of Democratic ancestry and affiliations have felt right at home in the New Right.

But I also mentioned leadership, and no account of the New

Right would be complete without mentioning the people and techniques that made it happen. Among our leaders, at least two—Reverend Jerry Falwell and Phyllis Schlafly—are already household words. Many others, like Paul Weyrich, Terry Dolan, and Howard Phillips, are also well known to the general public. The Heritage Foundation, led by its young president Edwin Feulner, regularly makes headlines, and may become to the Eighties what the Ford Foundation and Brookings Institute were to the last couple of decades. Reed Larson and the National Right to Work Committee are scoring considerable lobbying successes. Connie Marshner of Library Court has had a great impact in pro-family causes. These are only notable examples. In my book *The New Right: We're Ready to Lead* I have listed literally dozens of others.

Most of these people are generalists, which is to say they head organizations devoted to a wide range of conservative causes rather than single issues. Their efforts are building coalitions that will cut across party lines—doing to the Democratic Party what the liberals have long done to the Republicans.

A final element of our success has been our special medium, the one with which I personally have been associated: direct mail.

By now it has become commonplace to say that the New Right depends heavily on direct mail for contributions. But it is even more basic than that. Direct mail has been our basic form of communication. The liberals have had control not only of all three branches of government, but of the major universities, the three major networks, the biggest newspapers, the news weeklies, and Hollywood. You can hardly overstate their influence on public opinion—or the difficulty conservatives have run up against in their attempts to gain a serious hearing.

So our communication has had to begin at the grassroots level —by reaching individuals outside the channels of organized public opinion. Fortunately, or rather providentially, a whole new technology has become available just in time—direct mail, backed by computer science, has allowed us to bypass all the media controlled by our adversaries. We have built an eight- to ten-year lead over the liberals in the use of this technology, and we have most of the sexy issues right now to boot.

As a result, we have become as independent of the mass media as we are of the political parties. The old roles are reversed. Today they are coming to us. We have our own agenda, our own network.

We are making things happen through our own institutions. And for the first time in memory, the liberals and moderates are being forced to adjust to conservatives, rather than vice versa.

Even the liberals have realized deep in their hearts that America was never made up of 200 million liberals. Even at the peak of their power the liberals sometimes gave signs of worrying that they might face a massive uprising on the right. There has always been a market for conservatism, but it has usually gone untapped.

For years liberalism made war on private property, private initiative, private education, public morality, religion, and finally human life itself. Beginning with high taxes and ending with abortion, it violated the deepest aspirations and convictions of millions of Americans. Consider the liberal record in the areas of family life, crime, pornography, national defense, Communist subversion, government waste, inflation, the use of taxation for socialist redistribution, the use of the IRS to harass private religious schools. I believe our descendants will rub their eyes when they see how long and how far liberalism got away with immoral, destructive, and downright unpopular policies.

But why did it happen? Because despite the deep conservatism of the American people, there was no political vehicle for change. The Republican Party could have made tremendous capital out of the public's disgust, but was unwilling or unable to do so until the New Right showed the way.

Today the Republicans are disavowing any debt to the New Right and even denying that the New Right packs any significant political wallop. They are rapidly becoming a conservative party, while letting on that it was their own idea. But it wasn't. The real conservative leadership in this country has come from the New Right.

The proof is in the history of the last sixteen years. After Barry Goldwater's betrayal and defeat, the Republican Party was quick to learn the "lesson" of 1964, and slow to unlearn it. That "lesson" was that no conservative candidate could win a national election. The special circumstances of 1964 were ignored. But as William Rusher has recently observed, it is clear in retrospect that 1964 marked the beginning of a conservative upsurge, not the end of a conservative decline.

As early as the 1966 off-year elections, the country's second thoughts about the Great Society were becoming apparent. But in

1968 only George Wallace, who was himself no true conservative, saw and capitalized on conservative sentiment in the country. That sentiment was even stronger by 1972, when George McGovern, candidate of the majority party, got less than two-fifths of the popular vote. Even Jimmy Carter masqueraded as a conservative in 1976 when he beat out a field of liberal rivals for the Democratic nomination.

Throughout these years, the Republican establishment was too timid to make a strong conservative appeal. Once in a while it might do so for fund-raising purposes, as when it sent out a direct-mail appeal signed by Ronald Reagan denouncing the Panama Canal treaties—but even then, many Senate Republicans joined the Democrats in voting for ratification!

We should give Republicans some credit for discovering conservatism in 1980. But the Democrats are beginning to discover it too. The reason in both cases is simple: Conservatism is now bigger than either party. And the reason for that is the New Right, the real base of effective conservatism in the United States.

That's what I mean by leadership. For a while we in the New Right thought the country needed a third party. As I have said, we came to see that this was wrong. Under a two-party system, the parties don't really lead; they follow. Their business is not to form coalitions, as in Europe, within which they can keep their own shape and identity. In America their business is to build majorities, which means, very often, putting principles on a back burner.

So genuine principles have to find institutional support *outside* the parties in order to *influence* the parties. As long as only the liberals did this, they kept gaining relentlessly. The lack of real popular support didn't matter. A well-organized minority can often defeat an unorganized majority. In the words of William James, "A small force, if it never lets up, will accumulate effects more considerable than those of much greater forces if these work inconsistently."

But as soon as conservatives developed their own structures to match the liberals', it was no contest. James's words apply with special truth to organized minorities with genuine majority support. It is my hope that in America you will never find more people who want to kill unborn babies than want to save them.

Of course all sorts of things can pass if there is no opposition. As long as abortion is described in the media as "terminating a pregnancy" or "a woman's right to control her own body," it can hypnotize people into thinking it sounds reasonable. But the minute someone uses the blunt word "kill," the pro-abortionists' spell is broken and they are on the run. As long as socialism is described as "social justice," people will tamely let the government reach into their pockets. But when they hear the process of fleecing taxpayers for the sake of special interests described as "organized plunder," they will see it all in a different light.

Of course you have to make sure they hear the truth. The phrase "organized plunder" isn't mine. It was used by Frederic Bastiat in France over a century ago, and to this day most people haven't heard it. We don't need new ideas nearly as much as we need new techniques to spread tried and true ideas.

Politics used to be a pretty tame affair, with both parties representing fairly settled regions and interests. But in today's turbulent world, it has become much more a contest of ideologies and of publicity. If you lack access to a sophisticated communications system, you can forget about having any political influence.

The Left has used the media very effectively. Spreading leftist propaganda is called "consciousness-raising." But the Left's market was always limited, and by the mid-1970's they had pretty much shot their bolt. They still enjoy favor in the mass media, but not as much as they used to. And today their efforts are aimed at containing their losses rather than enlisting new recruits.

In developing its own media, the New Right has also won increasing attention and respect from the established press and networks, where hysterical attacks are slowly giving way to objective reporting. You still hear occasional talk of "hit lists," but basically, the major media are coming to see that the New Right is only working within the democratic process—albeit in new and often inventive ways.

In the 1960s the New Left emerged and proliferated into a mass movement with heavy support from the universities and the liberal media. By the 1970s many of the young radicals of the previous decade had settled into institutions like the left-wing Institute for Policy Studies, where they have influenced American foreign policy out of all proportion to their numbers.

We in the New Right hope to reverse this history in the 1980s. During the latest decade we have organized and found our "sea legs." During the next one we hope not only to help swing elections, but to guide public policy back into alignment with the wishes and interest of the American people.

Whether we succeed or not, we have already achieved a great deal. Leadership is like nuclear power; once you split that first atom, a chain reaction develops. The future will record that America's conservative renaissance began with a modest group of men and women known in their days as the New Right.

Jeffrey Hart

THE INTELLIGENT WOMAN'S GUIDE TO A MODERN AMERICAN CONSERVATISM

Today's reactionaries call themselves progressives and revolution-aries. No amount of hype can change their true nature, as Professor Hart, senior editor of National Review *and a Professor of English at Dartmouth College, points out.*

A conservatism that cannot face the facts of the machine and mass production, and its consequences in government and politics, is foredoomed to futility and petulance. A conservatism that allows for them has an eleventh-hour chance of rallying what is sound in the West.

—Whitaker Chambers (1954)

INTELLIGENT WOMAN: Young man, I find your title offensive, indeed downright sexist.

YOUNG MAN: I do not apologize, and new words like "sexist" are not used around here. My title, of course, alludes to a famous tract by George Bernard Shaw called "The Intelligent Woman's Guide to Socialism." The title is a sort of joke.

IW: But why do you want to tell this joke?

YM: Because we're going to run the whole socialist scenario backwards. We're going to reverse it right across the board.

IW: I gather that all this has to do with "conservatism"—that's in your title. But what about the words "modern" and "American."

YM: Those are key words.

IW: I'm not sure I understand quite why.

YM: Well, despite its recent victories, the conservative cause has been creating unnecessary difficulties for itself. Like everyone else, I draw on my own experience, and that is a professor of English at Dartmouth, a senior editor of *National Review,* and a conservative

37

activist. The fact is, a lot of my students are not sold on conservatism.

IW: Why?

YM: There's a short answer. They think conservatives are preppies who are against sex.

IW: Well, is there any basis for that opinion?

YM: Unfortunately, there is. In some visible cases, the main content of "conservatism" seems to be a refusal of experience. We have more than our share of young fogies. I could name some names, but what the hell. In my view, young-fogie American conservatives and American Catholics generally, place an altogether disproportionate emphasis on sex and sex-related moral questions. They all ought to remember where Dante placed his illicit lovers, Paolo and Francesca—in the outermost and most comfortable precincts of Hell. And Dante was orthodox. Had Paolo and Francesca confessed, they, like all the other illicit lovers, would have gone to the Purgatorio, and listened to the sweet music, and loved God too. Modern conservatives and Catholics too ought to remember what one might call the "proportions" of orthodoxy.

IW: Could you define a conservatism that would have wide appeal, that would get us away from the young fogies?

YM: I would certainly like to try. It seems to me that a modern American conservatism can command an overwhelming majority, both political and cultural, if it just crystallizes the correct identity. One of our problems has been with the way the idea of tradition has been articulated within American conservatism.

IW: Why has that been a problem?

YM: Because the American tradition is different from the European tradition, different from the British idea, or the French or the Spanish idea. To put it in a nutshell, Americans by and large think of themselves as optimistic and modern. They welcome new possibilities. They like to try things out. They are not hostile to science and technology. The European sense of tradition is more restrictive, more closed. It grows out of small, crowded towns, out of a long past whose lessons tend to be tragic.

IW: Do you mean that America and Europe are totally different?

YM: By no means. They are intertwined historically. But America's sense of itself is different. The emphases are different. An American in Europe cannot avoid a generalized sense of claustrophobia. Columbus didn't discover Europe. Gertrude Stein said many profound things, but one of her profoundest was her observation that America is the oldest country in the world because it was the *first* modern country. She meant that America, as the first nation to enter "modern" history, was therefore older than the other nations because they were born into modernity later, and usually incompletely.

IW: What has this got to do with conservatism?

YM: It has everything to do with modern American conservatism. The average American is a modernist in his bones. Americans believe in possibility, in "making it new," as Ezra Pound once urged. If conservatism is to be truly American, it must embrace that sense of possibility. We like to say that conservatism is the politics of reality. Well, that is the cultural reality. A truly popular American conservatism must be modern, because most Americans are modern. They do not live on ducal estates. They don't even go to Groton. And because they are modernizers they are also anti-communists.

IW: It seems to me that you've got something there. But why do other conservatives have trouble with such ideas?

YM: For both historical and ideological reasons. Some conservatives appear to confuse Victorian morality with the Western tradition, and even with Christianity. Would you believe, a prominent conservative recently, in all seriousness, tried to blame the great slaughters of the twentieth century—Hitler's, Stalin's, Mao's—on the expansion of freedom during the nineteenth century?

IW: Why?

YM: Evidently the idea of freedom gives him the willies, and he wants to badmouth it. But I would like to make a historical point here that seems to me important. Historically, the middle class was the great modernizing class. It burst through the feudal barriers and created capitalism. But it did not fully understand the relationship of capitalism to modernity. Capitalism freed the individual from the older ties to station and place. It created the city. But the older bourgeoisie tended to resist modernity—everywhere except in the economy and in science. Where the human spirit was concerned, the older middle class behaved like a lot of commissars. They banned *Sister Carrie*. They banned *Ulysses*. The very inventors of the modern took refuge in stuffiness. This represented a failure of analysis, a failure of intelligence.

Too many conservatives today are merely the intellectual descendants of that older bourgeoisie. They handle the idea of tradition as if it were something in the Smithsonian Institution, rather than a living and developing thing. They have not read their Newman and their Eliot. Tradition, viewed as an accumulation of human experience, is a very important thing. But it is not a set of static axioms. The tricky thing is to decide what weight to give to tradition when making a decision concerning a concrete situation —and it's tricky because the concrete situations are constantly changing. Tradition informs the understanding under concrete circumstances. It is not a set of axioms. It is not a cookbook.

IW: I would like to return to that later. But I am interested in your idea of the "modern," and of America as a "modern" nation. I'm not sure that I understand what that means, or how it applies politically. Do you mean that everything that has happened recently is somehow better than what happened earlier?

YM: By no means. The idea of the modern is very clear. It has hard edges. It is a particular political and cultural idea.

IW: I notice that in your writings you frequently use the word "modern." You refer to *The Waste Land* as a "modern" poem, even though it came out in 1922. And you have said that books of poems that were published this year are not modern. Frankly, this makes as little sense to me as birdsong. I'm all screwed up.

YM: First of all, the term "modern" as I've been using it is not a chronological word. Picasso's *Les Demoiselles d'Avignon,* though painted in 1907, is a work of modern art. Most of the work hanging in the galleries on 57th Street is not.

IW: Then the term "modern" has nothing whatever to do with chronology.

YM: Not exactly. It's more complicated than that. Where art and literature are concerned, the modern comes forward around 1895, though it has relatively distant roots in such works as Diderot's *Rameau's Nephew.* The modern mode dominates high culture from 1895 until around 1930, then recedes a bit; but modern works continue to be created until today.

IW: Then how am I to recognize a modern work? It all seems very mysterious.

YM: Not really. Modern works do not look like anything done before, usually. *Les Demoiselles d'Avignon* does not look like previous paintings. *The Waste Land* does not look like any previous poem, or, for that matter, any important subsequent one. In prose fiction this sense of difference is less dramatic, since a line of prose goes all the way over to the margin. But when you get *into* a modernist work such as *Heart of Darkness, The Sun Also Rises,* or *The Trial* you sense immediately the radical break with the past.

IW: Why is the break with the past so important to modern art?

YM: Again, the matter is complicated. First of all, the break has to do with the fact that modern art is centrally about *freedom.* The modern artist is concerned to assert his freedom, and that involves an adversary relationship to past conventions. To an unprecedented degree, a modern work creates its own conventions and does not take them over from previous works.

IW: But Conrad wrote in fairly normal prose, didn't he? Why is *Heart of Darkness* a work of modern art?

YM: Excellent question. Because of its complex and ambivalent attitude toward what might be called ordinary civilization and ordinary experience. Civilization in *Heart of Darkness* has a dead aspect. It is touched by the lie. It lacks authenticity. Mr. Kurtz, though guilty of unspeakable crimes, precisely does not lack authenticity. He dies, in Eliot's phrase, with "direct eyes." Marlow himself recognizes his own inferiority to Kurtz. Kurtz is the tragic hero—but hero nevertheless—of Conrad's story. Like Gatsby, Kurtz is worth the whole damn bunch of them.

IW: Wait a minute. Kurtz is an immoral man, and he goes savage. How can he be a hero?

YM: Conrad wants to stand Rousseau on his head. He gives us not a Noble Savage but a Savage Savage—and he sees the power of that idea. Around the same time, Picasso was getting interested in African art, you will remember.

IW: What other things are the modern artists interested in?

YM: Their rejection of past conventions is connected with their desire for intensity of emotion. You will notice that modern art is constantly changing. Joyce writes successively different books. Eliot's poetic forms constantly change. Hemingway does not write the same kind of novel twice. Picasso constantly reinvents himself. So does Stravinsky. So does Pound.

IW: I think I begin to see. But why did this unusual kind of art emerge around the end of the nineteenth century?

YM: This is a fascinating thing historically. The bourgeoisie was the first "modern" class. It developed technology as the dominant means of production. It shifted the social and economic focus from the countryside to the city. It tended to liberate the individual from ties of neighborhood and family. Rousseau, Pip, Julien Sorel, Gatsby and many others represent this bourgeois ability to invent the self as a social artifact. With the advent of the bourgeois, the sense of the "given" becomes progressively weaker, or the willed and created progressively stronger. The fact that official bourgeois culture took so long to recognize its modernist offspring is, well, one of the ironies of cultural history. Capitalism could well say with Ezra Pound, *Make It New.*

IW: So modern art is hostile to the past.

YM: Again, the matter is complicated. It would be more accurate to say that modern art is hostile to the conservative and static side of the bourgeois ethos. *The Waste Land* is a kind of echo-chamber of past literature. Eliot writes with "the mind of Europe, from Homer to the present," in his bones. In one aspect, *The Waste Land* is the most modern of poems, but it goes all the way back to the great myths, and it ends with a line of Sanskrit. Joyce's *Ulysses* and Pound's *Cantos* are both based on Homer. Matisse and Picasso constantly allude to the great masters. The point, however, is not that they imitate the past, but that they work out their own relationship to it and use it.

IW: We have been talking mostly about art. But does this art have any wider significance?

YM: Certainly. If you examine modern experience, that is, contemporary experience, closely you will see that it is *modern* in the sense in which I have been using the word in connection with art.

IW: Really?

YM: Yes. In a little while, I will ask you to have dinner with me. I will leave it up to you whether we go to a French, Greek, Chinese, or American restaurant. In the past, if you were in France, you ate French food. If you were in China, you ate Chinese food. But we are freer now than ever before in this and other respects. You can live in a Tudor house if you want to. A person in Tudor England had no other choice. Freedom implies an eclectic style.

IW: And much modern art is eclectic. *The Cantos, The Waste Land* . . .

YM: You're beginning to get the point, and we are going to get along very well together. If you look at other areas of life, you will see immediately that freedom advances inexorably. People can choose to have children or not to have them. The advance of technology

'rth of Louise Brown, and it will certainly press further.
, is a little frightening.

...d sometimes painful. The individual is also more isolated
...an in the past. His social experience is discontinuous in an unprecedented way. When you walk down a city street you see hundreds of people and events that you will never see again. Your
normal relations with countless people are usually "role specific,"
as the sociologists put it. That is the elevator man. He might also
be an expert lepidopterist, but you don't know about it. Over there
is the news dealer. We tend not to know people in their full existence. In an unprecedented way, our normal experience tends to be
discontinuous. It involves juxtaposition, rather than the older
"narrative" form of experience. In addition, social relationships
are changing in sudden and, inevitably, disconcerting ways.
Women, for example, find their options expanding. Some of them
are marrying later, maybe not at all. They are making the decision
to have children, or not to have them. Given this novel circumstance, the rules are of course changing, whether we like it or not.

IW: I'm not surprised that people find modernity uncomfortable.

YM: Certainly. The older bourgeoisie resisted it, as I've said. And
we constantly face reactionary attempts to return to a less in-
dividualistic and free existence. From this standpoint, Marxism
and all forms of socialism and communism are reactionary. Marx's
attack on capitalism is anti-modern. Mao tried to get back to a form
of the peasant commune. Of course, Marx, who also talked of "the
idiocy of rural life," had a modern urban sensibility, which con-
tradicted his doctrine. He was screwed up.

IW: So you think that the modern in aesthetics is the representative
form for our experience?

YM: There's no doubt about it. Freedom will advance unless it is
forcibly repressed. Naturally, the Soviets hate all forms of modern
art. They know what it means, and they fear it. They much prefer
John Steinbeck, Erskine Caldwell, or their own boy-meets-tractor.

IW: This is a startling idea. The Soviet Union claims to be a revolutionary society.

YM: All the great tyrannies of the twentieth century are mon-
strously reactionary. They are rear-guard attempts to hold back
the universal human desire for concrete freedoms. Naturally they
suppress modern art. They are puritanical about sex. From Hitler
and Stalin through Mao and the Ayatollah they have been desper-

ate attempts to re-establish a lost community. Society in the form of traditional culture is communal. It subordinates the individual, often ruthlessly, to the group. Its economy is static, closely tied to the vicissitudes and cycles of nature. Such a society lives by standards handed down through countless generations, sometimes codified in some holy book, sometimes merely customary. Social arrangements are usually hierarchical, with authority lodged in some kind of priest or holy man. Such a society is held together by powerful emotions, familial, communal, and religious; and such a society is almost necessarily xenophobic.

IW: I can see the power of such a society. But to tell the truth, I would hate to live in one.

YM: Historically, mankind has said the same thing. It always chooses freedom. Modernity offers a lethal challenge to a restrictive kind of society. The modernizing impulse places a very high value on the individual. Its economy is not static, but expansive. The medieval schoolmen, longing for stasis, considered the taking of interest unnatural. They were absolutely correct. An economy of possibility tends to liberate mankind from the natural cycle. From the taking of interest to walking on the moon is a shorter step than you may realize. From this perspective, a man like Mao Tsetung was one of history's great reactionaries. His "revolution" used the peasants against the hated city. Seizing absolute power, Mao tried to make China into a vast egalitarian peasant commune. Hitler was a curious amalgam of tradition and modern technology. His emotions were anti-individualistic, but he required a modern technology. In Iran, the Ayatollah represents a reactionary counter-revolution against a modernizing Shah. In the West, and the point should be underlined, Marxism, insofar as it has any appeal, exercises that appeal among the most backward economic and cultural groups, to whom it holds out the illusory hope of restoring a lost "community." Beyond that, Marxism appeals to a fringe of intellectuals who are attracted to the idea that they would enjoy power and status in the hierarchy of a new feudal, that is Marxist, state. A conservatism that is both modern and American understands all of that. It is a conservatism that would have very wide appeal, since it is coherent.

IW: I suppose the philosophers have written about this.

YM: Indeed they have. But these philosophers of course are not widely read, and even less widely understood. You might try

Nietzsche and Hegel. In his *Philosophy of History,* Hegel viewed all of human history as advancing toward freedom. Nietzsche projected modes of living under conditions of freedom, and this he saw requires the constant invention of the self. As Wordsworth said, "By our own spirits are we deified."

IW: In these philosophers, philosophy tends to dissolve back into, or fuse with, art. It becomes the "act of creativity."

YM: You have hit the nail squarely on the head. As Yeats asked in that great Nietzschean line, "How can we know the dancer from the dance?"

IW: I feel that I am sailing on uncharted waters.

YM: That is the modernist feeling.

IW: But what does modernism say about morality? About limits?

YM: Tradition has plenty to say about them—tradition correctly understood, that is.

IW: You said earlier that tradition is not a set of axioms. I think I can rebut that assertion.

YM: Really?

IW: What about the Ten Commandments?

YM: I would like to propose to you a somewhat surprising modernizer, none other than St. Paul. He is looked upon by many people as a pretty sour old rabbi, but he cut to the heart of the matter. He extracted the essence of Christ's teaching, or, to put it another way, he explicated the First Commandment as the controlling one and defined God as love. "Though I speak with the tongues of men and of angels, and have no charity, I am become as sounding brass or a tinkling cymbal." It is important to stress that in the decisive situations Christ did not enunciate axioms, he told stories, dealt with concrete circumstances.

IW: That all sounds very, well, *permissive* to me. You just do what you want.

YM: Not if you think about it. Making decisions in actual situations under the absolute imperative of love is hardly *permissive*.

IW: I see your point. But what is so different about modernism? Is there really something new about it, a distinctive new teaching?

YM: Not really new. I would call it a new emphasis—but a degree of emphasis that may make it qualitatively new. It is the central point of *Heart of Darkness,* or *The Waste Land,* or Joyce's "The Dead," or Tolstoy's *The Death of Ivan Ilyich*. It is something that everyone recognizes, in his or her own modern experience. Yet, as one looks at the modernist movement as a whole, it does propose a primary sin in its moral agenda.

IW: But what is that teaching?

YM: It teaches that there is a great sin: *the unlived life.* In Dante's line, "the great refusal." Almost all of modern art and literature tells the same moral story. It is the story, as Lionel Trilling put it, of "the moment to be snatched, the crucial choice to be made, and if it's made on the wrong [the safe] side, the loss of human quality, so that instead of a man we have a Success and instead of two lovers a Statue and a Bust in the public square." In however dim or vulgarized a way, that perception is now shared by millions. That is why the murder of John Lennon was such a moment of mass poignancy. Lennon's was not an unlived life.

IW: And what has this got to do with a modern American conservatism?

YM: Conservatives must comport themselves as if they understood all of that. The late George Apley passed away a long time ago.

IW: This form of conservatism sounds really interesting.

YM: We must learn to live amidst discontinuities, whose discontinuousness is transcended only by love. Art has entirely separated itself from morality, even from "content" as traditionally understood. The Newtonian universe is gone. The universe is a mathematical equation. The holistic world view expressed in natural law is fading; at the very least, the "natural law" will have to be reformulated. It is simply a fact that as most people live their lives under modern circumstances, sex is not very closely connected with reproduction. Modernity is a differentiating process, and a viable natural law will have to take that into account.

IW: Oh wow!

YM: I'm going to take you to a Polynesian restaurant for dinner.

Paul M. Weyrich

BLUE COLLAR OR BLUE BLOOD? The New Right Compared with The Old Right

One of the most powerful and vigorous political voices of the New Right, Paul Weyrich is among the few people I have heard whose practical statements are impressive in Washington but can be understood without translation in South Boston or West Virginia. Mr. Weyrich is Director of the Committee for the Survival of a Free Congress in Washington, D.C. How the Washington New Right developed and what it is trying to do on Capitol Hill is explained here with the clarity of a practitioner.

The phrase "New Right" was first used in 1975 by Kevin Phillips in a headline discussing the "Coors/Richard Viguerie/New Right Complex." The phrase was used to distinguish the coalition thus indicated from the network of older groups acting in the name of conservatism. From Phillips, the national media picked up the term, and introduced it into common parlance. One virtue of common parlance is that it can speak meaningfully of an entity which in scholarly parlance would be difficult to define. So it is with the phrase "New Right." A political observer could look at, for example, the Conservative Caucus, and say with promptness and accuracy that it is a "new right" group. Similarly, the observer could look at a well-known conservative journal, pronounce it "old right," and be equally correct. The observer might not fully understand why his nomenclature is accurate. It is the purpose of this essay to elucidate some of the points of distinction between the two political groups, which, let it be said at the outset, are not opponents in any important context.

The New Right differs from the Old in its political origins, its philosophical/political motivations, its strategic/tactical operations, and its self-conscious goals. The New Right shares with the Old a common adherence to general conservative principles; it differs, however, in articulation of those principles, and in the emphasis given them in the respective politics.

In speaking of origins of a movement, one is speaking of people. It is difficult to separate politics from the influence of social class and education, particularly in America. Prior to the 1970s conservatism tended very much to be a phenomenon of the upper classes, of the genteelly educated. That made for a highly intellectual strain, of which William Buckley's *National Review* is quintessential. Buckley has acknowledged that most of the *NR* circle had been brought up on James Burnham's *Suicide of the West* doctrine —a pessimistic, almost Spenglerian point of view—and that the possibility of arresting the decline of the West was not part of their consciousness at all. Despair, in varying degrees and countenances, was the logical conclusion. In 1978, William Buckley admitted to me that where political action was concerned, *National Review* had been guilty of the theological sin of otherworldliness: the belief that, as long as one's own life was free of sin, one needn't worry about the affairs of this world.

The Old Right was strong on intellectualism. This is worthy in itself, but unfortunately that was as far as it went. In criticizing proposed programs like the Great Society schemes, the Old Right could make its objections soundly and completely, in scholarly publications. The only problem was that it was not speaking in the language of the ordinary man. The language was incomprehensible, and what is incomprehensible is politically irrelevant. We need intellectual discussions, and studies, and experts who know their field through and through, no matter what it is. I believe in truth, and that we should in human affairs get as close to it as human nature will allow. But we also need someone to translate the significant points and the ramifications, if we are to pursue truth in political life.

The intellectualization of conservatism was particularly unfortunate because it completely lost touch with the other branch of the Old Right: working class anti-Communism. Call it knee-jerk, if you will; in truth a debt to Senator Joseph McCarthy must be acknowledged for his role in its political awakening. McCarthy had an enormous following throughout the nation. The tragedy was that that following was never made politically cohesive. When McCarthy died, that was it. Those people never got further into politics. And, to this day, the working class anti-Communist element has not been activated, due to lack of leadership.

I must fault Senator Barry Goldwater for that lack of leadership. Goldwater tried, he fought the good fight. He was vilified as was no other political figure in history. Certainly I do not want to diminish the merits of all that. Despite the vilification, he energized 27 million voters. But then—after the election—he left those 27 million hanging there. He disappeared from public view until he was re-elected to the Senate, as a personal vindication, but not as a leader. What could have been the beginning of a national movement of tremendous significance was nothing without a leader.

The intellectuals behind Goldwater, the Bill Buckleys and Brent Bozells, presented Goldwater as a standard-bearer of truth, a philosopher-politician. That was not the man. Fundamentally, Goldwater is a straight-shooting Westerner who wants to get the government onto a more sensible path. That's what he was in 1964. But those of us who were galvanized by that campaign expected him to be more; the people he drew to his cause then waited for him, or someone else, to continue to lead them. It didn't happen. Because it didn't happen the Right lost a generation of political achievement, of leadership, and of educating the nation.

The seeds of the contemporary New Right were sown by the Goldwater campaign. Most of us can, in our personal histories, mark that campaign as the beginning of the motivation that has never left us. Even if we did nothing but wear a Goldwater button, or attend a rally—and some of the New Right are so young   is all they did—it made a mark, and had an impact. To a limited extent, the organization of Young Americans for Freedom kept in touch with the young people who had been impressed by Goldwater, and kept them politically viable. *Triumph* magazine, which was founded shortly after 1964 by Brent Bozell, Goldwater's chief speechwriter, deserves mention for keeping the Catholic element politically together because it maintained some thread of continuity between the Catholics who had been Goldwater supporters and current politics. The previously existing Young Republicans became a battleground and a training ground for some of the young people who had been galvanized by Goldwater. But the YRs, like the larger party, by and large did not meet the standards of conservatism that Goldwater had set. For sure, the Republican Party had no idea of what it had launched, and reacted to Goldwater's defeat by being tremendously embarrassed, rather than by helping launch a movement.

I said earlier that the Old Right tended to be intellectual and upper class. It is as accurate a generalization that the New Right tends to be middle class, blue-collar and ethnic in its origins. Eighteenth century British economic theory did not pertain very clearly to a German workingman's family in the 1950s. Though the upper classes had more intellectual expertise, they tended to become deficient in something that was strong in the working middle classes: values. In blue-collar areas, especially among the first and second generation ethnics, be they Russian Jews or German Catholics, tradition was as real a part of life as paying taxes, and old world culture as close to home. Well-bred, well-heeled youth allowed right and wrong to become blurred, and tradition to become a romantic decoration. Respect among working people was a consciously instilled value, the cornerstone of everything else—respect for father and mother and grandparents, for priest or rabbi, for the institutions of society: teachers, police, law, government. Respect engenders discipline, and hard work was the means to achieve desired goals.

In the 1960s there was among ethnic Catholics a rush of enthusiasm to share in the Kennedy liberalism. President Kennedy was a Catholic, a Democrat, and was therefore loved as an adopted "favorite son" by most ethnics. By the 1970s, though, we were seeing a large-scale end to this honeymoon, as the bitter fruit of liberalism became known: the fostering and propagating of policies and values that were increasingly destructive to society, policies which are anti-family, anti-religion, and devoid of respect for traditional values. Few of the leaders of today's New Right, despite their often "ethnic" backgrounds, were ever on the liberal bandwagon. This fact, I suspect, had to do with farsightedness, or perhaps with history properly studied. Many of the Catholic New Right activists have a further element in common: Their parents were often faithful listeners to the radio broadcasts through the 1930s and 40s of Father Charles Coughlin, the noted political commentator.

Thus, the blue-collar, middle class origins of the New Right help explain its philosophical motivations. The New Right differs from the Old in its value-orientation, which translates to the "social issues" in the current political jargon. The Old Right gives a primacy to laissez-faire economics. To be sure, we of the New Right believe strongly in free enterprise and individual initiative, and we oppose the expansion of government interference with individual lives. However, the New Right also believes that the individual as an individual does have personal responsibility to society and that each individual has intrinsic moral worth. The Old Right's "live and let live" idea is not reflective of Christian social teachings. A common assumption of New Right activists is that government should support certain moral truths.

Having experienced life in working class America, the New Right leadership realizes that people have come to expect certain things of their government, and that it is possible to give those things to the people without destroying the free enterprise system. Christian social doctrine teaches that, just as individuals have a certain responsibility to individuals, so does government. We reject the total indifference advocated by libertarians, just as we reject the extremes advocated by liberals. I would, for instance, want to see government—through churches and private institutions—ensure care for the helpless. I want to see government by law protect the helpless, be they unborn or senile, against the self-interest of others.

Culturally destructive government policies—racial hiring quotas and busing come to mind as examples—are to the New Right more immediately important in the realm of action, since the damage they can do is enormous and practically irremediable. Given a choice between focusing attention and effort on the defeat of a pork barrel public works bill, and focusing effort on the defeat of an abortion funding bill, the New Right would work to defeat the abortion bill.

Through New Right efforts the Hyde Amendment was successfully preserved through the 95th Congress, something which had not been possible in the 94th Congress when the measure had first been introduced. What caused the difference? This first New Right success was a combination of the distinguishing factors I have described previously between Old and New Right. First, we did not see ourselves as a defensive force in a crumbling society. We expected to win, and we developed a strategy to win.

I came to Washington in 1966, hoping to be a support staffer to a conservative leader. The Senator for whom I worked was a fine conservative of the Old Right school of strategy and tactics. What were the characteristics of that school?

First, there was an actual absence of strategic thinking, by which I mean large-scale manner, long-range planning. On small matters, tactics, there was some activity, but even that was very limited. Conservative Senators on Capitol Hill did not understand or believe in organization. In part, I think this was due to their rugged anti-collectivist philosophy; in part it was also probably due to the lack of a leader around whom they could organize. Their activities were totally reactive. They didn't take the initiative to go out and make an issue, and then let the liberals start talking about *their* issue. Of course, to do that sort of thing pretty much requires some supportive structures. The liberals had their Members of Congress for Peace through Law, their Institute for Policy Studies, their Brookings Institute, their Democratic Study Group. Conservatives had nothing comparable, and prior to the late 1960s did not even have their share of aggressive staff personnel, which the liberals had been acquiring for a decade.

In working with these Senators, I noticed a reluctance to carry matters to their logical conclusion, a personal reluctance to push a point to its last step, an unwillingness, figuratively speaking, to go for the jugular. Part of this was a reluctance to take risks. A lot of this reticence was due to the Old Right's enormous fear of the media. I'll talk more about that later, because I think it's very critical.

For all these reasons, the Old Right was not taken seriously as a political force in Washington. To some degree that was the result of a self-fulfilling prophecy, since these conservatives viewed themselves as the last, futile fingers in the dike of rampaging liberalism. I emphasize the word futile. They had resigned themselves to the inevitable defeat of their principles. They were intending to go down gracefully, preserving the status quo of the nation a little longer, prolonging the death agonies of the American republic, lessening the pain of disintegration of American society.

That was how they viewed themselves. I know that because I had conversations with them, and upon occasion tried to initiate some action, tried to get them to have a more positive approach to things. And I was not successful.

During the height of the anti-Vietnam activism, the Left was bringing up its issues, such as the various end-the-war amendments, time and time and time again. They were always defeated, but by smaller and smaller margins each time. Our people were able to observe the other side practicing this routine, but did not emulate it. Our Senators would bring their issue up for a vote. They would have marshaled their colleagues for a single loss, and that would be the end of it. Six months or a year or two years later if someone suggested, "Why don't we try this?" the decisive answer would be, "Oh no, we tried that a year ago and it didn't work." Period. End of discussion. Here is what I mean by a lack of strategy resulting from a sense of resignation to Fate.

Let me tell you an interesting story, of the one conservative victory our side had during this Old Right era. This was when we managed to stop President Lyndon Johnson from naming Abe Fortas as Chief Justice. It was actually a double victory, because if Fortas had become chief justice, LBJ had a liberal Texas judge lined up to appoint to the Supreme Court. As it turned out, Justice Douglas did not step down, so Fortas was not named Chief Justice. The irony is that this whole effort was engineered by Senator Robert Griffin of Michigan, a moderate Republican, not a staunch conservative. Griffin had gotten 27 Senators to sign a pledge to oppose Fortas's nomination. When the going got tough, just before Johnson gave in under the pressure, a number of Old Right Senators wanted to cave in and give up fighting. It took Griffin to hold them in line. That's what I mean about not being willing to carry things to their logical conclusion. It reminds me of the old joke that the Republican Party is so good at snatching defeat from the jaws of victory. It was a case of that almost happening. (Of course, the Left got its revenge. When Richard Nixon was President, the embittered Senate refused to consent to the nominations of Carswell and Haynesworth in direct retaliation for the blockage of Fortas.)

I think a lot of the Old Right reluctance to engage in visible activity was motivated by a genuine fear of the media. These were people who had been burned, and burned badly, in the McCarthy era. As a result, they did everything in secret. If they had a regular meeting at the same time each week, and a reporter found out about it, they would cancel the meeting. We of the New Right have a far different attitude toward the media. We invite them to our meetings if they want to come. The Old Right Senators did not understand that you can get fair coverage if you handle the reporters fairly. The media want and need access to the newsmakers. They want to feel they can ask you about something. If a Senator is cold and unfriendly to a reporter, the reporter will know it, and is likely to reciprocate.

Also, I think the Old Right did not know how to do and say things in an interesting way. When I was a news reporter on the City Hall beat in Milwaukee, I didn't want to give coverage all the time to the liberals. But they were the ones who were holding press conferences, who were saying quotable things, who were voicing opinions that were newsworthy. So I had to cover them. The Old Right, whether intentionally or not I can't be sure, did not do things that were newsworthy. Of course, there was not much intrinsic news value to preserving the status quo. Innovation is always more interesting, which was a natural advantage for the Left. The Old Right did not understand anything at all about mass psychology, since they came from a different, pre-television era. It never did much good to try to persuade them to be dramatic, to think big. There was also a barrier to using technology. The New Right recognizes that technology, like the media, is morally neutral and exists to be taken advantage of by anybody. The Old Right seemed to have had the idea that because the Left had exploited the media they could not exploit it themselves without danger of moral corruption. It was a confusion of ideology with an application of technology.

The difference in coverage given the Old Right and the New Right is considerable. In quantity, first of all—media coverage of the Old Right was scarce as hen's teeth. We get a lot of it. For instance, on the day President Jimmy Carter announced he was selling out Taiwan, right away on the AP wire, left-wing Senator Alan Cranston had 500 words' worth of coverage, applauding this decisive move and so forth, as was only to be expected. But also . . . Representative Philip Crane had 500 words on AP! Equal coverage, you could say. That's evidence of progress. *The Washington Post* in its front page story mentioned the Committee for a Free China, the New Right organization long dedicated to preserving Taiwan's freedom. That's evidence of progress, too.

In 1978, the New Right set up a Truth Squad, aimed at exposing fallacies behind the Panama Canal Treaties. We held press conferences wherever we went, and welcomed inquiry from reporters on any subject. One of the questions that reporters will always ask is, "How are you funded?" Now, the Old Right, even assuming that they undertook or participated in such a venture as the Truth Squad, would have been defensive about that question, and responded with some remark amounting to "It's none of your business." This, naturally, would have been the beginning of a big story for some newsman. Not so with the Truth Squad. In the press kit which we routinely handed out was an enumeration of the organizations contributing financial support to this endeavor. Sure enough, at the very first press conference, that question came up. We were able to say, "Uh, fellas, it's in your press kit." So the question never came up again, in all the trips we made. Five years ago, that question would have been the beginning of a juicy story about right-wing finagling and secrecy. But since we engaged in no secrecy, there was no evasion, and hence no adverse publicity.

Another great advantage of the New Right derives, again, from another of the factors which distinguish our general outlook from that of the Old Right. We are not speaking abstractly of the decline of the West, but concretely about preserving values we know are revered by other middle class Americans.

I think the fact that the New Right does speak the language of the common man helps explain the facility with which we can get coverage when we want it. It is like the analogy of differences between the Roman Catholic and Orthodox theologians. Now, everyone can understand the question of whether you recognize the Pope or not. Things get much more subtle and hard to follow when you start getting into the significance of the epiclesis and *filioque,* and so forth. Ordinary folk can't understand these problems so readily. I'm afraid that conservatives have had more than their share of *filioques* in secular politics. It's a distinction the Left has long understood. For a long time, the measures to force oil companies into vertical and horizontal divestiture were being discussed at high levels, but were not generating much publicity. Then some sharp speechwriter coined the phrase "obscene profits," which Senator Henry Jackson began using. Immediately, that phrase gave a handle to the issue, which gave a boost to the clamor for divestiture. The oil companies cannot get over the impact that polemical phrase had on their life history.

New Right campaigns in 1979 used very emphatic language in establishing their issue positions. Senator Gordon Humphrey of

New Hampshire has been criticized for his "strident right-to-life rhetoric." Maybe it was strident, but it made the point. It was down to earth and simple, and that's what matters in getting the message across. After all, getting one's message across is the whole point of politics.

To me—and I think most other New Right leaders would share this perception—politics is activity in relation to power. To the extent that power in the American system resides in legislative bodies, politics focuses on the election of those legislators. Power is also vested in the executive, i.e., the President; hence the electoral fever every four years. Increasingly, however, power resides in the echelons of the Executive Branch which are not affected by a change of administrations. Both the Right and Left realize this. But only recently has the Right—and that which is generally characterized as the New Right—acted in a manner calculated to directly affect the bureaucratic power structure. "Who will draft IRS regulations?" is as portentous a question today as "Who will be President?" was a century ago. "Who controls the drafting?" is a question that may not even be answerable—regardless of the *de jure* reply.

The Constitution vests the Judiciary with power that was intended, at least to some extent, to be an arbiter of matters assigned to it by the Constitution. The New Right recognizes that the courts are far from immune to the currents of contemporary dispute. In fact, since the establishment of publicly funded legal services programs with a definite advocacy bias, the court process has become directly manipulated by power politics. Because of this advocacy element, the judicial process today is simply not what the Constitution envisioned. The appellate jurisdiction has given the courts a veto power that supersedes legislative will and even executive directions. The abortion decision in 1973 is an example of the courts making the law of the land rather than simply resolving disputes over it.

Power is located in other places today, and a realist recognizes that politics can not ignore the innovations of progress. The Constitution could not have anticipated the electronic media, or the power of the press. The Framers did not expect a national public education system, and certainly did not provide for the nationalized public education system sought by the Left. Yet those institutions have tremendous sway over the thoughts of the millions of citizens who ultimately cast the votes in the electoral aspect of the American political system. Late nineteenth century reformers recognized the power vested in the patronage systems of that era and moved to counter it. The New Right observes that potentially corrupting influence on the governing process is no less today because it comes from a government agency rather than from a Big Boss wardheeler. The control may be more respectable coming from a federal representative than from a ward politician, and he is certainly harder to unseat. But that influence is no less a distortion of constitutional and legislative intent.

When I, and others like Howard Phillips, Ed Feulner and Richard Dingman, came to Capitol Hill, we were looking for a Senator or Congressman to whom we could attach ourselves in a support capacity. We were looking, in other words, for leaders. But we quickly found that there were none. Goldwater had provided some leadership in the early 1960s as had Senator Strom Thurmond and a few others in isolated instances. But by the late 1960s there was no such leader. The Left, I believe, has had Congressional leadership consistently over the past two decades. Men like Senators Birch Bayh and Wayne Morse were politically substantive individuals in and of themselves. To be sure, they had good staff, but the staff could hitch themselves to left-wing stars because they were already there, and doing much of the orchestrating themselves.

Conservatives, by the 1970s, were on the way to forming the organizations necessary to launch and keep afloat a political movement. The Left had the Democratic Study Group in the House of Representatives, an ultra-liberal, member-formed backup operation for left-wing issues, dedicated to cranking out research, thinking up strategy, writing speeches, doing footwork, causing things to happen for the Left in general. There was no comparable conservative operation at all until 1973. Until 1970, conservative members of Congress barely met with each other at all to talk politics and strategy. When Representative Floyd Spence came to Congress on January 1, 1971, he initiated formal meetings among conservative members. By 1973, the Republican Study Committee had been formed; by 1974 the Senate Steering Committee, a comparable body on the Senate side, was in operation.

Once there was a coordinated conservative effort on the Hill, we became sharply aware of how little organized effort there was to help elect specifically conservative Senators and Representatives. So the political action groups began to be formed, the Committee for the Survival of a Free Congress in 1974, the National Conservative Political Action Committee in 1975, and others thereafter. Historically, thus, the New Right started on Capitol Hill. No longer is the Hill the core of New Right operations, however. In further emulation of the Left, we had to begin our own think tanks, our own public interest legal operations, our own grassroots organizations, and even our own lobbying efforts. Common cause is made with "like-minded single-interest groups" whenever possible. The right-to-life issue has what one unsympathetic reporter described as a "symbiotic relationship" with the New Right. Whether they want to or not, right-to-lifers find they have to work with New Right activists, simply because nobody else cares about protecting the unborn.

The right-to-work cause is one which frequently comes into the coalition. Most of our fathers belonged to unions. We are anti-big business. The problem is that big unions turned into part of the problem. The New Right does not believe that unions *per se* are evil, as did the economic purist conservatives of the 1930s; we do not want to abolish unions. We merely recognize that today's big union leadership is unrepresentative of union membership, and, worse, uncaring of membership's concerns. We see that the big union bosses abuse members' hard-earned contributions. When people do not want to be forced to join a union, where else can they turn for help but the National Right to Work Committee? Further, the Right to Work Committee also supports pro-free enterprise measures, and opposes further power grabs by regulatory agencies and big labor.

As circumstances dictate, the single-interest groups organized around anti-busing, tax resistance, defense issues, parents' rights, private school survival, energy selfsufficiency, and other major problems find they are able to make common cause with the New Right, because the New Right is a political force which shares their concerns on these issues. There is nothing underhanded, nothing conspiratorial, nothing sinister about this: It is simply the exercise of practical politics, as predicted by Hamilton, Jay, and Madison in *The Federalist Papers.*

One very interesting and promising development is the broadening of the New Right appeal from strictly Republican lines. In their resigned defeatist attitude, the Old Right had totally written off whole chunks of American life: the Democratic Party, labor unions, most churches, and for that matter, most of the working class. The New Right realizes that the participation of all these groups is necessary to forge a coalition for victory. Conservative influence in the Democratic Party is increasing steadily—some of it planned, some not. The Committee for the Survival of A Free Congress, for example, offered a workshop for conservative Democrats at the 1976 Democratic Convention. We had a major role also in the election of conservative Democrat Kent Hance (Texas 19th), and thus in the defeat of liberal, establishment Republican George Bush, Jr. That Edward King could be elected Democratic Governor of Massachusetts in 1978, being the genuine social-issues conservative that he is, is a tribute to the accomplishments of the New Right coalition. Many of his workers, for example, were trained by the right-to-life movement and his election demonstrated the effect of the working class anti-busing movement at the polls. But more than that, Ed King's election is indicative of a new and promising trend in the electorate. The populace is turning away from worn out liberal appeals, looking to the conservative answer.

At the start of the 1980s, it can be said that the New Right has managed to establish the institutions necessary to have impact on the entirety of the political process. We have within our grasp the mechanisms needed to achieve our goal. That goal is not merely to oppose, but to govern. Unlike the Old Right, which saw as its destiny the supervising of the dissolution of the American nation, we see as our goal a new direction for the American republic. We believe we can achieve this goal, provided the Left does not put us out of business before another few years have passed. (That is no idle possibility: Federal financing of House and Senate campaigns would be a major step in that direction. The elimination of single-issue interest groups, a high priority of the Left in the 96th Congress, would be a *coup de grâce* to the New Right coalition.)

If we, or others of our philosophy, had done ten years ago what we are doing now, the situation for the nation as a whole would have been much better. In so many ways, America is limited now, and will be for a long time to come. Militarily, we are weak; we are energy-dependent; our foreign policy is under many constraints. In the last ten years, the years in which conservatism skipped a generation, we have lost so much time that when the New Right does come to power, as I and my co-workers believe it will, things will be much limited by circumstances beyond our control. The Panama Canal has been given away, Taiwan is gone, the Middle East is going.

Despite all this, I am not despondent. It is basic to my philosophy that God's truth ought to be manifest politically. Collectivism, which is what the Left is ultimately advocating in a thousand guises, is an error. The New Right coalition is the only organized substantial effort opposing and speaking truth to its power. I believe with truth on our side we have great cause for hope.

Samuel T. Francis

MESSAGE FROM MARs: The Social Politics of the New Right

Dr. Francis discusses the general confrontation of class and values which lies behind New Right politics, and his exposition makes clear the importance of the New Right in keeping this struggle in the political arena. Dr. Francis is Legislative Assistant to Senator John East of North Carolina.

The label "New Right" is at best a confusing one. In the first place, what the label represents is not entirely new, since many of its themes, values, and interests have been expounded to one degree or another by the Old Right of the 1950s and 1960s. In the second place, it is not entirely "Right," since other ideas and values associated with it have seldom been expressed by conservatives of any generation. The New Right is perhaps best known for its populism and its heated contempt for elitism and "limousine liberals." Its polemical exchanges with the Left (and even, sometimes, with the Right) often display a bitterness that was lacking in the amiable sparring bouts of Mr. Buckley and Professor Galbraith. Moreover, the New Right voices no small amount of anti-business (not to say anti-capitalist) rhetoric. Bankers, multinational corporations, Big Business, and The Rich occupy a distinct circle in the New Right vision of the Inferno. The symbols of wealth are also important in its demonology: the Ivy League, the country club, and the Trilateral Commission. Orthodox conservatives of the Old

Right generally deprecate, smile at, or strain themselves ridiculing such gaucherie.

Yet, if the New Right is often the victim of its own rhetoric, it can, in 1981, lay claim to something that the Old Right never had. Political commentators will no doubt debate for years to come whether the Republican capture of the White House and Senate in 1980 was or was not due to New Right efforts alone, but they have never debated, and never will, whether the Old Right elected Barry Goldwater in 1964—or Robert Taft in 1952—or Herbert Hoover in 1932. The New Right in 1981, and for some years to come, has what the Old Right could never achieve: a national constituency, and the clear possibility of political victory, if not political dominance, in the United States for the remainder of the century.

Despite the incoherence of its name and sometimes of its message, the New Right—so this essay and presumably the others contained in this volume will argue—represents far more than a political ideology or an electoral coalition. The New Right is the political expression of a profound social movement that reflects the dynamics of American society and that promises to dominate not only politically but also perhaps socially and culturally. The origins of the New Right in a social movement explain why its political message often appears to be incoherent, contradictory, or simplistic. What the New Right has to say is not premeditated in academic seminars, calculated with precision in the inner sanctums of tax-exempt foundations, or debated in the stately prose of quarterly and fortnightly journals. The contents of its message are perceived injustices, unrelieved exploitation by anonymous powers that be, a threatened future, and an insulted past. It is therefore understandable that the New Right has less use for the rhetorical trope and the extended syllogism than for the mass rally and the truth squad, and that some of its adherents sometimes fantasize that the cartridge box is a not unsatisfactory substitute for the ballot box.

The social movement that the New Right expresses—and whose values, resentments, aspirations, and fears it tries to articulate—is composed of what sociologist Donald I. Warren calls "Middle American Radicals"—MARs. This movement, in Warren's description, is less an objectively identifiable class than a subjectively distinguished temperament, yet it possesses verifiable features that set it apart from other social groups and formations. In the mid-1970s, MARs had a family income of $3,000–$13,000. There was a strong presence among them of northern European ethnics, although Italians tended to account for more MARs than other groups. MARs were nearly twice as common in the South as in the north-central states. They tended to have completed high school but not to have attended college. They were more common among Catholics and Jews than among Protestants, and among Mormons and Baptists than among other Protestant sects. They tended to be in their thirties or in their sixties and were "significantly less likely to be professional or managerial workers" than to be "skilled and semi-skilled blue-collar workers."[1]

Yet these statistical features do not define MARs. What defines them as a movement is an attitudinal quality, and what Warren finds most distinctive about them is their view of government and, in a broader sense, of the "establishment" and their role in it. Unlike the Left, MARs do not regard the government as favoring the rich and, unlike the Right, they do not regard the government as giving too much to the poor. According to Warren,

> MARs are a distinct group partly because of their view of government as favoring both the rich and the poor simultaneously. . . . MARs are distinct in the depth of their feeling that the middle class has been seriously neglected. If there is one single summation of the MAR perspective, it is reflected in a statement which was read to respondents: *The rich give in to the demands of the poor, and the middle income people have to pay the bill.*[2]

This attitude is resonant with significant social and political implications. It points to a sense of resentment and exploitation, mainly economic but also broader, that is directed upward as well as downward. It points to mistrust of decision-makers in state and economy as well as to fear of the economically depressed. It points also to the frustration of aspirations, to an alienation of loyalties, and to a suspicion of established institutions, authorities, and values.

The economic frustrations of MARs, as represented in the above quotation, spill over into political, cultural, social, and moral expression. The objective features of the MAR profile, coupled with awareness of MAR political ferocity in New Right protests from the anti-busing movements of the early 1970s to the Panama Canal and anti-ERA mobilizations of 1977–78, should substantiate the movement as social rather than political in a narrow sense. MARs form a class—not simply a middle class and not simply an economic category—that is in revolt against the dominant patterns and structures of American society. They are, in the broadest sense, a political class, and they aspire, through the New Right, to become the dominant political class in the United States by displacing the current elite, dismantling its apparatus of power, and discrediting its political ideology.

"Ruling classes," wrote Gaetano Mosca, the great Italian political scientist of the early twentieth century,

> do not justify their power exclusively by *de facto* possession of it, but try to find a moral and legal basis for it, representing it as the logical and necessary consequence of doctrines and beliefs that are generally recognized and accepted.[3]

The current elite in the United States, which has held both political and social power since the 1930s, is no exception. Its ideology or political formula, by which it rationalizes its power, is generally known as liberalism—a set of ideas and values that ostensibly eschews power and upholds equality, liberty, and the brotherhood of man but which is amazingly congruent with and adaptable to the political, economic, and social interests (the structural interests) of the groups that espouse it.

This elite seized power in the political and economic crisis of the Depression. The chief instrument of its rise to power, then and in the following decades, was the state, especially the federal government, and more especially the executive branch. Through the state, it made common cause with certain mass organizations—large corporations, labor unions, universities, foundations, and the media—and has generally favored their expansion and strengthening at the expense of smaller-scale units. In domestic affairs it has favored federally enforced economic planning and social engineering for the purpose (at least ostensibly) of realizing its liberal ideology. In foreign affairs, it has until recently favored international activism through similar large-scale organizations and transnational alliances that seem to promote global fraternity and the disappearance of international distinctions and differences. In political theory it abandoned the ideal of a neutral government based on impartial laws and administering equal justice and associated itself with a concept of the state as intimately involved in social and economic processes and as an architect of desirable social change. This concept has been buttressed by a variety of pseudo-scientific ideologies: psychoanalysis, behaviorism, legal positivism, applied sociology, Marxism *manqué,* educational progressivism, etc.—most of which are logically incompatible with liberalism but are nevertheless abridged, distorted, and popularized into congruence with current ideological fixations.

It is in its cultural and social ideologies and lifestyles that the new elite has developed what is probably the clearest indicator of its dominant position. The lifestyles, aspirations, and values of the current elite are bound together, rationalized, and extended by what may be called the "cosmopolitan ethic." This ethic expresses an open contempt for what Edmund Burke called the "little platoons" of human society—the small town, the family, the neighborhood, the traditional class identities and their relationships—as well as for authoritative and disciplinary institutions—the army, police forces, parental authority, and the disciplines of school and church. The cosmopolitan ethic, reversing a Western tradition as old as Aesop, finds virtue in the large city, in the anonymous (and therefore "liberated") relationships of declassed, desexed, demoralized, and deracinated atoms that know no group or national identities, accept no given moral code, and recognize no disciplines and no limits. The ethic idealizes material indulgence, the glorification of the self, and the transcendence of conventional values, loyalties, and social bonds. At the same time, it denigrates the values of self-sacrifice, community, and moral and social order. Its most perfect (though extreme) expression is perhaps Mick Jagger, but a more typical and vapid form is portrayed in advertisements that tell us What Kind of Man Reads *Playboy.*

The ideology or formula of liberalism grows out of the structural interests of the elite that espouses it. Liberalism barely exists as an independent set of ideas and values. Virtually no significant thinker of this century has endorsed it, and many have explicitly rejected, criticized, or ridiculed it. Internally, the doctrines of liberalism are so contrary to established fact, inconsistent with each other, and immersed in sentimentalism, resentment, and egotism that they cannot be taken seriously as a body of ideas. Liberalism flourishes almost entirely because it reflects the material and psychological interests of a privileged, power-holding, and power-seeking sector of American society.

In the early twentieth century, the increasing massiveness of

American society appeared to demand new organizational forms of
control. The imperatives of mass scale in the economy, in government and politics, and in social and cultural life gave rise to a new
elite that found its principal power base in bureaucracy. In both
the public and private sectors, the bureaucratic organization of
power and control appeared to be the only means of ruling modern
mass units. In the private sector the evolution of bureaucratic
dominance followed the "separation of ownership and control" in
the large corporations and took the form of managerial direction
of large corporate firms. In government, modern bureaucracy developed in a more sudden and revolutionary way in the crisis of the
Depression. Yet there was no fundamental difference between the
interests of the two bureaucratic realms. Both sectors shared a
common mentality: a rationalistic faith in administrative and
manipulative techniques as a means of holding and exercising
power. Both sectors, perhaps more importantly, shared certain
common material interests: the more massive the scale of organization, the more imperative the bureaucratic-managerial form of
organization.

The same or similar interests and imperatives pertained in all
mass-scale organizations, and the same dominant bureaucratic
function developed in control of the mass unions. Similarly, but
more recently, the media of mass communication (in almost every
form—book publishing, news reporting, entertainment, documen-
taries, etc.) have displayed the same dynamic of elite formation, as
have, most recently, the instruments of legitimate force—the
armed forces and the larger metropolitan police departments. Unlike the older, more localized and personal elites of American society, the new elite possesses a more uniform mentality and a more
homogeneous interest: the expansion of mass units of organization
under the bureaucratic forms of governance, animated by an ideology of manipulative, administrative social engineering.

From its very nature, therefore, the new elite found liberalism
a useful and indeed indispensable formula for rationalizing its
existence and power. Modern liberalism allowed for government
on a mass scale and for bureaucratic manipulation of social and
economic processes. Liberalism allowed for an economy led by mass
corporations, themselves governed by "progressive" executives
whose positions depended on merit and schooling in managerial
sciences, and not on inheritance, experience, or the virtues of the

Protestant ethic. Liberalism championed schooling itself, especially education (also on a mass scale) that emphasized the practical disciplines of social science, public administration, and modern
business management. Finally, liberalism, at its very center, articulated a vision of man that not only allowed for bureaucratic
manipulation of his environment but also laid the groundwork for
the cosmopolitan ethic. The great value of this ethic in the rise of
the new bureaucratic elite was to discredit the formulas and ideologies of its older rivals. Liberalism and cosmopolitanism were able,
through their immense appeal to an intelligentsia, to portray local-
ism and decentralized institutions as provincial and a mask for
bigotry and selfishness; the small town, the family, class, religious,
ethnic, and community ties as backward, repressive, and exploita-
tive; the values of work, thrift, discipline, sacrifice, and postpone-
ment of gratification (on which, as values, the moral legitimacy of
the older elites rested), as outmoded, absolutist, puritanical, superstitious, and not infrequently hypocritical.

A more direct connection between the material interests of the
new elite and the semi-collectivist ideology of liberalism exists also.
The mass economy of the twentieth century requires a mass level
of consumption for the financing of its productive capacities. Due
to the inability of lending institutions in the Depression to mobilize
sufficient credit for the resumption of production, the federal government undertook labor policies, transfer programs, and pension
policies designed to ensure sufficient demand for the mass economy
to function. The immediate beneficiary of these policies, of course,
was the impoverished underclass of American society, but the ultimate beneficiaries were the new managerial and bureaucratic
elites in corporations and government. The stimulation of demand
through government policy—a policy financed by the middle class
taxpayers and consumers—ensured the existence and dominance
of the mass organization of government, corporation, and union
and their managerial elites. At the same time, this policy cemented
an alliance not only among the different sectors of the new elite,
but also between the new elite as a whole and the proletariat of
American society—against the remnants of the old elite and an
exploited and excluded middle class.[4]

The new elite, following a pattern that has been repeated
many times in human history, also found that the aggrandizement
of the federal executive branch was conducive to its revolution. The

older elites were based mainly in local and state governments and in the Congress. The Caesarist political style of the new elite made use of the Presidency, under Roosevelt and Truman and their successors, to attack, wear down, usurp, and discredit the authority and powers of both state and local bodies and the Congress. In this new political style, the rising managerial elite was following a pattern evident in the careers of Pericles, Caesar, Henry Tudor, Louis XIV, and Napoleon Bonaparte. Older elites, entrenched in established institutions, are attacked by newer social formations that make alliances with charismatic leaders exercising autocratic power and with an underclass that receives material benefits expropriated from the old elite. New, centralized institutions controlled by the new elite develop in place of the localized institutions of the old rulers.

A pattern often associated with this "sandwich" attack on an old elite by an alliance of underclass and autocrat is an activist and expansionist foreign policy led by the new men in opposition to the passive, often isolationist policies associated with the old ruling class. Thus, Pericles promoted Athenian imperialism through enfranchisement of the lower-class crews of the Athenian navy and against the interests of the landed, inward-looking Attic oligarchy. Caesar's revolution in Rome, made possible by his patronage of the lower classes, was to be extended in imperial-military adventures in the East, but this was cut short by his assassination. The Tudors, Louis XIV, and Napoleon all embarked on expansionist foreign policies that sought to benefit the aspirations and interests of the new elites on which their own power was based. The older elites oppose expansionism because their own power bases are not equipped to profit from it and indeed are frequently threatened by the rise of new powers and forces in the newly acquired territories.

This pattern also was present in the revolution of the managerial elite of the Depression–World War II era. The Old Guard of the Republican Party, representing the old elite, was isolationist in both World Wars. The new elite found that both its economic and political interests benefited by an activist, globalist foreign policy. The new political structures revolving around international and regional blocs, new markets and trade arrangements, and new internal institutions for international relations and conflict were all congruent with the interests of the new elite in government, industry and finance, education, and labor.

It is against this new elite—which Irving Kristol and others somewhat belatedly call the New Class, but which James Burnham more accurately (and much earlier) called the "managerial class"[5] —that the New Right with its MAR social base operates. It would be tendentious to claim that the ideologies and institutions of the managerial class are purely self-serving while claiming also that those of the MARs are objectively true, public-spirited, in the general interest, and morally pure. The MARs form a socio-political force now coalescing into a class and perhaps into a new elite that will replace the managerial one. As a rising political class, the MARs have their own interests, aspirations, and values, and these are not intended to benefit the nation, society as a whole, or humanity. Nevertheless, the structural interests of the MARs—what is of benefit to them because of their position and functions in American society—may be beneficial to America as well. The MARs, and similar social forces now developing in the Sunbelt, promise a new dynamism in America—economically as well as spiritually—in place of the now decadent and moribund managerial elite. They offer also a discipline, a code of sacrifice for something larger than themselves, and a new purpose that are beyond the reach of the jaded, self-indulgent, increasingly corrupt elite of the present day. The MARs are not better or worse than other human beings in other social formations, but the objective interests of their formation appear to dictate a social order quite different from, and probably better than, that designed, manipulated, and misruled by the managerial class and its cohorts.

What the MARs and the New Right seek, then, is the overthrow of the present elite and its replacement by themselves. This is a revolutionary goal, no less so than the goal of the rising managers of the early part of the century. It is revolutionary not in the sense that its realization will require violent rebellion, mass liquidation, or totalitarian rule—these are not envisioned by the New Right and would be antithetical to MAR interests—but in the sense that the replacement of one elite by another almost always leads to a cultural renaissance, to new and dynamic forces that alter ideas and institutions, and to an efflorescence of material and spiritual life.

Yet the New Right will not be the spearhead of the Middle

American Revolution if it is concerned only with politics in its narrow, formal sense. It must go beyond the tactics of electoral coalitions and roll-call votes and develop a strategy for the seizure of real social power. Real power is not limited to control of the formal apparatus of government but extends to the levers by which human societies are controlled—to the media of communication, the means of production, and the instruments of force. At the present time these levers of social control and real social power are almost entirely dominated by the managerial elite or are negated by it. Formal control of the political apparatus will not alter this fact.

The New Right–MAR coalition must seek to dismantle or radically reform the managerial apparatus of social control, and this objective means a far more radical approach to political conflict and to contemporary institutions. The strategic objective of the New Right must be the localization, privatization, and decentralization of the managerial apparatus of power. Concretely, this means not only a dismantling of the corporate, educational, labor, and media bureaucracies; but a devolution to more modest scale organizational units; and a reorientation of federal rewards from mass-scale units and hierarchies to smaller and more local ones.

To include the large corporations in the "enemies list" of the New Right may strike many adherents of the Old Right as odd or even as subversive. Yet libertarians have long recognized that large, publically owned, manager-dominated corporations have interests and political orientations quite different from those of small, privately owned and controlled enterprises. As G. William Domhoff, a radical sociologist, has recognized,

> the businesspeople who were most isolationist, antiwelfare and antilabor were more likely to be in NAM [National Association of Manufacturers] and to be associated with smaller and more regional corporations. Those who were more moderate [i.e., liberal] were more likely to be in CED [Committee for Economic Development] and to manage larger companies. More recently, our study of the corporate interlocks of CED and NAM leaders revealed the same large/small dichotomy. For example, NAM's directors for 1972 had only 9 connections to the top 25 banks, whereas CED had 63. Similarly, NAM had but 10 connections to the 25 largest industrials, while CED had 48. The findings were similar for insurance, transport, utilities and retails.[6]

The present managerial elite, whether in the public or private sector, has a vested interest in centralized decision-making and collective organization. The dynamic of MAR interests dictates ultimately a policy of localization and privatization of real social power in both the public and private sectors. Only by unleashing the now over-regulated, over-taxed, and unrewarded MAR social and economic forces can their innovative and productive potential be developed. This unleashing of MAR forces can come about only by dismantling the managerial power structure.

To call the New Right "conservative," then, is true only in a rather abstruse sense. Its social and cultural values are indeed conservative and traditionalist, but, unlike almost any other conservative group in history, it finds itself not only out of power in a formal sense but also excluded from the informal centers of real social power. Consequently, the political style, tactics, and organizational forms of the New Right should find a radical, anti-establishment approach better adapted to the achievement of its goals. Ideologically, much in the formulas and theory (insofar as there is any) of the New Right derives from exponents of the Old Right. Yet the premise of almost all Old Right publicists has been that the values and institutions they were defending were part of an establishment that was under revolutionary attack. For much of the period in which the Old Right flourished, this premise was correct. Today, however, and since at least the mid-1960s, the revolution of mass and managers has triumphed, entrenched itself as a new elite, and, indeed, has revealed strong signs of ossification and decadence. The Old Right failed to arrest the revolution mainly because it lacked an adequate social base. Its powerful, well-honed, but esoteric critique of liberal ideology appealed to few save the most sophisticated intellectuals and the declining entrepreneurial elite whose interests and values were reflected in conservative theory.

The New Right must consciously abandon much of the inertial conservatism of its Old Right premises. It must cease congratulating itself on its ability to raise money and win elections within the system developed by the present establishment and begin to formulate a strategy for besieging the establishment. With its MAR social base, the New Right is in a strong position to develop such a strategy, and there are signs that some parts of it are doing so. Some New Right groups have successfully politicized sections of

American society. Smaller businessmen, broadcasters, clergy, parent groups, and other institutional representatives have played an active and important role in New Right political campaigns. However, a key element in the success of the New Right will be its ability to focus on how the establishment uses its apparatus of power in the media, corporations, schools, etc., for political domination and exploitation. This has been made reasonably clear with regard to the bureaucracy and the unions, but other institutional supports of the liberal managerial elite need exposure as well.

In economics, the Old Right has consistently defended the free market. While there is much to be said for the renaissance of free market ideas led by von Mises, Hayek, Friedman, Laffer, and others, it is doubtful that the MAR coalition and its allies in the Sunbelt entrepreneurial regions will continue to focus on this classical liberal principle. It is more likely that MAR-Sunbelt interests require a strong governmental role in maintaining economic privileges for the elderly and for unionized labor (where it now exists), that they will also require (or demand) subsidization of construction and perhaps of characteristic Sunbelt enterprises (energy, defense and aerospace industries, and agriculture). One New Right tactic would be payment of these subsidies and privileges out of the proceeds of taxing the Frostbelt and reorienting economic policy and legislation toward the South and West. For the New Right to embrace such a tactic openly (as well perhaps as a more favorable attitude toward protectionism) would be a frank recognition that the classical liberal idea of a night-watchman state is an illusion and that a MAR elite would make use of the state for its own interests as willingly as the present managerial elite does. MAR resentment of welfare, paternalism, and regulation is not based on a profound faith in the market but simply on the sense of injustice that unfair welfare programs, taxes, and stifling regulation has bred. The central focus of MAR–New Right political economy is likely to be economic growth, a value often confused with, sometimes encompassing, but not identical to the free market.

Clearly, economic growth involves the lifting of most legal and administrative restraints on enterprise—the demise of environmentalist legislation and OSHA, the sale of federally owned land in the Far West, etc. But it would also include government assistance to dynamic but underfed sectors of the economy—e.g., the space program and new technology forms. The role of government in stimulating growth is no less inconsistent with free market ideals than its role in retarding growth, and since the social forces of the New Right would have a strong interest in the former role, there is little value in their adherence to a strict laissez-faire ideology.

The promotion of a "no-growth" cultus by powerful elements of the current liberal managerial elite is strong evidence of its decadence and ossification. The "selective isolationism" in foreign policy, the withdrawal from the Third World and the conflict with the Soviets, and the guilt experienced for our past foreign policy are also indications of decadence. The fundamental reason for the fall of Vietnam, the U.S. retreat from Angola, the betrayal of Somoza, the desertion of Taiwan, and the collapse of the Shah (as well as the weakening of our commitments to other Third World allies) lies in the inability of our present elite to deal effectively with the often brutal realities of the Third World, in the failure of the liberal formulas of the elite to rationalize necessary and desirable policies for dealing with these realities, and in a preference by the elite to deal with other elites similar to itself in developed regions (Japan, Western Europe, and the Soviet Union). The rationalistic, administrative, and technical skills on which the power of the managerial class is based are of little value in underdeveloped regions, especially where violent resistance to planning and manipulation requires a more coercive response than managerial ideology can justify.

Moreover, the material interests of the elite, as well as its psychic interests and ideological orientation, impel it toward the developed world. Ideologically, the current elite distrusts nationalism and favors internationalist and regionalist units of organization (the UN, the Common Market, the British Commonwealth, the Atlantic Community, etc.) This preference is in accord with its cosmopolitan ethic, but it also accords with the economic interests of the large corporate entities. Free trade, the integration of international markets, and the stabilization of international relations all reflect the interests of the transnational elites that dominate in the developed countries. In contrast, smaller producers situated in the Sunbelt require protection against cheap imports and access to the raw materials and resources of the Third World, and they are less committed to international stability than to the continued predominance of the United States.

The foreign policy of the New Right, then, reflecting the interests and values of its MAR–Sunbelt–neo-entrepreneurial base, is likely to endorse a new nationalism that insists on the military and economic pre-eminence of the United States, on international activism (and even expansionism) in world affairs, on at least some measure of protection for domestic producers, and on far more resistance to Third World arrogance, aggression, and barbarianism. The controversy over the Trilateral Commission, whatever its merits, reflects this conflict over foreign policy between the social forces of the dominant elite and those of the New Right. The Commission is essentially the forum of the elite and its multinational components; as such it has become a symbol of the resentments of MARs and the forces of the Sunbelt.[7] Moreover, the nationalism of the New Right will probably replace the anti-Communism of the Old Right as a focus of foreign policy. While the Soviet Union, Cuba, and their allies remain the principal threat to the United States and our predominance, New Right elements are likely to focus on the threat itself rather than on the ideological origins of the threat. The distinction between the nationalist focus of the New Right and the anti-Communist orientation of the Old became clear in the opposition to the Panama Canal Treaty. While Old Right anti-Communists sought to protray the late Panamanian dictator Omar Torrijos Herrera as a Marxist, this was a far less effective tactic than Ronald Reagan's New Right, nationalist slogan on the Canal—"We built it, we paid for it, and it's ours."

The nationalism of the New Right points to what is perhaps its best known characteristic, the rejection of the cosmopolitan ethic of the managerial elite and a thunderous defense of moral and social traditionalism. The most offensive component of cosmopolitanism to MARs is its abstract universalism, its refusal to make any distinctions or discriminations among human beings. The brotherhood of man, egalitarianism, the relativization of moral values, and the rejection of conventional social and cultural identities as obsolete and repressive all derive from this universalist tendency. In its place, the central formula of the rising MAR-Sunbelt elite is likely to form around what may be called a Domestic Ethic that centers on the family, the neighborhood and local community, the church, and the nation as the basic framework of values. The values associated with the Domestic Ethic will contrast sharply with those of cosmopolitanism: the duty of work rather than the right of welfare; the value of loyalty to concrete persons, symbols, and institutions rather than the cosmopolitan dispersion of loyalties; and the social and human necessity of sacrifice and deferral of gratification rather than the cosmopolitan-managerial demand for immediate gratification, indulgence, and consumption. The Domestic Ethic may also lay the basis for a more harmonious relationship between employer and worker, since the place of work itself can be portrayed as an institution no less central than the family or the local community. The common interest of workers and employers in opposing the restrictive, stagnationist policies of the managerial elite is one element of New Right rhetoric that could develop into this harmony, and the explicit approach to blue-collar workers by recent New Right candidates appears to confirm this trend.

Out of the structural interests and residual values of the MARs, and similar forces in the Sunbelt and in new entre-preneurial forces throughout the country, the New Right can con-struct a formula or ideology. This formula will reflect the demands for economic growth, a more aggressively nationalistic foreign pol-icy, and an assertion of traditionalist ethics and loyalties. It will not be conservative although it will encompass some ideas of the Old Right and reject others. It will in fact be a radical formula, demanding changes not only in the formal appearance of power but also in the realities of the distribution and uses of power in its social forms. As a radical movement, representing rising social forces against an ossified elite, the New Right must abandon the political style of the Old Right. That style, based on the premise that the Old Right represented an establishment, sought to defend the intermediary institutions against the Caesarist, leveling forces of the new managerial class. The managerial class, however, has long since become the establishment and shows signs of abandon-ing the executive branch as a spearhead of its power-seizure. The New Right, therefore, should make use of the Presidency as its own spearhead against the entrenched elite and should dwell on the fact that the intermediary bodies—Congress, the courts, the bu-reaucracy, the media, etc.—are the main supports of the elite. The adoption of the Caesarist tactic by the New Right would reflect the historical pattern by which rising classes ally with an executive power to displace the oligarchy that is entrenched in the intermedi-ate bodies.

Jeffrey Hart has suggested this idea of a New Right–Caesarist style based on the Presidency, but apparently without attracting broad support.[8] While the New Right can expect to make gains in Congress and state and local governments, only the Presidency— as Nixon and Agnew showed—has the viability and resources to cut through the intractable establishment of bureaucracy and media to reach the MAR social base directly. Only the Presidency is capable of dismantling or restructuring the bureaucratic-managerial apparatus that now strangles the latent dynamism of the MAR-Sunbelt social forces. The key to this Caesarist strategy is that the New Right does not now represent an elite but a sub-elite, that it must acquire real social power and not preserve it in its current distribution. The intermediate institutions of contemporary America—the bureaucracy, the media, the managerial hierarchies of the mass unions and corporations, the universities and foundations, the urban conglomerates—are not allies of the New Right and are not conservative influences except in the sense that they serve to protect established powers. Hence, the New Right should not defend these structures but should expose them as the power preserves of the entrenched elite whose values and interests are hostile to the traditional American ethos and which is a parasitical tumor on the body of Middle America. These structures should be leveled or at least radically reformed, and only the Presidency has the power and the resources to begin the process and to mobilize popular support for it.

The characterization of the New Right presented in this essay is unconventional and will perhaps be controversial. The New Right is not merely an electoral coalition concerned with winning elections and roll calls; it is the political expression of a relatively new social movement that regards itself as the depository of traditional American values and as the exploited victim of the alliance between an entrenched elite and a ravenous proletariat. Viewed in this sociopolitical perspective, the New Right is not a conservative force but a radical or revolutionary one. It seeks the displacement of the entrenched elite, the discarding of its ideology of liberalism and cosmopolitanism, and its own victory as a new governing class in America. The New Right is able to aspire to these ambitions because, unlike the Old Right, it has a viable social base in the Middle American Radicals and in the dynamic economy of the Sunbelt.

If the New Right is not conservative, it should be clear that it will need a new ideology, formula, or political theory that can win the loyalties and represent the interests of its social base and which can rationalize its quest for social and political power. The primary justification of its quest for power must be the corruption, decadence, incompetence, oppressiveness, and alienation of the old elite that it is seeking to displace. This elite—identified here as the managerial class that rose to power in the government bureaucracy, large corporations, and other modern mass-scale organizations since the 1930s—is clearly foreign to the bulk of the nation in its lifestyle, values, and ideals. Yet these lifestyles, values, and ideals cannot be simply discarded by the old elite; they represent a logical outgrowth of its own structural interests: large, social-engineering government in alliance with corporations, universities and foundations, the mass media, unions, and other bureaucracies. Only the cosmopolitan ethic and liberal ideology described above can rationalize these structural interests of the entrenched elite. The fundamental problem therefore is not the ethic or ideology of the elite but the elite itself; and it is the elite and its apparatus of power that must be the main target of the New Right attack.

The principal values to which the New Right should appeal in this attack differ from those defended by the Old Right as well as from those articulated by the managerial elite. In place of the free market of the Old Right or the "stabilization" of the present elite, the New Right should center its economic aspirations on the concept of economic growth. Clearly, the concept of growth involves a dismantling of the bureaucracy, regulation, fiscal and environmentalist policies, and a decentralization and privatization of economic forces, but this reorientation toward a freer economic climate is incidental to the central idea of economic growth, expansion, and dynamism. In place of the strictly anti-Communist foreign policy of the Old Right or the selective isolationism of the decadent managerial class, the New Right should assert a foreign policy founded on a new activist and expansionist nationalism—a policy that would necessarily encompass Old Right anti-Communism but would also respond to rising non-Communist threats. In place of the hedonistic, pragmatist, relativist, and secularized cosmopolitanism of the present elite, the New Right should expound without compromise the ideals and institutions of the American ethos: hard work and self-sacrifice, morally based legislation and policies, and a public commitment to religious faith. In place of the faith in Congressional supremacy and established intermediary institutions that characterizes both the Old Right and the entrenched managerial elite, the New Right will favor a populist-based Presidency able to cut through the present oligarchical establishment and to promote new intermediary institutions centered on Middle America.

The conflict into which the New Right is entering is a complex one. Because of its complexity, the political expression of the MARs cannot take forms that are entirely consistent in ideology or that are calculated to please everyone within its own ranks. Because the issues and values are real and not the product of abstract cerebration, there will probably be no monolithic movement under the New Right aegis. There will be a coalition that will often find itself split, and the opponents of the New Right will of course seek to take advantage of these splits. Hence, the political movement requires, more than is customary in American political history, a discipline, a leadership, and a formula that will promote its cohesion, its electoral advantages, and its objectives.

The late Carroll Quigley argued that new civilizations form themselves around dynamic, innovative social forces, which he called "instruments." As these instruments develop, they acquire vested interests that retard their dynamism and slow their innovative capacities. The instruments then become ossified "institutions" that oppose the rise of new forces and, unless challenged, lead to civilizational decay.[9] The managerial elite as described in this essay began its history as an instrument and is now in a stage of what Quigley would call institutionalization. In its youth it was a force for much innovation, expansion, and cultural dynamism. In its senescence it is a force only for itself and for the cultivation of self-indulgence, both material and psychological. Its power is being challenged by a new force, also described above; if victorious, no doubt the MARs themselves will exploit their rivals and, like all men, have much to answer for. No doubt also the new elite that they will form will someday degenerate and itself be challenged by new dynamic forces. But the choice between the present elite and its challengers is not merely between one power and another. It is a choice between degeneration and rebirth, between death and survival, for survival is not a right or a gift freely granted by the powers that be. Survival, in the jungle or in political societies, is a hard-won prize that depends ultimately on power itself. In this world, wrote Goethe, one must be the Hammer or the Anvil. The essence of the message from MARs is that the messengers want to work the forge.

ENDNOTES

1. Donald I. Warren, *The Radical Center: Middle Americans and the Politics of Alienation* (Notre Dame and London: University of Notre Dame Press, 1976), pp. 23–29.
2. *Ibid.*, p. 21.
3. Gaetano Mosca, *The Ruling Class (Elementi di Scienza Politica)*, ed. by Arthur Livingston, transl. by Hannah D. Kahn (New York: McGraw-Hill Book Company, 1939), p. 70.
4. The alliance of elite and underclass against the middle class—what I have here called the "sandwich strategy"—has been noted by, among others, New Right political theorists Robert W. Whitaker, *A Plague on Both Your Houses* (Washington and New York: Robert B. Luce, 1976), ch. 4 *passim;* and William A. Rusher, *The Making of a New Majority Party* (Ottawa, Ill.: Green Hill Publishers, 1975), pp. 33 *et seq.*
5. See Irving Kristol, *Two Cheers for Capitalism* (New York: New American Library, 1979), especially ch. 2. Kristol's idea of the "New Class" is apparently limited to the public sector and media and does not extend to large corporations. James Burnham, *The Managerial Revolution: What Is Happening in the World* (New York: The John Day Company, 1941), despite its age and problems, remains to my mind the most accurate and comprehensive account of the New Class, its ideology, interests, and dynamics. For a fuller discussion of the New Class, see *Society,* XVI, 2 (January/February, 1978), pp. 14–62.
6. G. William Domhoff, *The Powers That Be: Processes of Ruling-Class Domination in America* (New York: Random House, 1978), p. 85; see also John Chamberlain, "The New Enterprising Americans," *Policy Review,* No. 13 (Summer, 1980), p. 4, on "the preponderance of small-scale Middle Western enterprises on the board of trustees" of conservative Hillsdale College, Michigan, and their criticism of Big Business.
7. Thomas Ferguson and Jack Rogers, "Another Trilateral Election?", *The Nation,* June 28, 1980, pp. 783–84.
8. Jeffrey Hart, "The Presidency: Shifting Conservative Perspectives?", *National Review,* November 22, 1974, pp. 1351–55.
9. Carroll Quigley, *The Evolution of Civilizations: An Introduction to Historical Analysis* (New York: The Macmillan Company, 1961), pp. 73–74.

Robert J. Hoy

LID ON
A BOILING POT

Everybody in power today has the idea that, in the end, blue-collar workers and hard hats are patriotic, and will therefore rally to anyone who waves the flag. They are right about the first point, wrong about the second. Those who rule are increasingly perceived as aliens who have made the American flag a symbol for something which many patriots feel is inimical to them.

Bob Hoy, a freelance photo-journalist who has worked for The Washington Star, *gives a first-hand view of the dangerous frustrations implied elsewhere in these papers. Many a refugee has told us, "I simply couldn't believe that it could happen in my country." Surely things could not go "that far," or someone would have seen the danger. If this be alarmism, it is an alarm worth hearing.*

"When a boat's taken on too much water, all the bailing in the world isn't going to keep it from sinking."

> —*Young American worker during the 1980 election campaign, commenting on the state of his nation*

When Americans look to the future, ever larger numbers don't like what they see. A recent Gallup Poll showed that, for the first time ever, a majority of Americans see the coming decade as worse than the preceding one. A 1975 survey indicated that roughly one-third of white Americans feel that violence against the federal government will eventually prove necessary to save "our true American way of life."

Just below the surface, powerful currents are stirring. Growing millions of working- and middle-class Americans feel betrayed by a system which they see as ever more alien.

As an eager participant and an empathetic observer, I was intimately involved for several years in a nationwide populist struggle by angry and forgotten Americans.

These people love America because they *are* America. But they need to feel that Washington and New York and Harvard and Hollywood represent them—that those to whom they have delegated power stand for America. They desperately want and badly

85

need new political and social leadership which understands their hopes and shares their dreams.

My close ties to an authentic American populist movement have convinced me that the emerging New Right faces a tremendous challenge to restore America to its people, and an opportunity to take and hold political power. The forgotten Americans are slow to anger, but even harder to placate once they have been aroused.

For unless major changes are made soon, the lid on top of the boiling pot will explode.

In December 1973, a lot of truck drivers were fuming over soaring fuel prices. But Mike Korotasy and three other independent midwestern truckers decided to do more than complain. Over their CB radios, they organized a protest strike action to dramatize their anger.

"We didn't want trouble," Korotasy said later, "but we decided that if somebody had to be the first, it would start with us. When we crossed the Connecticut line on I-84, we pulled our four rigs together and blocked the lanes. Right or wrong, we did it." By the next morning, truckers from New York to California had heard of the blockade by CB radio.

Soon, thousands of truckers had highways tied up at a dozen points. The largest blockade was at Berlin Heights, Ohio, where a thousand trucks snarled traffic for 112 miles. Violence erupted when state police and National Guardsmen confronted truckers who would not disperse. The shutdown lasted eleven days and pulled one-third of the nation's 100,000 independent truckers off the road. Four truckers died in the struggle. This wildcat "citizens' strike" was the first of many which a new generation of populists would wage in battles against an unresponsive establishment.

The new year, 1974, opened with a second and better organized blockade, coordinated by Mike Parkhurst, the publisher of *Overdrive* magazine. Within two weeks, the governors of more than twenty-five strike-crippled states issued proclamations of emergency and pleaded for help from Washington. As severe food shortages struck one city after another, Attorney General William Saxbe cried, "We cannot allow the truckers to bring this country to its knees."

It's not surprising that truck drivers kicked off the new populist revolt. As masters of their rigs, truckers have long prided themselves on their independent spirit. As the populist revolt grew, the truckers were joined by farmers in tractorcades, "roving pickets" of mobile coal miners and others who helped make the highway a focal point of protest.

Some have called this populist struggle the "CB revolt"—and with good reason. The Citizen's Band radio is Middle America's secret weapon. This alternative media network, which is restricted to police use in many countries, is what makes coordinated strike tactics possible. The vast CB underground also allows over thirty million Americans to exchange views and ideas banned from most of the semi-controlled conventional media. During every phase of the populist struggle, the CB network has served as an ad hoc communications system. In June, 1979, for example, some two hundred trucks appeared without warning outside of Washington and Baltimore. Their drivers threatened to invade the downtown areas, park their rigs in the middle of intersections, and walk away with the keys. Only a hastily organized police blockade of key highway entrances into the cities prevented the threatened action.

For myself and several friends, the truckers' strike was a call to organize. On New Year's Day, 1974, just after the first big truck blockade, Bob and Brigitte Whitaker and I set up The Populist Forum. Our aim was to provide writing and press relations services to populist movements. We did not seek to tell them what to say, but to help them get a hearing. Our shoestring operation was successful because no group ever had reason to complain that our work ever represented anything but their own sentiments expressed in media or magazine language. Our first goal, joining the anti-busing and textbook protests against the education establishment in a common march and press conference, was accomplished in five months.

It was our conviction, for example, that the average striking trucker had a lot more on his mind than fuel prices, regardless of what he might self-effacingly say when put on the spot by someone with a more formal education. The pervasive note of bitterness which we detected in many working men seemed to reflect their unfocused and hence all the more frustrated awareness of larger, more pernicious forces at work in American life. Might not their growing obstinancy, which was being laid conveniently at the feet of day-to-day economics, actually be more of a slow psychological distillate, the residue of galling minor incidents and grievous major trends which almost defy enumeration? By making personal involvement the hallmark of The Populist Forum, we got close enough to many Middle Americans to see our intuition abundantly confirmed.

In his paper, William Rusher states that the achievement of overriding importance of the Goldwater campaign was to introduce American conservatives to each other. In the same vein, it fell to The Populist Forum to bring social and economic conservatives together. Even more importantly, they made social issue groups— like West Virginia textbook protesters and the Boston anti-busing movement—aware of each other's existence and the possibilities and strengths arising from cooperation. Even as early as 1975, The Populist Forum held joint press conferences for "single-issue" social conservatives.

We spent several years trying to channel the energy and resentment of many sporadic uprisings against the establishment into some kind of enduring alliance. Wildcat miners, textbook protesters, despairing farmers, opponents of busing: These and others came under our purview.

We sympathized heartily with the pressing concerns of these grassroots activists, and made it an unvarying point of honor to begin by asking each group, "What can *we* do for *you?*"—especially since no one else had dreamed of asking them that. In the back of our minds, however, we maintained perspective. When the time was right, when fearful hearts and minds were at least partially won, we began prodding: "What can *you* do for other groups around the country which share a common neglect? What can the miner do for the farmer? How can the busing foe in South Boston express solidarity with the textbook protester in West Virginia?"

We posed these questions sincerely because we were always looking for the formula which would unify the disparate protest groups into something lasting and cohesive. We saw The Populist Forum as a vehicle for unity—a catalyst for unifying those we had brought together. Beyond a certain point, people must make things happen for themselves—or you're talking some brand of elitism, not populism.

Besides bolstering morale and functioning as an introduction service among otherwise isolated groups around the country, The Populist Forum arranged extensive media coverage. The attention we generated was hostile as often as friendly, but even that was preferred by protesters to the previous silence. The *Washington Star,* for which I had once worked as a photographer, ran a lengthy article dealing with our efforts to reorganize "the old alliance of Southerners and urban ethnics now that the Democratic party no longer represented the working people of America."

The Communist *Daily World* attacked The Forum as a well-organized, effective extremist group. The National Education Association cited us as part of "a highly sophisticated, well organized right-wing extremist group . . . an organization of nationwide proportions and a broad financial base."

In his recent book, *Thunder on the Right* (Pantheon, 1980), Alan Crawford maintained, with only slightly greater accuracy, that The Forum "operates to aid and abet any and all spasms of anti-establishment behavior, apparently without discrimination."

Actually, The Populist Forum was a tiny organization that operated from our homes. We had an impact far out of proportion to our size only because, at that time, almost no other organization in the nation's capital was speaking up for a vast bloc of alienated American working people. An article by Bob Whitaker in the *Conservative Digest* (July 1975) outlined the tactics of populist revolts:

> Social conservatism—populism—will triumph only when it is built on local struggles.
> The establishment, for all its wealth and power, is in precisely the position of a large nation challenging a guerrilla force—which in a sense we are. We know our community, we live here, we can keep a campaign headquarters open and be a thorn in their side.
> Like guerrillas, we require only on-the-job training. The establishment, however, must come in like an outside army, with support troops and support costs hundreds of times what we must spend for the same results. And always, the outsider in our community, however he poses, is the invader.

William Rusher, the publisher of *National Review,* applauded our efforts. Mr. Rusher worked to get populist ideas heard in New Right outlets and wrote an enthusiastic foreword to Whitaker's *A Plague on Both Your Houses* (Robert B. Luce, 1976), which articulated the social and political implications of the new populist revolt.

This book was decisive in winning acceptance for our ideas in New Right circles. *National Review* (June 1978) called Whitaker, one of the three leading spokesmen (along with Kevin Phillips and William Rusher) for the idea of a populist-conservative New Right coalition of productive Americans.

Governor George Wallace, in many ways the progenitor of the new populism, noted that *A Plague on Both Your Houses* "accurately describes our populist struggle: the battle of the middle class against its twin exploiters, the corporate establishment of wealth and the leftist education-welfare establishment."

The Populist Forum's first major campaign was in mountainous Kanawha County, West Virginia, where we joined the parents of "Concerned Citizens," who demanded that textbooks which they considered obscene and mocking be removed from school classrooms. The protest, which dragged on for more than two years, was marked by shootings, brutal beatings, firebombings, violently enforced school boycotts, wildcat coal strikes and economic boycotts.

The people of Kanawha County saw the struggle as a question of community self-determination and cultural integrity. The Federal government and the liberal newspapers portrayed the conflict as an issue of book censorship and resistance to progress towards a pluralistic America.

The Populist Forum helped to transform the controversy from a local dispute over a few textbooks into a debate with national implications about basic questions of power and cultural destiny. When one young Maryland father was confronted by school materials which deeply wounded his sense of decency, he could only despair for the present, yet vowed to defend his legacy: "They can do anything they want to me," he said, "but they had better leave my kids alone." Perhaps the publicity surrounding the West Virginia battle had forced this man and others to take stock of how endangered their standards had become. We certainly had people like him in mind as we tried to maximize national media coverage for the uprising, and as we persuaded the aggrieved to take their feelings directly to Washington.

One who took little persuading was the fiery preacher Avis Hill. Speaking before a gathering of 5,000 parents during our third march on Washington, "little Avis" warned: "If they can break us in our mountain home, if they can break us in the farm towns of Jefferson County [Kentucky], if they can break us in the streets of South Boston, then they can break us anywhere." The Populist Forum helped Pastor Hill to record and produce an album which set his people's case to bluegrass music. *The Washington Post* denounced a song I wrote as an unfair attack against liberals, the National Education Association, communists and the Supreme Court. Actually, the point of my song, entitled "Kanawha County Uprising," was precisely that these great powers, and a number of others, were united against a relative handful of parents in one rural county of America.

The exquisite hypocrisy shown by some liberals during the textbook protest was epitomized for me by the editor of the Montgomery County, Maryland *Journal*. He ridiculed the actions of those who opposed certain textbooks because of their obscene passages. Yet when confronted by a local parents' group, he refused even to publish those portions of the textbook being criticized—because, he explained, they were too vulgar to print in his newspaper. That is, too vulgar for his adult readers in one of the most sophisticated counties in America, but not too vulgar for nine-year-olds in West Virginia!

Hypocrisy was no less plentiful in the bitter controversy over forced busing, a conflict absolutely central to the new populist revolt. Wealthy white liberals told their less well-to-do kinsfolk, in effect, to "do as I say, not as I do." Today the dreaded buses still roll, but we in The Populist Forum look back on our participation in that struggle as among our proudest moments.

We worked closely with the two most active anti-busing groups in America, "Restore Our Alienated Rights" (ROAR) in Boston, and "Union Labor Against Busing" (ULAB) in Louisville. We served as the Washington liaison between these groups and the "Concerned Citizens" of Kanawha County, and helped to forge a united front. One protest motorcade of Louisville parents went to West Virginia to lend support to Avis Hill and his followers, and their cars stretched along the highway for over twenty miles.

The three marches on Washington for which we provided publicity each brought together some 15,000 parents from across America and attracted major media attention. What we sent into the streets of the capital was a microcosm of the base of the Democratic Party: urban Catholics and rural Protestants, "white ethnics" of nearly every stripe and stipple, union members and small businessmen, farmers, factory workers and housewives. Few of these people had previously been political conservatives, but, with their voices unheeded by establishment liberals, most would soon be voting that way.

The often violent response by parents to forced racial integration during the heyday of the anti-busing struggle is well known. But it's one thing to read or hear about the desperate resistance put up by the people of Boston, Louisville, and a dozen other cities, and quite another to experience it personally as we did. Participation in the struggle destroyed irrevocably the faith of tens of thousands of Americans in the basic reliability and honesty of the complex thing we call the "system."

For Harold O'Brien, a South Boston demonstration "marshal," only the feelings associated with warfare were comparable. "I was in Korea," he stated, "and I killed people for less than what they've done to our neighborhood, to our wives and to our children."

Like its predecessors, this new populist awakening was not confined to the great cities. Discontent in rural America boiled into sometimes violent revolt under the banner of the American Agriculture Movement (AAM). The American family farm had been dying for decades. Now, the last of a hardy breed were threatened with extinction. Even competent, normally successful family farmers were going broke.

The high point of the AAM revolt came in the winter of 1977–78. After the harvest was in, thousands of tractors from across the land converged upon Washington like an invading army. Most of the 40,000 farmers had driven hundreds or even thousands of miles —from the Midwest, the Deep South, and the Northwest—in tractors with top speeds as low as twenty-five miles per hour.

I'll never forget the cold dark morning when we mustered our forces on our Manassas Battlefield, Virginia staging grounds. Thousands of tractors lumbered into Washington like tanks. I rode with a Southern contingent under the leadership of Georgia farmer Tommy Kersey.

The tractorcade returned the next winter, but in smaller numbers. The winter following, the ranks were thinner yet. I joined them each time. The plight of the family farm was not lessening. Rather, the despair of the family farmer was growing.

The Populist Forum also played a key role in publicizing the coal miners' strikes of the late 1970s. In 1976, for example, I arranged for a group of British journalists to meet secretly with the underground leaders of the West Virginia wildcat strike. Later, I helped a BBC television crew produce a documentary about the area. The Populist Forum helped arrange other important media coverage, and produced a bluegrass album about the populist struggle, for which, in spite of the *Post*'s earlier criticism, I wrote six songs.

Various Communist organizations tried to exploit the strike. One of them, an outfit calling itself the "International Workers' Party," even put out a bluegrass strike album of its own. Speaking to a rally in Charleston, West Virginia, one IWP spokesman attacked The Populist Forum as made up of the kind of people "who spend enormous energy to keep people from learning what Communism is."

What bothered Communists—from the tiny IWP to the *Daily World*— was that we were treading pretty effectively on their turf. I was regularly able to get into places where neither Communists nor even regular union leaders could gain access. Conservatives were upset by many of our activities, as was Alan Crawford, because our interest was not in the ideology of the grassroots protest, but in giving voice to protests which genuinely were from the grassroots and which lacked access to public expression of their grievances. The Communists prefer that these dissatisfactions remain voiceless, so that they can exploit them. Conservatives avoid most such risings, thereby giving the left—and the Klan and Nazis —precisely what they desire.

Later, we took on a cause which infuriated just about everybody. The 1978 wildcat coal strike upset the United Mine Workers, whom it defied; industry, against which it was directed; the government, which forebade it; conservatives, who like workers quiescent; and liberals, who want workers to keep their mouths shut unless their union tells them to say something. If The Forum had not provided its services, the strike would have taken place and ended without the views of the strikers being aired.

A leading miners' organizer tipped me off that the upcoming coal strike promised to be a long one. Certainly its success depended on prolonging it. I quickly got in touch with AAM farm leaders and urged a coordinated effort to emphasize the common plight of America's basic producers. The farmers understood their identity of interests with the coal miners and the importance of more than token collaboration.

The farm leaders made calls around the country and arranged

for a large donation of food from AAM members. I next contacted some of our old independent trucker buddies and they agreed to donate their time and rigs to form "CB convoys" to transport the donated food. The truckers picked up the food from locations as far afield as Texas and western Canada, and moved it to distribution centers set up by the miners' relief committees. The largest of the convoys delivered more than 75 tons of food to Central City, Kentucky, and Beckley, West Virginia, in March 1978. This alliance of anti-establishment miners, farmers and truckers powerfully demonstrated the self-reliance and independent organizing ability of Middle America, its capacity for constructive self-help campaigns as well as protest actions.

For me, this food relief operation was the most exciting expression of the populist rejection of both union and governmental establishments which had ceased to represent them. Far more than mere demonstrations against the existing order, the operation manifested the willingness and ability of populist America, if necessary, to go its own way.

The populist unrest of the late 1970s had its roots in the Wallace upheaval of the late 1960s and early 1970s. Millions of members of the traditional "New Deal" Democratic party alliance had bolted to support a man portrayed in the media as a boob, a racist, and a closet fascist.

While the media depicted George Wallace as a kind of political Tyrannosaurus Rex, his candidacy actually served as a safety valve for streaming populists. By getting his followers to "Send Them a Message," he channeled a growing bitterness back into the electoral process and helped to reaffirm the flagging faith of millions in the system's ability to redress their grievances.

In 1968, Wallace captured an impressive ten million votes (14 percent of the national total) while running as a third party candidate. In 1972, he won several major Democratic primaries, including Michigan's, before an almost successful assassination attempt cut short his campaign.

As the Governor lay near death, I kept an all-night vigil with other Wallace campaign workers. The despair of these young activists portended a more militant populism that would not confine itself to due process. When Wallace was shot, millions of Americans saw their last hope pass from the political stage.

The liberals and leftist militants who captured the Democratic party in 1972 chose to ignore the populists whom Wallace had championed. George McGovern, the party standard-bearer, seemed to epitomize everything that Middle America detested. Not surprisingly, the populists abandoned their traditional party in November to reelect Richard Nixon and deal the Democrats their most crushing presidential defeat ever.

A number of perceptive writers dissected the phenomenon of the new populism, and the frustrations behind it. As early as 1969, Kevin Phillips explored the estrangement of working-class white Americans from the Democratic party's traditional New Deal coalition. His book, *The Emerging Republican Majority* (Arlington House, 1969), dealt with the shift of political power from the Northeast to the Sun Belt states. He foresaw the winning combination that would later propel Ronald Reagan into the White House.

William Rusher went a step further with his discerning work, *The Making of the New Majority Party* (Green Hill, 1975). Robert Whitaker's previously mentioned *A Plague on Both Your Houses* provocatively examined the depth of populist disaffection, and pointedly warned of the dangers which ignoring the problem would bring.

According to the official media line, "rebelliousness" only occurs among nonwhites, or on college campuses. The establishment looks on the Middle America that supports it financially very much as slave holders looked on the "happy darkies," and the French and Russian aristocracies looked on the peasants shortly before their respective Revolutions. If Harlem were to give an avowed Communist two percent of its vote in an election, the press would immediately recognize dangerous frustrations. But the fact that the official Nazi Party, swastikas and all, never gets less than five percent of the vote when it fields a candidate is looked on as a sign of irritating restlessness on the part of the peasants.

Like their Czarist and Bourbon predecessors, today's ruling class sees the surly peasantry as another demonstration of the need for a firm hand. Wildcat strikes, protest demonstrations, and Nazi votes are merely proof to them of the fundamental depravity of the mass of Americans. If a black man votes Communist, it merely confirms what they have always said, that America is not spending enough on social programs. If a white man votes Nazi, it shows the same thing, that social engineering has not gone far

enough. What those surly peasants need, the media experts con-
clude, is another sight of the whip.

Those of us who have seen this building frustration first-hand
view today's politics differently from either liberals or conservatives. Conservatives think of President Reagan as answering all
the problems. They feel all people want is a little less government
and less taxes, and maybe some laws on social issues, and everybody will be happy. Liberals think of Reagan as a temporary revolt
against the natural rule of the liberal establishment, after which
business will be as usual. Populists tend to think of the conservative swing as the letting off of a little steam from a pot which, if
Reagan continues business as usual, will continue to boil toward
the explosion point.

The New Right, under attack by everybody else as asking for
too much, concerns us only in asking too little. Many a Southerner,
after the Civil War, wished he had listened to some of those who
wanted a gradual abolition of slavery. Likewise, pre-Revolution
"radicals" were remembered wistfully by exiled aristocrats from
France and Russia. By the same reasoning, of course, it is hard to
believe that the New Right will not be forced to trim its sails and
be "reasonable," as most of the radicals in 1789 France, 1850
Georgia, and 1916 Russia had to do.

Donald I. Warren, a professor at the University of Michigan,
explored the extent of Middle American frustration in his detailed
study, *The Radical Center* (Notre Dame, 1976). Professor Warren
wrote that the alliance of the West Virginia anti-textbook struggle
and the Boston anti-busing battle at a Washington march in early
1975 had symbolized the beginning of a new "Middle American
Radicalism" (MAR). Since this act of unity was arranged by The
Populist Forum, it seems clear that the people whom Warren calls
MARs overlap greatly with those whom we call populists.

Warren presented the findings of an extensive Cambridge Survey. It showed that MARs (populists) constituted 31 percent of the
white American population, up from 29 percent in 1972.

The Survey asked white Americans to agree or disagree with
this statement: "The true American way of life is disappearing so
fast that we need to use force to save it." Forty-three percent of the
MARs, and a quarter of "other whites" agreed with the statement.
This means that roughly one-third of all white Americans foresee
the necessity of using force to maintain the "true American way

of life." A substantial majority of these saw "the American government," "politicians," "the President," "radicals," and "big business" as the primary targets of such force.

Warren grimly concluded:

> No democracy can tolerate that kind of dissatisfaction and not stumble into great danger. For a while MARs may indeed be subdued and less able to carry out via a party, a program, or a leader what is implied in their anger and dismay with the course they see American society following. But unless bridges are formed and policy adjustments are made, the MAR perspective may grow to the point where it begins to pervade society and to affect the political and social fabric with possibly drastic consequences.

The social dissatisfaction which Warren recorded in 1975 has unquestionably grown since then. America is that much closer to the "drastic consequences" which he foresaw.

What factors have brought about the alienation and frustration that manifest themselves in the new populism? Economics is only a part of the problem. Living standards have actually risen slightly in the last twenty years. In the past Americans have solved economic problems far greater than any we face today. It is rather that the entire social and political system has grown increasingly unresponsive and even hostile to many of the most basic needs and ideals of the great majority of the American people.

During the election campaigns of the 1960s, crime was a major issue. Since then, the crime rate has increased to epidemic levels. But it's not much of a campaign issue today because the government has shown that it cannot or will not bring itself to act with the severity necessary to deal with the problem. When a government fails to enforce its most basic laws, it forfeits the moral right to demand loyalty or obedience from its citizens.

Indifference in Washington is exceeded only by hypocrisy. Congress exempted itself from the "affirmative action" employment laws it forced on the rest of America and voted itself salary increases far in excess of inflation while exhorting everyone else to sacrifice and belt-tightening.

Not surprisingly, the percentage of eligible Americans who vote has been declining steadily for three decades. Political apathy among young people is especially endemic.

The electronic media controlled from New York and Washington barrage America with a storm of fads and novel ideas that undermine faith in tradition, in the future, and in ourselves. Novelty is praised as a virtue unto itself. As a result, our sense of identity becomes warped and many of us clutch at straws of emotional security. The mass media are a kind of collective mirror. But the image of ourselves we see reflected there is contemptible and hideous.

The experience of the Vietnam war did much to disillusion and embitter my entire generation. During my one-year tour of duty in Vietnam as a civilian contractor, I saw how the U.S. government squandered the sacrifices of Middle America. The administration that sent young men to die in that war actually *boasted* that they gave their lives not for America, but . . . for the Vietnamese! Everything that the United States was doing in Vietnam, President Johnson repeatedly told the world, was being done to bring security and happiness not to our country but to South Vietnam.

Nothing has contributed more to white populist disillusionment than the breathtaking hypocrisy and condescending arrogance shown by the establishment over the race issue.

Infuriated South Boston residents booed and threw tomatoes at Senator Edward Kennedy when he made a rare public appearance to defend the hated racial busing program. "We cannot have one set of laws for Mississippi and another set of laws for Massachusetts," Kennedy once said. But no Kennedy has ever had to experience the horrors of having himself or his children bused into the ghetto. The Kennedys of America have their own double standard: one set of rules for their own wealthy class, and another for the middle and working classes. They created a system whereby the rich could *buy* their way out of racial trauma.

David Cohen, responsible for enforcing federal busing orders through the U.S. Civil Rights Commission, advised local school boards around the country to simply ignore protesting parents: "Let them blow off steam," he instructed, "They'll learn to accept busing." But under intense questioning, Cohen admitted that his own children attended an exclusive private school.

No wonder millions of populist Americans lost confidence in government leaders like Kennedy and Cohen who reserved privileges for themselves that they denied to others. While the wealthy remained immune, populist Americans have been expected to welcome the social and racial experimentation which bodes only disaster for themselves and their communities. Those who resisted or fled forced busing weren't asking for special favors or economic privileges. They only wanted a little social and cultural stability for themselves and their families.

No wonder vast numbers of white working-class Americans have come to believe that the federal government holds them and their children in something approaching contempt. These Americans spend their lives on the economic and psychological brink, and lack the resources to make the expected generous sacrifices to social progress. All too many of them are heaved off their tenuous perches by uncaring, do-gooder politicians who consider them expendable.

Government racial regulations sometimes reach absurd limits. A Wisconsin manufacturing firm, for example, was denied a defense contract because it employed no blacks. When the company explained that no blacks lived for miles around, the Defense Department curtly replied: Import some blacks—if you want defense contracts. The commander of a U.S. Army base in Germany was reprimanded after he tried to make his Hispanic troops speak English—while on duty. A Texas court has ruled that American taxpayers must finance the schooling of illegal alien children.

As basic social institutions deteriorate further, we can expect populist disaffection to manifest itself in growing political extremism, territorial dissolution, nihilistic "survivalism," and extralegal militancy.

Recent years have already seen a sharp rise in extremist political activity. After a long period of decline, the Ku Klux Klan is showing new signs of life. In 1980, a self-avowed Nazi won 43 percent of the vote in the Republican primary for Lieutenant Governor of North Carolina. A few months later, another "neo-Nazi," Gerald Carlson, actually won the Republican primary in Michigan's 15th Congressional District. In a solidly Democratic district, Carlson polled 32 percent of the vote in the general election against a longstanding incumbent. Tom Metzger, grand dragon of the California Ku Klux Klan, likewise rolled to victory in a Democratic Congressional primary.

While still a peripheral and negligible phenomenon, white racist political activity will grow in the years ahead unless the frustration it symptomizes can be directed into regular political channels.

For the first time since the Civil War, regional separatism and

Balkanization have become plausible possibilities. The example of Quebec, and growing disaffection with Washington and the dying Northeast have encouraged discussion in the West and South about breaking away from federal rule. Some see the United States splitting along racial lines. Militant Chicano leaders talk of taking back the Southwest United States for "La Raza." Federal bureaucrats who give taxpayers' money to La Raza insist that the title just means "people," and that Spanish doesn't have a separate word for "race." This is an insult to the Spanish language, which has words for "people," and also a word which means "race." That word is "raza." La Raza Unida means "the united race." It is hard to imagine federal money today being given to a white, or even a black group with such a title. Kevin Phillips examined the separatist phenomenon with remarkable insight in "The Balkanization of America" (*Harper's,* May 1978).

The rapid growth of the "survivalist" movement in recent years underscores the extent to which Americans have lost confidence in the future. Anticipating complete social, economic and political collapse within the next few years, "survivalists" are moving to the countryside, hoarding food supplies, and arming themselves with a vast array of weapons. They are not alone in their apprehension. Over half of the American people now own guns.

The system's response to the black riots of the 1960s and 1970s betrayed a dangerous lack of self-confidence with sinister implications for the future. In response to the civil uprisings, the government and numerous large corporations poured untold billions into black communities. But behind all the rhetoric about "compensation" and "economic justice" was the vivid lesson that groups using violence could successfully extort money from the establishment.

The result, of course, has been increasing contempt for a system that indirectly rewards those who violently break the law. We have come to accept and even expect extra-legal political extortion as a reality of American life.

These lessons have not been lost on populist militants. Following a campaign of violent resistance by the parents of Kanawha County in 1974, officials withdrew the offensive textbooks. In 1976, the government rescinded all fines and injunctions against strike leaders after 150,000 coal miners began a wildcat strike in their defense. During the coal strike of 1978, the government proved unable to enforce its own Taft-Hartley "back to work" rule.

Kenneth Underwood was the School Superintendent of Kanawha County—until he hastily resigned and fled the state following a school board meeting at which a group of angry mothers got physical. "These people don't just make threats," he whined. "They mean what they say." During the AAM tractorcade marches on Washington, I repeatedly heard comments that farmers would not get a hearing until they began to make trouble as the blacks did in the 1960s.

The rise of populist militancy suggests that America may be entering a pre-revolutionary era. Historically, revolutionary situations have arisen not as a result of poverty or even oppression, but only when the possibilities for further progress within the system seem exhausted. Certain disturbing parallels can already be drawn between our own age and the decades preceding 1917 Russia, 1789 France and 1775 America. Whether or not our era culminates in revolution will depend on the response of our political leadership.

The political implications of the new populism are awesome for liberals, and the Old Right, and, most of all, the New Right.

The 1980 election of Ronald Reagan represented a stunning rejection of liberalism. Although Democratic officials seemed surprised, only the aberration of Watergate had delayed the debacle so long. For millions of Americans, liberalism has become identified with the enormous problems which liberals seemingly created. Liberalism, for many, has come to stand for all that is sick and alien about our society. Except for militant minorities and a dwindling remnant of party loyalists, liberalism has been thoroughly repudiated. As George Will has pointed out, not since the 1964 Lyndon Johnson landslide has a Democratic presidential candidate received a majority of the white vote.

Another bastion of liberalism, organized labor, has been steadily losing populist support since the 1950s. I remember when national AFL-CIO officials refused to meet even briefly with Jim Luckett, president of the largest union local in America (with 17,000 electrical workers), because he represented the anti-busing parents of Louisville. The 1976 "issues convention" of the national Democratic party refused even to consider busing as a serious issue.

Many liberals pretty much concede that the great experiment has proven a social, cultural and political failure. In his last days, even liberal stalwart Hubert Humphrey was given to musings like,

"I can't believe everything we did was wrong." It is difficult to see how liberals can ever hope to resurrect the New Deal coalition, because modern liberalism is inherently unable to genuinely represent populist America.

The Old Right has traditionally distrusted the working class and feared the populist movement. In the 1960s, many large corporations donated millions to black areas as a kind of extortion payment. During the great anti-busing struggle, even the Catholic church, with only negligible exceptions, betrayed the South Boston Irish who had built and sustained the church for generations.

On several occasions, I tried to arrange meetings between prominent conservatives and populist leaders, but without success. After one such effort, I returned empty-handed to the AAM farm leaders. I told them of the conservative fear that the farmers' strike was some kind of socialist plot. One farm leader replied sardonically, "If we don't get help soon, we won't have a plot to piss in."

Populists are not traditional fiscal conservatives. Many of them revere the memory of Franklin D. Roosevelt and admire George Wallace. For years they were aligned with the liberals. And although populists feel betrayed by liberalism, conservatives make a big mistake if they take populist support for granted. The populist backing for Ronald Reagan is only tentative and conditional upon performance. If his conservatism is limited to Old Right concerns, it is doomed. He can build a new political movement by embracing populism, but he will have to come out of the conservative Rose Garden to do so. Populism is not an historical aberration or a form of political extremism. It is a traditional and genuinely American political phenomenon. An American who ignores it is not a conservative, but an elitist of the right.

Populist America today lacks political leaders of its own. Its power is currently undirected and dissipated. Therein lies the great challenge and opportunity for the New Right, which is the only political current in a position to concentrate and direct that power. This opportunity is also an enormous responsibility, because it's hard to see how America can survive unless the New Right seizes this historic moment.

Neither liberals nor old-line conservatives are in a position to successfully articulate or manifest the frustrations of Middle America. The New Right is. It can tap into a tremendous reservoir of frustration, which can mean political power. Or it can misread the wave of anti-establishment feeling as a temporary aberration which an improvement in the economy and a partial dismantling of the federal government will dispel, as the Old Right and the neo-conservatives have done.

Populists are as alienated and frustrated today as their forebears were in the years just preceding the American Revolution. Many are just as radical and ready for violence. I have witnessed numerous acts of populist rage a great deal more dramatic than the Boston Tea Party.

The first American Revolution began when government troops trying to seize two illegal weapons collections were fired upon by farmers at Lexington and Concord. A hundred such incidents are waiting to happen today.

Tommy Kersey, the AAM farm leader, was explicit in comparing today's populist struggle with the one fought some two centuries ago. "The American Revolution was fought by farmers who farmed in the summer and fought in the winter. Well, that's us. We're the winter soldiers." American populists made one revolution in 1775. If no alternatives are offered, they can make another one today.

We stand now before a national crisis as pregnant with revolutionary change as any in history. Politics as usual is proving utterly inadequate to the challenge. Our New Right political response must differ fundamentally from those we have been used to.

The question is not whether Middle America will become more radical. That is inevitable. The question is whether the New Right will rise to the challenge posed by the process of radicalization. To borrow a phrase from the leftists, that means "seizing the time." It means articulating the frustrated hopes of Middle America and *leading* that process.

As happens so seldom in history, destiny holds out the hand of tremendous opportunity. Woe to us if we do not accept it!

NEW
RIGHT
ALTERNATIVES

Clyde N. Wilson

CITIZENS
OR SUBJECTS?

Clyde N. Wilson has seen America from many angles—he was a textile mill worker, police reporter, and is presently Associate Professor of History at the University of South Carolina. His observations, both historical and contemporary, describe a situation where political revolution is necessary, and its ugly alternatives—lasting submission or violence—real possibilities. Clyde Wilson is also the editor of The Papers of John C. Calhoun.

During the past half century a struggle has been going on to decide whether America will remain a republic or become an empire. Almost every political, cultural, social, and even economic issue that has been fought over is subsumed in this larger struggle. The forces of imperialism have seemed to have history on their side and have almost, but not quite, prevailed. The forces of republicanism are battered but not quite vanquished.

The 1980 elections were the *beginnings* of a last great counteroffensive by the republicans. The war will probably be decided within the next decade. The outcome will determine whether the descendants of the present generation of Americans will be free citizens of a proud republic or merely ciphers in a faceless mass of imperial subjects. The slender hope of avoiding the latter end depends in the short run upon the foresight, morale, and determination of the republicans and in the long run upon the ultimate survivability of American institutions.

An empire is not to be distinguished from a republic by the

extent of its overseas commitments or the possession of foreign colonies or the size of its military forces. It is possible, though not necessarily easy, for a people to remain republican while engaging in extensive trade, military campaigning, and even colonization overseas. An empire is differentiated from a republic by the nature of its domestic society and by the purposes which inform its official and public activities.

Nations come into existence when a unique identity is fused by history out of a particular group of people, a particular land, and a particular culture. In unusually fortunate circumstances, a nation emerges with institutions of self-government, institutions in which political power originates within and is widely dispersed among the community—a republican society. Such institutions appeared naturally among the British colonists of North America and were legitimized by the Revolution and the Constitution.

The Founding Fathers knew that republican societies were fragile. History taught them that republics, and particularly large and diverse ones, tended to degenerate into empires. Their best thought and effort were directed at means of enhancing and prolonging the life of those self-governing institutions of which Americans had fortuitously found themselves in possession. The fear of degeneracy loomed so large that how to avoid it was the source of the sharpest disagreements that occurred among the founding generation.

At the heart of their dissensions was the confusion engendered by the paradox of liberty and order. But all agreed that political liberty was a meaningful concept only within an ordered community. Self-government was of value only to one who was indeed self-governed. That is, only a virtuous people could be republican. Virtue was defined according to stern Roman values, with something of the sober English ones thrown in. A society of men who did not govern themselves could not be self-governing. Republicanism was not a benefit bestowed from above, a decree of government that magically guaranteed freedom and equality to all warm bodies. Self-government was a blessing that flowed to people who, both by their efforts and by the kind of people they were, established communities in which self-government became possible and reasonable, communities in which there were moral resources sufficient for the strenuous task of reconciling liberty, order, and popular rule. Men did not become good citizens by having democracy. They had democracy because they were the stuff of good citizens.

Further, a society of men who did not value their self-govern-ment enough to make sacrifices for it could not long remain self-governing: sacrifices not only in what was necessary to defend against foreign dangers, but also sacrifices in self-discipline and self-denial of those indulgences and laxities that accumulated to the degeneracy and subversion of republicanism.

The benefit of republicanism, the reason why it justified these sacrifices, indeed, the very definition of self-government, was the superiority of the community to its rulers. In a reversal of the common pattern of mankind, rulers (a necessary evil) became dele-gates of the community, temporarily assigned to look after the public business, rather than the community existing chiefly as a source of gratification and support to the rulers. The rulers were "responsible," a word used often by the Founding Fathers—"re-sponsible" to the community which designated them and to which they would retire, in time, to share as ordinary citizens in the benefits or burdens following upon their administration. This was the difference between a republic and an empire.

"Responsibility" was an intensely moral concept. Responsibil-ity in the officeholder entailed being under the law, scrupulously staying within the limits of delegated authority, being the agent of the community rather than its master. "Responsibility" had an-other moral sense, as well. The ruler, while staying within the limits of his authority, carried out within those limits the duties of his office as vigorously and effectively as possible. A republican statesman was the trustee of the community. A sense of honor kept him in obedience to those who elected him. While observing the limits of delegated authority, he was expected to have the high moral and intellectual qualities required to discern the long-range interests of the community and to govern effectively.

The key to republicanism, then, is the precedence of the com-munity over the government. America, at least republican Amer-ica, is not merely an accidental collection of individuals dependent upon a particular government. The American community is the expression, at this moment in time, of that unique synthesis of people, culture, and land that occurred in the emergence of the nation. Communities have forebears and descendants. Their politi-cal acts are governed in the consciousness of these as well as of present necessities. Empires, on the other hand, are governed by the momentary necessities or even the whims of rulers. In an empire, by the calculus of the Founding Fathers, the rulers were the opposite of "responsible." They were corrupt and dangerous in two senses: They were usurpers of authority over (against) the rights of the people, that is, the community; and, they were incompetent in carrying out the high and necessary functions of government. One needs only to read over the indictment of George III in the Declaration of Independence to see how the two evils went together in the American mind.

The Founding Fathers, drawing on their understanding of English history, had a terminology for the contrary tendencies to which government was subjected. There was the "court party," which was devoted to the interests of the rulers, and the "country party," which sought to defend and preserve the community. The court party represented and favored the pressure toward the degeneracy of republicanism, that is, it represented an imperialist thrust. The country party's main duty was to guard against the cunning usurpations of the court. Allegiance to the "country" party rested upon an assumption that society took precedence over government, that government existed only to preserve and enhance society.

The "country" philosophy was also a philosophy of individual liberty. One of the many plausible guises under which evilly motivated rulers sought to undermine or overthrow the limitations put upon government by republicanism was that of protecting the individual from the community. But to the "country party" there was no contradiction between the liberty of the individual and the liberty of the community. Indeed, the liberty proclaimed by Revolutionary Americans encompassed both meanings. The separation out of individual liberty and the placing of it in conflict with the community by modern political philosophy has been the greatest asset imperialism has enjoyed—it has provided imperialism with its strongest motivating drive and its most powerful legal weapons. Government has aggrandized itself by posing as the defender of the individual against the community.

To the Founders the community was the context into which the individual was born or admitted, a context which provided him with a secure identity and the possibility of realizing his potential as a human being. Community implied a degree of homogeneity and stability, of givenness. Cultural activity was an expression of the personality of the community. Political activity, in a healthy and republican community, was the effort to enhance the well-being of the community in regard to its domestic peace and its freedom from the foreign enemy.

As understood by the Founders, individual liberty could only occur in an ordered community. While the group, in the final analysis, took precedence over the individual, the individual's existence, including his exercise of freedom and his possibilities for individual expression and achievement, was given a framework of relevance only by his membership in the community. One must be a member of the community, he must share in its culture and tradition by birth or active allegiance, before he could be a free and self-governing citizen. In practice in early America, citizenship was not bestowed upon the immigrant by the government, but by the community. Immigrants voted in some states before being granted federal naturalization. The government merely registered that the mutual adoption had taken place.

Individual liberty was thus a byproduct of membership in good standing of a free community, not a grant from government. Therefore, individual liberty was much more effectively guaranteed by limitation upon government than by grant of rights. To assume any other grounds for republican citizenship was to assume (and a great deal of what passes at present for democratic political philosophy does so assume) that man derived his worth from government, that he had no intrinsic value. This may indeed be true of imperial man. It is not true of republican man. Even man's relation to the Almighty, while transcending nations and cultures, has no means to express and perpetuate itself except through the personality of a particular community.

To put it another way, limited government is synonymous with republicanism. The limits have not to do with abstract mechanisms, checks and balances (which are merely incidental, though they make up almost entirely the modern pseudophilosophy of democratic government), or even with constitutions, which are not the substance of a republican society but simply the register of its existence. Republicanism consists essentially in the inviolability of the community, its superiority over the machinery of government. Individual liberty and the postulated equality of citizens before the law are not gifts of the government but products of the precedence of the community over the government, indicating the limited and secondary standing of the latter.

An empire, on the other hand, functions in indifference to both the individual and the community. It reverses the precedence of community and government. An empire may originate in the colonizing or military efforts of a particular people. Its institutions may reflect, palely, the institutions of the communities out of which it arose. Its founding people may remain on hand as a ruling caste in the empire, but in that case they will have become merely a class and not a people. Their identity will depend upon their political position in the empire, not their membership in a nourishing culture.

The republic passes over into empire when political activity is no longer directed toward enhancement of the well-being of a particular people, but has become a mechanism for managing them for the benefit of their rulers. That is to say, an empire's political behavior reflects management needs, reflects the interests of maintaining government itself, reflects the desires of those who happen to be in control of its machinery of administration, rather than the personality and will of the nation being governed. The government of an empire is abstract, manipulative, a government of, by, and for the government, not of, by, and for the people. Power flows downward rather than upward.

In an empire all institutions receive their legitimacy from the approval of government, rather than government being a means to nourish and protect institutions. In an empire the government is the basis of all things, in a republic the community. In an empire the genius of the people, as the American Founding Fathers called the particular native social fabric, no longer matters because an empire consists of many peoples, or, in effect, none. It consists of subjects, interchangeable persons, having no intrinsic value, to be manipulated in the interests of that abstraction, the empire. Subjects, for instance, whose neighborhoods or schools may be turned over to criminals should the rulers prefer to placate criminals rather than punish them. Subjects whose hallowed notions of family and morality may be put officially on a par with debased forms invented by diseased personalities. Or whose culture can be treated as inferior to some other that has been or is to be imported and officially recognized.

Or subjects whose lives may be expended in wars the relationship of which to the security and welfare of their community is tenuous. Thus imperialist foreign policy (like imperialist domestic policy) is "irresponsible" in the republican sense. It reflects the vagaries of mind or the assumed self-interest of the imperial class. It has no point of reference, such as is axiomatic to a republican society—the well-being of the community. Republics go to war to defend their interests or presumed interests, including possibly their honor. Empires go to war because going to war is one of the things that "irresponsible" rulers do. Since imperial rulers are not responsible, they have power but not moral obligation, and represent themselves and not communities. They are capable of going to war for subjective self-gratification, making a remote land "safe for democracy," for instance. They are equally capable of ignominious retreat on the flimsy grounds of the evaporation of their fantasy. They choose illogically to ignore communism ninety miles away and fight it five thousand miles away—it is, after all, the duty of subjects to obey, not to question. The obedience of subjects to their rulers is easily distinguishable from the obedience of republican citizens to the laws and deliberate decisions made by their community.

The New Right, it seems to me, may best be understood as a largely spontaneous and as-yet-imperfectly-articulated defense of the American community (or rather communities, for there are several) against the inroads of imperialism. It has been forced out by a sense of alarm that the balance of power has shifted away from the community and toward an imperial ruling class, and a sense of fear that such a shift represents a malignant condition for a republican society. That is to say, viewed in the light of the Founding Fathers and of the instinctive feeling of Americans about what it means to be American, the trends of recent decades forebode the end of the republic and anticipate the termination of a unique experiment in the self-governance of communities and the limitation of rulers.

The fact is that the balance of power *has* shifted against the people and in favor of the court; that government policy, both domestic and foreign, has for some time now been directed more and more by the interests and opinions of the class that dominates the centers of power, official and unofficial, and its clients, and less and less by the well-being or beliefs of the people.

Most of the ills facing American society today can be viewed simply as the varied manifestations of the growth of what I have called imperialism. It is the onset of imperialism that accounts for the widespread sense of powerlessness and decline felt by Americans today, a malaise far deeper than that experienced in major crises of the past like the Civil War or the Great Depression. The trends of recent decades, unchecked and unreversed, foretell the transformation of republicanism into something else—the familiar, ancient forms of servitude, the end of liberty and dignity, except for the imperialist class—those lucky, ruthless, or cunning enough to belong to the court rather than the country.

That the form of republicanism remains intact, apparently, is of little significance. It is the substance which ought to be our concern. That members of the imperialist class, floating on a sea of luxury and irresponsibility such as was never known before in the world, do not see the degeneracy of the times, does not matter. The average American, rooted in the reality of work, responsibility, and survival, knows that he is not as well off, not as secure, not as proud or as easy as he once was.

It was the boast of the Founding Fathers and subsequent generations that America was the best country in the world for the common man—that was one of the meanings of republicanism. It may still be true, but how much longer? With the value of labor eaten away by inflation, neighborhoods threatened, education deteriorating, the minimal conditions of civility disappearing, the American, except for favored members of favored minorities, sees his hopes slipping away. Dimly, he apprehends a sinking from citizenship into peasantry, that he has become a subject rather than a citizen. His unease arises not only from a sense of deterioration but from the instinct that his rightful inheritance, as an American, is to be a proud and self-governing being.

The American body politic is now divided into a country party and a court party, republican and imperialist camps. Republicans are those who place their primary allegiance in the American community—its traditions, values, its very unique reality. They stand distinguished from those who are primarily motivated by the interests of the court and its clients. The latter dominate equally the Left and the Old Right and appear in various guises, as expediency dictates, but most often as adherents of the ideology of "liberalism."

What is today called the New Right is thus not a new but a very old phenomenon in American history and tradition. It is the American country party, provoked into militancy. The tendency, the preference, the despairs and hopes which the New Right signifies are deeply, fundamentally, originally, anciently American. They are not recognized as such, perhaps, because most of our history and political philosophy in recent decades has been imperialist, has been distorted so as to mask the will to power of the court party by an abstract and mechanistic discussion of a disembodied "democracy." The regime has ignored, as much as it could, the interests, even the survival of the living community of republican Americans. The New Right is purely and simply the revolt of the community against the threat to its dignity and self-determination posed by imperial rule. Its mission is to reorient American politics, domestic and foreign, around a clear and simple objective, the well-being of the American people.

The common man's instincts come far closer to the understandings of the Founders than do the apologists of received wisdom. Our course in recent decades conforms perfectly to the scenario familiar to the Fathers as the decay of republicanism by usurpation. Imperialism, remember, is not just bad policy, to be cured by a repair of mechanism or a change of leaders. Imperialism is a condition, a state of decayed responsibility with implications for every part of society. Its ravages are evident everywhere in America today.

There is hardly anyone who has not been aware of the flow of power to Washington in the past few decades. More recently, almost everyone except paid apologists of the imperial class has become aware of the inefficiency, fraud, and waste that have accompanied that flow. Yet the discussion of this issue has been too trite and narrow. It is not a question of redistributing a given quantity of "power." Imperialism should be looked at within the framework of republican responsiblity. The imperialist arrogance of Washington and its minions and the decay of will in the community go hand in hand. The social fabric has deteriorated as power has drained away from the community. The court has gathered power as it has shucked off responsibility. We are governed more, and less well.

Power has been shifted away from the voters and officers of the community, but responsibility has not gone with it. Washington is not "responsible" to those it rules, because the ruled cannot reach it, cannot exercise any effective authority over it. They are subjects, not citizens. Often no one knows who issued the directives that have impinged upon the community, and if they are known, they are out of reach. And Washington is not responsible in the sense of governing effectively either. None can be found to take the responsibility when the directives prove to be onerous. From representatives expressing the will of their people, the local fathers have become leaders in securing acquiescence in what nobody wants but nobody seems to know how to avoid, in what government does *to* us.

Even Congressmen no longer go to Washington to deliberate and achieve a consensus and decree the will of the people to the government. They have been tranformed from delegates of the sovereign people into imperial lackeys. Their primary "responsibility," except possibly on election day, is to the bureaucracy. They maintain themselves by sitting atop and taking credit for the flow of government manna back to their communities. It is beyond the Congressman's power to be "responsible" in the republican sense because it is beyond his power to make the will of his community felt and beyond his power to prevent usurpations by the rulers except in small and incidental ways. Seeking to serve the people, he becomes frustrated or impotent; or else he becomes a willing and well-rewarded camp follower of the imperialists. Many thousands of bureaucrats and judges not "responsible," in the understanding of the Founding Fathers, to the public and even unknown to it, exercise power greater than Congressmen. They even, in many cases, enjoy pay and perquisites superior to those of the elected delegates, as complained of as the latter are. The Founding Fathers would have recognized this immediately as the rule, in all but name, of a "court" party.

But the decline of power and will in the community, the transfer of local authority and responsibility out, does not have a benefit in the increase of the individual liberty of the citizen vis-à-vis the community. Ordinary citizens have never been less secure in their incomes and persons, never had a harder struggle to maintain a sphere of decency for their families, never had less freedom to come and go without fear, never had less liberty and means to undertake enterprises independent of government authority. They are less free and happy, their aspirations in humane terms are lower than when affluence was much less in evidence.

Ordinary Americans, particularly in the largest and most liberal cities, are no longer proud members of self-governing communities. They are cowering nobodies, faceless interchangeable beings without a notion of being masters of their own fates. All this under an imperialist regime which seeks "quality" and "equality" with immense expenditures and police powers, yet is increasingly incapable of guaranteeing minimal conditions for civilized life, indeed often becomes the enemy of private efforts to maintain those conditions.

Another indicator of the state of decay which is imperialism is the shift of emphasis from production to consumption, from work to amusement, such as has taken place since the middle 1960s. It reflects an assumption of power by an irresponsible court party. "Aristocrats" concern themselves with what is due to them, not with the sordid details of providing it. All the emphasis is on distribution, none on production. The courts, the bureaucracy, and a careless Congress have erected so many lavish entitlements that society is threatened with bankruptcy on one side and disappointment of immense proportions on the other.

With typical imperialist behavior, the rulers have taken credit for the distribution and eschewed responsibility for the production. Distribution, no matter how irresponsible, is moral, production contemptible. Our rulers are inundated in a sea of money which they are ready to spend on themselves or for any purpose they see fit without any verifiable distinction between private greed and public need. It does not occur to an imperialist President that the public does not owe him a landing field on his ranch. It does not occur to an imperialist scholar that the government should not subsidize his viewpoint. The line between private appetite and public purpose has nearly ceased to exist.

It is not enough to blame bureaucracy. Bureaucracies have tendencies to self-aggrandizement that need to be watched, but they can perform useful and necessary public functions. The point is that our institutions are now managed in the spirit of and for the interests of the imperial class. The institutions exist primarily to perpetuate themselves and to provide sustenance for those who belong to them, not to fulfill clear and limited goals related to the well-being of the community. The community provides tribute, the rulers dispose.

The New Right, I believe, starts from a real if poorly articulated instinct that economic problems are at base problems of morale, that is, of morals. The well-integrated community produces its needs and a surplus. Only when the community becomes embattled, sees its production preyed upon by nonproducers and nonmembers, does economic morale begin to sag, with all the dire consequences—especially dire in a complex and a distribution-oriented economy. Of all the dire consequences of irresponsible distribution, inflation is the worst. Inflation is not a technical problem, it is a moral problem, a failure by rulers which takes the form of oppression of the prudent and productive. Communities with governments that take responsibility for their actions can control inflation.

Imperialism is not only a political phenomenon. The pervasive and progressive loss of function characteristic of our economy and of local and state government spills over into every area of life. The abandonment of responsibility to remote and abstract power is simultaneous with the decay of will and identity in nonpolitical institutions. Increasingly, all our institutions exist primarily to perpetuate themselves and provide employment rather than to perform the functions for which they were established. Do not deteriorating goods and services and corporate bailouts tell us that, even in business, responsibility decays? A society in which clergymen don't save souls, school children don't learn to read, reporters can't distinguish facts from feelings, tanks break down on their first run, jurists substitute whims for legal learning, has already gone a long way down the road to imperialism. We no longer judge by result and results no longer depend upon will and effort. In more and more areas of life success depends upon political manipulation, luck, and advantage. Cunning and bluster, the hallmarks of politics, become more important than accomplishment in more and more areas of life, as these are increasingly politicized.

Republican societies reconcile individual ambition and social good by providing scope for the former and harnessing it to the benefit of the latter. One burns to make more money, another to compose a symphony, another to invent a new device or technique, another to fly farthest or fastest, all to do something well for the love of that thing or the distinction that doing well brings. Such achievements derive part of their meaning from being contributions to the common good by people who feel a sense of belonging to the community.

Thus a sound community automatically generates leadership. The very fact that it provides a meaningful framework for existence arouses ambitions and encourages talents. To lead the nation, to enhance its well-being, becomes the end of existence for the maturest and highest minds. To achieve honor and position within the community informs the efforts of the young. This is not merely political but affects every activity of life—business, professions, culture. Integrity is encouraged because it has an observable value in fundamental life relations with a given people, and is respected. Excellent performance is recognized, not just by a technical group or a government committee, but as a contribution to society. Thus the strongest individual ambitions and the strongest social instincts are reconciled. A free and flourishing society is possible. In the republican community, an approximate if not absolute relationship between reward and effort prevails. But in an empire success consists of access to the levers of political power, which accounts for a progressive decline in performance in all areas of life. Only in sports and to some extent show business does the desire for excellence still reign supreme—the circuses of the masses have to be good as the quality of bread declines.

One of the keys of republicanism, as understood by the Founders, was that rulers were temporary and delegated. They could be reduced regularly to the ranks of the people to take the consequences of the laws they had made. But in imperial America special privileges and immunities characterize the "court party" and its adherents. The erection of special privileges, in fact if not in name, is the sure sign of the rise to power of an imperialist class. Just as rulers cease to function responsibly, so do they aggrandize themselves. There is one law for the peasant, another for the lord. The imperialists decree busing for our children but not for theirs. They create inflation against which they are guarded by automatic raises while the rest of us survive as best we can. They decree permissiveness for criminals but expect protection for themselves. They subsidize schools of Hindus in California and ersatz Muslims in Detroit and suppress Christian schools set up by tenth-generation Americans in North Carolina. In the name of equality they destroy the safety and homogeneity of other people's neighborhoods, not their own.

The Founding Fathers realized that republican societies had a particular tone or atmosphere that differed from that of aristocratic or monarchical states. Republican citizens gave respect to leaders for their services. Imperial subjects, on the other hand, gave flattery to rulers because they were rulers. The immense sentimental adulation that surrounded the Kennedy family during the 1960s and 1970s is perhaps the most pointed evidence that can be produced for the pathological state of republicanism. The Kennedys demanded and received honor not for what they had done, but for what they *were*. A fawning press hid their indiscretions and sang their hosannas in a spirit that would have disgusted Washington and Jefferson, or even Franklin D. Roosevelt. A rather similar treatment was extended to Martin Luther King, and poor Mr. Nixon's troubles resulted largely from his pathetic efforts to secure similar status. Observing the special privileges and glamour surrounding some people, and sought by others, the Founding Fathers would have unhesitatingly diagnosed America as being in a "monarchical" frame of mind, hardly any longer possessing the spirit necessary for a republic.

The Founding Fathers realized that republics could not be proclaimed in a vacuum, but depended upon a republican social fabric. Lack of virtue in the people called forth corruption in the rulers. And corrupt rulers communicated their moral deformity to the entire social fabric. At the heart of the failure of republican responsibility is the substitution of alleged political virtue for private virtue, a failing that has had an irresistible appeal for a certain type of American since the pre-Civil War era and has occasionally burst forth into a predominant mode, as it did in the 1960s and 1970s.

The increasing deterioration of private virtues, the increasingly small number of people who can shoulder mature responsibilities, private or public, is evident in American society and in some of the more modern parts is epidemic. It relates directly to the style of the imperial class, typified by the Kennedys—the making of a ritualistic pronouncement as a substitute for the exercise of virtue and responsibility. By this style, once the proper incantation is said, one is entitled to reward. Government will now magically solve the problem. Day care centers will substitute for unloving mothers and unsustained marriages. Rehabilitation programs will solve the problem of "citizens" who destroy their brains with drugs. More lenient laws and more generous handouts will cure the widespread disrespect for law. This is a profound and devastating kind of loss of responsibility.

The New Right is based on the areas of American life where private virtue is still practiced or at least still recognized. Where the ability to speak the truth, to keep commitments, to exercise moral restraint, to labor productively, to take responsibility for work, family, and community, are taken for granted not only as values but as necessities. Ordinary decent citizens understand instinctively what the Founding Fathers recognized and articulated. Republics depend upon the virtue of the people. To put it another way, morality, a high moral tone, is the *sine qua non* of a republic. Self-government is for the self-governed. While some of the better parts of the Old Left and Old Right still maintain a vague sense of social responsibility and private decency, it is a flabby and attenuated sense, no longer relevant to the real condition of American society.

The New Right knows, for instance, that family is the indispensable basis of all civilized life. Whatever may be wrong with the American family at this moment in history, it is all we've got. Sound communities can only be built upon strong families. Alternative lifestyles do not constitute emancipation and progress, they constitute malignancy. New Rightists, perhaps, do not agree on every nuance of the abortion question. But they do agree that the cavalier attitude toward life, even unborn life, manifested by the liberal lifestyle, is retrogression, not progress. Much the same may be said about "gay rights" and the "alternative family." We have been shocked into reaction, not so much by the manifestations of sickness around us, as by the official sanctioning of it.

It is not a question of a government neutral toward lifestyles. It is a question of whose lifestyle will predominate, a question made by the imperialists with their relentless attacks on decent America. Nor is it a question of oppression or suppression of alternatives. It is a question of not permitting what is tolerable as a fringe of society from becoming the average. Our imperial governors, with characteristically cavalier disdain for consequences, have elevated the immorality that occurs at the fringes of any society and those lapses all flesh is heir to into programs and campaigns, into equality with—no, into *de facto* superiority to—those norms that not only enjoy divine sanction but without which society crumbles. Pluralism calls for tolerance, not disintegration.

At the bottom of the New Right movement lies a vague but deep sense that the worldview of the ruling imperial class in its social manifestations marks a pathological degradation of humanity. Its emphasis on supposed rationalism and openness have reached the point where they threaten the mysterious sanctities without which life loses meaning and becomes mere animal existence, a state in which tolerance becomes a perverse weapon and citizenship impossible. To put it another way, our leading class is decadent and must be replaced by fresher, stronger minds and spirits if we are to survive. It may be that abrogating the narrowness of small town morality was at some point a good thing. But liberation has not brought the Acropolis to Main Street, it has brought the Massage Parlor. The freedom sought by the imperialist is the wrong kind of freedom. It is not the freedom of self-governing republican citizens who prefer to be their own masters. It is the tired throwing off of responsibility, the decadent resignation of aspirations to higher humanity, that characterizes the subject. This point is grasped instantly by the ordinary citizen, but only with the greatest difficulty, if at all, by the liberal imperialist who sees what he has been taught to see, not what is there. It was this phenomenal blindness on the part of our rulers to the real consequences of their positions that to Alexander Solzhenitsyn was the most striking characteristic of American society.

It would be possible to draw out at much greater length the ramifications of our imperialist state, of how our malaise is related to usurpations of power that are easily comprehensible as the degeneracy of republicanism in the light of the wisdom of the Founders. But it is necessary here to anticipate the objections of liberals, including certain New Leftists who have eloquently diagnosed the pathology of American imperialism without realizing that they were a part of it. They will contend that government is not their primary value, that it is merely auxiliary to the democracy, equality, social progress, they wish to achieve.

The answer is that we must look at what they do, not at what they say. Modern liberalism has had only one empirically verifiable manifestation—the use of the government to manipulate and alter the community (which incidentally is often highly profitable, or at least gratifying, to those doing the altering). The manipulation may be deliberately punitive, as in the case of busing, or ostensibly benevolent as in the case of various kinds of "aid" that impinge upon the community. In either case it cannot be other than manipulation because it is done in accordance with some special vision entertained by the liberal of a better community, a vision outside of history and without specificity, a vision of a society endlessly open and malleable that never did and never can exist, a myth. If the liberal ever bore any relation to the real American community, he ceased to do so a long time ago.

Such a vision always entails the precedence of government over people, the means of manipulation over the community in being. The louder and more often the liberal talks about the people, the less specific he becomes—the further from the community of real people, the more abstract, the more imperialist. To him the people is everybody, that is, nobody. Whatever may be postulated about individual rights, in practice the individual ceases to have any significance except in the official hierarchy of manipulation. In the glossary of the Founding Fathers, the liberal is immediately identifiable as an "aristocrat," not a republican, a member of the "court" and not the "country."

I will also anticipate here the objections of libertarians, who will wish to brand the New Right, with its emphasis upon morality and patriotism, as just one more form of statism. Libertarianism, while encompassing some responsible criticism and high ideals, is an insufficient philosophy, though it is one that understandably flourishes among people who wish to be free of the burdens of a government that is becoming imperial rather than republican. The New Right differs from the Old Right and libertarianism essentially in understanding that economic problems are not technical problems but problems of morale, that is, essentially moral problems. The destruction of value by inflation and falling productivity and the loosening of bonds of contractual obligations are necessary and coterminous accompaniments of the loss of virtue in the community and in its rulers, not simply the direct result of too much government.

Free enterprise is a part of the genius of the American people, possibly a part of the genius of any dynamic and progressive people. The right to exchange goods and services, develop new enterprises, compete in the marketplace, is essential to material well-being, technological progress, and individual self-realization. There is no single social generalization applicable to the twentieth century world that is more easy to demonstrate than this.

Nevertheless, to the New Right, free enterprise is not an absolute. It is a means, not an end. New Rightists, including those who devote their lives productively to free enterprise, do not intend to establish a religion of the dollar bill. This clearly distinguishes them from certain elements of the Old Right and from libertarians. New Rightists have no intention of having their neighborhoods turned over to pornographers and dope peddlers, their natural resources controlled by foreign corporations, their national honor understood chiefly as a matter of dollars and cents, their labor cheapened and culture undermined by the removal of barriers to immigration, all in the name of the free market. They understand that such things as public morality, public responsibility, exist. Not only exist but are *sine qua nons* of a free society. Individual liberty flourishes not in a vacuum but is a possibility within a particular social context. Destroy that context by anarchy *or* oppression and individual liberty, as fundamental as it is to man's moral and material well-being, perishes along with every other humane value.

I wish to avoid the alleged besetting sin of the New Right, over-simplification. Thus, let us not exaggerate the ravages of imperialism. Its victories have not been pervasive. Much of the American community remains intact. But one must look beyond local and temporary setbacks and note the overall trend, which, previous to November 1980, had been steadily in favor of the imperialists. The 1980 elections, as yet, are only a check, not a defeat, for the imperialists. Their defeat remains to be consummated.

In further devoir to the dangers of over-simplification, it must be said, that there are two sides to every question. The increasing imperial arrogance of the governing class and its clients and the deterioration of will and identity in the community feed upon each other. The growth of imperialism is not simply the result of the machinations of evil men (though in a political regime that has produced several Supreme Court justices whom no prudent man would trust with the administrations of his children's estate, evil machinations cannot be entirely discounted). Imperialism is a result of, as well as a cause of, the deterioration of community, though in the last quarter century overt government action has greatly accelerated the deterioration of community by magnifying the unhealthiest elements of society and besieging the best.

There is a real question whether the American community is indeed viable any longer in other than an imperial form. Or, as the Founders would have put it, whether the people yet possess sufficient virtue to govern themselves. I believe we can give a cautious affirmative to the query. And I believe that the New Right represents that affirmation—an outpouring of positive belief in the people, an expression of the popular will that has risen above the routine of hog-trough politics—one might say, a resurfacing of the lost tradition of Jeffersonian democracy.

It is true that the multinational corporation, the industrial revolution, and what Joseph Wood Krutch called the "modern temper"—the dislocation of traditional morals, faith, relationships, and ways of life—have worked to undermine the viability of the republican community. The problems that afflict the American family today, for instance, can be blamed only in part on liberals and government. Such problems are not chiefly political problems and do not have chiefly political solutions. The greatest danger that faces the New Right is to avoid the trap of seeking a political solution to nonpolitical problems. To make the social issues primarily matters of political manipulation will be to play into the hands of imperialism. But here is a case, fortunately, where reform and liberty go together. We are once more happily in the place where the answer to many of our problems is not a grant of more power to the government but a limitation upon it, not politics but an end to politics.

New Right politics, then, do not or should not offer to solve such problems as the disintegration of family. What they can offer is the only hope for the political preconditions that will allow the family to save itself. To get the government off the backs of the people, as Mr. Reagan has so happily put it, to deter it from its abetting of social disintegration so that the healthy forces of survival and reconstruction natural to normal individuals and real communities can have scope for their work.

As the Founders recognized and often repeated, usurpers frequently seek to surround their activities with an aura of glamour and mystery, which lends them prestige and covers their shortcomings and greed. This phenomenon was explored with great insight by Jefferson and John Adams in their philosophical correspondence late in life. The clamor raised by the imperial class and its lackeys against "over-simplification" is a perfect example. The implication is that only they are wise enough to understand the complexities of the modern world, and that the common citizen, or even the well-informed one who does not share their particular view of life, had better keep his mouth shut. But republics can only achieve satisfactory decisions by open and honorable deliberation, something which the imperialists suppress by their control of the media and their penchant for branding all disagreement as stupid or evil.

The fact is, a little simplification such as is posed by the New Right is just what we need. We need to return to a simple republican form of government, a form which exists for one purpose—to enhance and defend the community. One of the reasons for our failures, social, economic, diplomatic, military, is that we have lacked a simple point of reference. The heads of our rulers, of the Left and the Old Right, have been full of idle ideologies and pretensions to imperial glory, of everything except the welfare of the American community.

All the great men of the world have been great because of their capacity for profound simplicity. And great issues are simple ones. Or at least, the first step in the solution of great problems is to grasp their simple essentials. The reason our problems seem complex is that they lack a point of reference. To the New Right, evils such as inflation, proliferation of crime, uncontrolled immigration, decay of civility and morality, and inertia in the face of foreign threats are not "complex problems" to be left in the keeping of shamans who worry them around but never solve them. They are the direct effects of "irresponsible" rule in the sense of George III. As such, they can be reversed.

What the New Right calls for is the reorientation of the government in accordance with American republicanism. The starting point of all policy should be the health of the American community in being, the enhancement of its domestic peace and harmony and its security from the foreign enemy. If the issues are viewed from a republican perspective, they *are* simple—what best will preserve and enhance the American people and their descendants. Such a formula will not solve all problems, of course, but it will provide the starting point for their solution. Republican American will be neither ashamed nor incapable of taking the steps that are necessary to secure its economic, moral, cultural, and physical well-being, and that of its posterity.

The republican restoration faces formidable opposition. Imperialism, in all the unbridled arrogance of its privilege and pretension, is deeply dug in in the leadership of both political parties, in the federal courts and bureaucracy, in the media and educational establishment, in the purlieus of inherited wealth. Still, there is much reason for optimism.

Our task is a largely negative and limited one, to curtail the imperial class and liberate the community's powers of creation and restoration. The Iranian crisis has renewed a widespread sense of patriotism in a way that could not have been foreseen. Mr. Reagan is the first President to come to office in more than a half century without the sanction of the court party, and he exhibits an almost providential ability to perceive simple truths and stick to them. Most important, perhaps, is that new generations have the capacity to see the world through different eyes.

All these things work in favor of the restoration of the republic, and suggest that the time is ripe for that periodic returning to our roots that Mr. Jefferson so earnestly recommended. What the future will resemble if we succeed in the renewal of the republic cannot be predicted, because for communities of self-confident, self-governing citizens, the future is open. If we fail, the future is certain to be shaped by the sad, sullen outlines of servitude.

Ronald F. Docksai

THE OTHER SECTOR

Paul Weyrich pointed out above that the New Right insists on public provision for the needy, and for other public needs, but that these things should be done so far as possible by private nonprofit institutions. This discussion, by a senior staff member (Majority Health Director) on the Senate Committee on Labor and Human Resources, covers the practical potential of such private effort. It also shows the consistent nature of developing New Right thought.

S olomon was right. There is nothing new under the sun.
        If any of us hard-thinking individuals had the chance to live the whole course of the last couple thousand years or so, we would probably witness a continuity of themes in the public debates. Man's greed (i.e., *our* greed), God's role and existence, social contracts, the integrity of the family—and we are talking here about the really important things. Institutions come and go or at least their names change. There are and have been peaks and valleys for one kind of social and economic relationship or another, but the basic question remains: How is wealth generated, and how should it be distributed?

Historically, capitalism, socialism and any one of the other theories about how economic systems should be organized and behave have never been applied in pure form. The euphemism, "mixed economy," can in different degrees be applied to every recorded political-economic system. This is especially so within our own country.

Thoroughbred "socialists" or "capitalists" can be found on many American college campuses, on prime-time television and in Greenwich Village. If the U.S. Census Bureau treated them as population categories, conceding a social cohesion which does not exist, they would nevertheless still only comprise a tiny minority within the broad and diverse American population. This is not to denigrate them nor to discount the theoretical influence particular ideologues can have on opinion makers or on those who make public policy. It is simply to recognize that we are not an ideological population. Foreign hosts who greet Americans as tourists think of us as pragmatic, as principally concerned with the practical consequences of whether something will or will not work. We tend to view results as the sole test of the validity or truth of one's political or economic beliefs. Let a few of us agonize over why something is done, but the majority of us are concerned with how. We hold the whys to be implicit. Take welfare, for example.

There is an unspoken, though nonetheless understood and overwhelming belief in the United States that welfare and free enterprise are compatible. So far, history has shown that they are. We don't talk about it, which is why there is an *implied* premise. The premise is that society owes an obligation to secure to all of its citizens a minimum standard of living, independent of each person's ability to provide for him or her self, by the fruits derived from his or her labor, the standard of social and economic security necessary to fulfill the minimum level compatible with the dignity and worth of each individual as a human being.

The protection of women and children, factory and mine safety laws, maximum hours-of-labor standards, sickness and accident insurance, workmen's compensation, old age pensions for workers and white collar employees and the other major social reforms of the nineteenth and early twentieth centuries are historically chronicled as controversial. But while they were controversial among some of the factory owners or managers who generally opposed them and the small group of workers who successfully agitated for their implementation, the vast majority of Americans by every record or index we have to go by thought these "radical" policies eminently reasonable and worthy of supporting. These were, after all, public sector extensions of what Americans were by-and-large already doing.

In the 1870s a post-war depression left millions of Americans without jobs. It was the worst economic upheaval we as a nation had to date experienced. Yet as much as the federal and state governments did to provide economic assistance, which by their standards, seemed like a lot, the welfare effort was unmatched compared to what was performed by groups of individual Americans. Soup kitchens were set up in every American city, foodlines and free lodgings were organized by religious and fraternal civic associations which also distributed coal, clothes and cash to the poor. Msgr. William J. O'Ryan of St. Mary's Roman Catholic Cathedral, Rev. Myron Reed of the First Congregation Church, Dean H. Martyn Hart of St. John's Episcopal Cathedral, Rabbi William S. Friedman of Temple Emanuel, all under the leadership of Reverend Stephen Humphreys Gurteen launched America's first Charity Organization Society in 1877, in Buffalo, New York. It coordinated the work of existing relief organizations, while guarding against duplication and waste. By the turn of the century, there grew to be C.O.S. organizations in 138 communities. The effort has geometrically increased many times since as community needs arose, and it is known today as The United Way organization.

Lord James Bryce, whose best-selling *American Commonwealth* made him the English Alexis de Tocqueville, saw all of this going on in 1887, when he wrote, "In works of active benevolence no country has surpassed, perhaps none has equaled, the United States. Not only are the sums collected for all sorts of philanthropic purposes larger relatively to the wealth of the Americans than in any European country, but the amount of personal effort devoted to them seems to a European visitor to exceed what he knows at home."

In 1917, Henry P. Davison set a goal of $100 million for the American Red Cross, fifty times the total Red Cross had spent in the three previous years combined. This goal was exceeded, and in 1918 it doubled, a year in which the organization had 21 million members. This effort, like the organized campaign described earlier, illustrates a seldom spoken but deeply implanted part of our American culture. In fact, its roots predate not only the American revolution but perhaps all Western culture if one is to account historically for the first time anyone came to the aid and comfort of his neighbor. It is the sector of our American economy which is taken for granted, perhaps because, despite the unmatched size of its public involvement and unparalleled scope of its work, its efforts seem dissipated or scattered.

THE INDEPENDENT SECTOR

I am talking about the nongovernmental, nonprofit provision of services, from churches to education, from The United Way to The United Negro College Fund. This huge and uniquely American complex points the way to providing for the social welfare and other needs of Americans while avoiding both the inefficiencies and the dangers of big government.

One of President Reagan's goals is to assure that local government performs as many functions as possible without federal interference. This is a matter of principle, of adherence to the federal system, as well as one of efficiency, obviating the cost and distortions caused by an extra layer of Washington bureaucracy.

On the same conservative policy basis, private efforts should be utilized fully before government programs are instituted. It is a matter of principle, of our preference for private as opposed to governmental initiative. But, as I will explain, it also leads in the direction of efficiency.

This is especially important for the New Right. Unlike libertarians, we want to ensure that the basic needs of poor people are provided for. The Third Sector offers a traditionally American way of supplying this and other services. If governmental action is necessary, it should, so far as possible, act through the Third Sector.

Unfortunately, this is not the way bureaucratic imperialism has led. Powerful lobbies and ambitious bureaucrats have used their influence to take as many programs as possible under federal control. Far from aiding nongovernmental, nonprofit efforts, they have concentrated on taking them over. If we reverse this process, not only can many present programs be returned to the private sector, but even programs begun by government could be handled better at that level.

When it is talked about, it is loosely referred to as The Voluntary Sector, The Charitable Sector or The Nonprofit Sector—all in the effort to distinguish it from the public (government) and private (for profit) sectors of our economy. More than anyone else, the man who has been its most articulate promoter and chronicler, Richard C. Cornuelle,[1] is responsible for its name, The Independent Sector:

> I found that we Americans once proudly solved most of our common problems outside government, through a rich array of institutions, neither commercial nor governmental, which I am suggesting we call "The Independent Sector." In the generations when The Independent Sector had great vitality, human needs were met without adding to the power of government. In the twentieth century, however, this huge potential force has fallen behind the surging vitality of private industry and ambitious government . . .
>
> Today, I believe, The Independent Sector is on the brink of a great renaissance. It can again become the most vital element in our national life. Our most urgent task is to bring our independent institutions to the full capacity our abundance makes possible. They can do much more of the country's serious business, with more efficiency, precision and understanding. They can break the bitter stalemate between doctrinaire conservatism and dogmatic liberalism. If we exploit their potential in a tough and practical way, we can reclaim the American dream.

As Cornuelle describes and as the history of America's tradition of voluntary action demonstrates, our country has never been and is not now prepared to be overtaken by a purely capitalist or socialist mentality. It has always been the congenitally moderate quality of our politics that when we as Americans symbolize our practical view of what society sould be like, it is a vision of a society which is *both* free and humane. For most of its life, the U.S. Congress recognized this, and encouraged voluntary giving. This is why there exists a provision for making foundations tax-exempt as 501(C)3 organizations, and why as far back as 1894 a law passed exempting charitable organizations from the income tax.

The Independent Sector provides something government cannot. Its private foundation assets are free of commitments to specific operating programs or projects, a freedom permitting foundations a relative ease in shifting the focus of their interest and financial support from one charitable area to another. Private charity is noncoercive, thereby reflecting the cumulative choices of individual citizens for how social welfare objectives can be met in a way special-interest beleaguered congressmen or other public sector servants cannot. It also makes provision for the charitable funding of the minority. It provides for the financial support for people, projects or causes which might not otherwise pass the public sector scrutiny of the tax-paying majority. In Grand Rapids, Michigan, we have a case in point in the form of The Dyer-Ives Foundation.

In its brochure, this community-based project is described as "a catalyst and stimulator for innovative projects in educational, social and cultural fields in the Greater Grand Rapids area." In a word, it provides the funds to do things government would never fund. Founded ten years ago by the family of a well-to-do furniture manufacturer, the foundation last year spent $34,651 on twenty-two different projects, with grants ranging in size from $276 to $5,000. It built a solar-powered shower at Wabasis Lake campground ($1,045.), funded a poetry contest ($955), gave $1,000 to a local high school program on jazz, ragtime and the blues, and spent $3,550 to assist in the printing of five booklets dealing with the history of the Ottawa, Chippewa and Potawatomi Indian tribes which originally settled the area. The dispensers of federal money would cite such projects as unimportant, and that is exactly the point.

These nonprofit, privately funded projects were described by a local politician critical of charitable giving as "whimsical." Government grants would seldom be as whimsical. They would seldom take chances. It took chances to sink over $32 million into the Jonas Salk experiments in the search for the cure of a seemingly incurable disease. In large part, this is why not the Federal Government, but the privately funded March of Dimes is responsible for the Salk vaccine which effectively eradicated polio.

The Salvation Army beds and feeds six times more people who would otherwise sleep hungry on the street than the sum of all the federally supported welfare projects in New York City. It was a private effort, marshaled by The Upjohn Foundation working with the Systems Development Corporation, which first worked out a national campaign to train the structurally unemployed, and it is still doing it more successfully then the federally funded Comprehensive Employment and Training Act (CETA) projects.

America's 350,000 churches with 122 million members own assets worth $31 billion. With this, they tutor underprivileged children; work to improve neighborhoods; fund low-cost, low-income housing projects; and foster home health care projects. Last year,

Americans spent $6.2 billion on the elderly relatives living with them, senior citizens not wanting institutionalization in a nursing home which is often seen by these senior citizens as a prelude to death. Despite institutionalized Medicare/Medicaid incentives for such nursing home institutionalization, making it more economically attractive to go the nursing home route, these citizens chose private action.

Kiwanis, Rotary, Civitan and Lions clubs; Chambers of Commerce; Masonic lodges; Knights of Columbus; the Church of Latter-Day Saints; and hundreds of other religious, civic and fraternal service organizations with over 48 million members work more than bankers' or civil service employees' hours to improve their communities and nation. Hundreds of labor unions with 21 million members not only bargain with their respective bosses, but run hospitals and nursing homes, build retirement centers, fund civil rights projects and hold community fund drives.

There are 650,000 organizations in the United States, all of which file with the Internal Revenue Service every year a statement of their receipts, expenses, assets and liabilities. The total assets of all of these nonprofit organizations (excluding corporations) is $531 billion, using 1979 figures. They perform various kinds of charitable work, projects of a greater variety and scope than the conventional images we associate with the word charity would reflect. We are not only talking about hospitals, churches and the Salvation Army. We are talking about country clubs, agricultural marketing cooperatives, professional advancement organizations, trade associations and the multiplicity of other 501(C)3 organizations which provide benefits not only for their members but for the community at large.

DOES ANYONE HAVE A MONOPOLY ON COMPASSION?

John Kenneth Galbraith in *The Affluent Society,* and other equally prominent liberals, have argued for varying forms of *de facto* socialism for a variety of reasons but all based on a common indictment of the private sector's failure. Its incomparable wealth-generating power and tendencies for innovation aside, the private, for-profit sector has at least one unremitting failure. It provides less than the needed quantity of collective goods for which consumers are willing to pay for the cost of production. Because the public sector can compel payment for the production of particular services which the private sector perceives to be unprofitable to finance, government is seen as the institution which can overcome the apparent private sector failure to provide for the common good in at least commonly recognized cases.

Yet for very different reasons, the public sector is at least equally deficient in the role of society's collective agent. Peter Drucker, in his masterwork, *The Age of Discontinuity,* observed that in his own long experience as an organizational manager and public administration consultant, he believed that government was only capable of doing two things well. It could collect taxes and make war, with Vietnam calling the latter into question.

The public sector's two chronic conditions which compromise its effectiveness as a social arbiter are: 1) its lack of information about consumer demands; and 2) its incorrect economic incentives. Briefly examining the first of these, neither theology nor science has yet produced a means by which a government or any other publicly supported organization with a comparable societal unity of command can know all the choices or predict the fancies or even basic needs of its product-consuming and service-soliciting population. (Extreme cases often make lousy analogies, but always serve as good illustrations. On a U.S.-commissioned trip to the Soviet Union five years ago, I inadvertently bumped into a warehouse in the southern Siberian city of Alma Atah. The warehouse had an unlocked door, my use of which brought me into a shiny plastic-coated cavern extending for as far as my contact-lensed eyes could see. I looked at the artificially colored purple, orange and green cylindrical columns for some minutes before I could make out what it was I had come upon. It was later explained to me by a Rumanian economist—whom I found to be less Marxist than cynical in his predisposition—that I had come upon hula hoops: thousands, perhaps millions of perfectly stacked hula hoops! Somewhere in whatever the Soviets call their ministry to determine the current flavor of consumer tastes, some alert micro-economic analyzer read about the hula hoop craze in the West. He or she read in a back issue of *Time* or *Life* magazine that every third American was buying a wooden, plastic coated, three-foot-diametered hoop with which one played homegrown varieties of hoochie-koochie. Those of us living in America at the time can remember the craze which must have lasted as long as six months in the middle 1950s before it petered out, and which has never been heard from since. The American magazine our Soviet Ministry for Consumer Tastes official must have been reading was probably published during the second year of President Eisenhower's first term. Perhaps the passing scene contributed to the fact that the 1973 Soviet manufactured hula hoops never became a big seller. It might also suggest why the 1980 Soviet-made Zils, purported to be the Mercedes Benz of the Volga, looks like a 1952 Chevrolet; why Soviet shoes look as if they were made for Disneyland cartoon characters; and why Soviet toothpaste tastes like plaster. This is not meant to be an exercise in cruelty, but to provide less than subtle examples of why Soviet five-year plans, or the less obvious Westernized forms of central planning, are grossly inefficient means of gauging what it is people really want to buy.

Then there is the matter of incorrect economic incentives. Particularly in democratic societies like our own, there is a tendency to give public support only to those projects and institutions which further the prevailing attitudes, tastes, mores and prejudices of the majority. The Independent Sector, however, is not bound to give only to those people or programs finding favor with the establishment. During the last several years, we have all read or heard about popular causes which early on started out as the nonprofit sector funded projects of voices crying in the proverbial wilderness of government and private sector apathy. The successful Wilderness Society (Independent Sector) project to save the American bald eagle came in the wake of a federally funded Department of the Interior study maintaining that it was too late and that for all practical purposes, America's high soaring symbol was moribund.

Until Martin Anderson's celebrated *The Federal Bulldozer* was published and its criticisms officially accepted and digested, the federal government's answer to urban housing decay was "urban renewal." It was a polite euphemism for bulldozing flat the homes and tenements of a community comprised of residents who did not want to leave, suddenly forcing them to live as urban refugees in spanking new super-apartment house buildings they hated, though most people would have seen them as an improvement. It was years before the public sector authorities caught up with Independent Sector projects organized early, like Thomas A. Matthews's urban city renovation companies. Borrowing construction money at below market interest rates from predominantly Black owned and managed banks, Matthews's Harlem-based operation built or renovated two-family homes which were in turn sold to buyers on the lower economic end of the scale for less than prevailing market prices.

In short, the Third Sector allows Americans to organize to influence every conceivable aspect of the human condition. The National Center for Voluntary Action estimates that 45 to 50 million Americans volunteer annually. That is roughly 24 percent of the population. Americans donated $35 billion to causes in 1977, an increase of 9.5 percent over 1976. Contrary to popular belief, only 10 percent of this came from corporations or foundations.

Estimated in terms of total hours spent and dollars collected, the aggregate figures on nonprofit, Independent Sector activity break down like this: Hospitals (9.2 percent); Other health related fields (8 percent); Education (21.6 percent); Social or Welfare work (19.8 percent); Recreational (5.3 percent); Civic or community (12.7 percent); Youth activities, including Boy/Girl Scouts (19.6 percent); all other, (3.5 percent). It could do far more, better, and more cheaply than government programs do.

Less obvious than the good works performed by the Independent Sector is the significance of how they are performed. These are all projects, we must remind ourselves, organized, funded and performed in three out of four cases by individuals within their own communities. We all need communities in which to relate, giving us our sense of belonging and worth. In performing community work, a citizen is working in proximity to real problems, knowing and feeling strongly about them because he is a part of the community. It is one thing to chart the progress of a retirement plan on a flow chart on the sixth floor of the U.S. Department of Labor. It is quite another to administer such a plan within the corporation or labor union in which the plan's beneficiaries work, wondering out loud how today's work might also impact on oneself when it is one's own turn for application. Throughout our national history, we have gone through one important change after another in which private citizen groups took the lead and the politicians followed. Not even the most saintly, socially minded member of the American public sector hierarchy can be much more sensitive to shifting needs and demands than are the Soviet consumer watchers, whose Five-Year Plan products are outdated and unwanted even before they leave the assembly line. The broad history of Independent Sector action teaches us that it has unexpected, unpredictable strengths. The compassion demonstrated by employees of the government is impersonal and secondary in importance when matched against the concern, resourcefulness and creativity of the much wider audience of private citizen volunteers engaged in social and economic projects within their own communities.

THE PREVAILING PROBLEM

The nation's capital was once charitably defined as an enclave surrounded on four sides by reality. Those of us who spend our professional lives there generally work long and hard, and if one were forced to choose only one criticism of the many which could be leveled against us it is that we cannot see the forest for the trees. You can work so long and so hard and so intensely that you do not have the time, the energy or, after a while, the disposition, to *really* hear and see what is happening elsewhere in the republic.

For the most part, the image of the Independent Sector even among those in government who should know better, connotes foundations like Ford, Carnegie or Rockefeller. These Fortune 500 members of The Independent Sector actually account for relatively few of the people, resources or moneys comprising the whole of America's nongovernment, nonprofit economic sector. Nevertheless, philanthropic activity and nonprofit foundations still get a bad press, particularly within the realms of the Treasury Department and the Internal Revenue Service.

In the wake of The Tax Reform Act of 1969, a bill later enacted into law for the redesignation of portions of the Internal Revenue code, there came to be born Section 4940 of the IRS Code. This section, which makes provision for taxing all investment income earned by nonprofit foundations, was designed by those IRS officials who believe that private foundations should share in some of the costs of government. The original idea, reasonable enough, was that foundations would pay some of the administrative costs of government required in order to insure that their funds were being used for charitable purposes. As often happens in the legislative process, however, the precision defining this proposal got lost on the cutting room floor of some House or Senate committee, so that we now have an increasing number of voluntary corporations or nonprofit enterprises closing up shop in light of the federal disincentives.

There is also the problem of Form 990. IRS Form 990 PF, on which private foundations write their tax returns, makes it impossible for an accountant to distinguish government grants from other sources of financial support. While slightly helpful to tax attorneys—who are given more work to do in the wake of this government form's complexity—990 PF is less than helpful to everyone else. It is also symbolic of the federal obfuscation which every day in every way is making it officially more blessed to receive than to give, citing the work of the nonprofit sector, Independent organizations and the public sector's natural predisposition to co-opt their work.

The solution to the problem briefly described above is less legal or legislative than it is educational. There are anti-philanthropy attitudes held by a majority of the key public sector decisionmakers within the federal government, even in the wake of the Reagan revolution of November 1980. Primarily civil servants of the GS-100 category, they believe that if any social service or facility or cultural program is to be provided, it should be by the state through tax moneys. One thinks of the king of Sweden, the country in which one must first have a permit approved by a five-man board before one can repaint one's house with a different color. Not long ago, the king was publicly rebuked for his audacity in offering to provide from his own pocket funds to help carry out some worthy civic project. We have not yet come to that state of mind in America. And yet it is clear that all too many who call for pluralism in society and proclaim their support for free enterprise lack an understanding of the critical importance of private initiatives for the public good.

The Independent Sector is perhaps America's most promising and least recognized resource. It is the basic weave of the broadcloth of our social and economic history. This is a history of barnraisings, of children's aid societies, of The United Way Campaign, of The American Cancer Society, agricultural cooperatives and innumerable other examples of a form of economic enterprise which is neither private-for profit nor publicly owned. It is the abiding strength of the American mainspring of human progress. It is the willingness of citizens to come to the aid of their fellow man within their own homes and communities, which separates the good from the bad social system, the workable from the dubious economic order, and the successful from the moribund society.

ENDNOTE

1.   See Richard C. Cornuelle, *Reclaiming The American Dream* (New York: Random House, 1965); and as additional statistical bibliography, William H. Smith and Carolyn Chiechi, *Private Foundations* (American Enterprise Institute, 1974); and the earlier case made for philanthropic giving, Richard Ellis, *Corporation Giving in a Free Society* (New York: Harper, 1956). See also Burton Weisbrock, *The Voluntary Nonprofit Sector* (New York: Lexington Books, 1977).

William A. Stanmeyer

JUDICIAL
SUPREMACY

The rise of judicial rule means the decline of government by consent. To put the situation in historical perspective, one must remember than an early act of the New Deal was to restrict federal court jurisdiction. The Dred Scott decision was reversed only by the Civil War.

Formerly a college Instructor in Ethics and Political Theory, Law Professor Stanmeyer has taught jurisprudence and constitutional law at Georgetown Law Center and Indiana University School of Law and written widely on Church/State and other First Amendment questions. Presently, he directs the Delaware Law School Government Law Program.

Quis custodiet ipsos custodes?

*"For myself it would be most irksome to be ruled
by a bevy of Platonic Guardians, even if I knew
how to choose them, which I assuredly do not."*
Judge Learned Hand,
The Bill of Rights

THE NEW LEGISLATIVE JUDICIARY

A revolution in the process of governing America has occurred. To some, this revolution portends a coming millennium of equality, fairness, and liberty. To others, this revolution portends an increase in arbitrariness, confusion in administration of schools and prisons and in the distribution of public services, and growing rule by an oligarchic elite coupled with growing frustration on the part of an impotent electorate. But whatever it portends, that a revolution in governance has taken place is a fact no longer seriously controverted. *For the ultimate legislative power has passed generally to the Federal Judiciary, specifically to the Supreme Court.* Even the defenders of this transfer admit as much.

The United States Supreme Court now sits as the ultimate legislature in the country. It sits, as well, as a Continuing Council of Revision of the Constitution. Therefore, it is a body of men who are under no rule but their own will. If somehow its nine members

143

could be compressed into one person, we would behold the functional equivalent of a King—and the unrestricted judicial power the Court wields would be called, as it was called in the 17th Century, "the Divine Right of Kings."

This conclusion is not original. On the contrary, it has become the continuing theme of a sizable group of scholars whom one could hardly stigmatize as being "conservative" in any but the most elemental classic sense, viz., desiring to conserve whatever is perennial and valuable in past sociopolitical arrangements. Many of these writers are, in terms of the issues that agitate Congress and the electorate, largely "liberal" in orientation. Still, they are profoundly disquieted by the ominous concentration of power in the hands of unelected officials with lifetime tenure.

A lengthy compilation of their names and writings would unduly extend these remarks, so I will mention only a few. Thus, Adolph A. Berle, a Franklin Roosevelt appointee to the State Department, later a distinguished law professor, states candidly:

> The thesis can be briefly stated. Ultimate legislative power in the United States has come to rest in the Supreme Court of the United States.[1]

Again, law professor Louis Lusky acknowledges quite openly that the Supreme Court is "ready to engage in freehand constitution-making"[2] in a way which he shortly later says "betokens the deliberate determination to impose on the nation the will of seven men who have not been elected by the people."[3] And the Harvard emeritus professor, Raoul Berger, author of landmark studies on the limits of executive privilege and on the constitutional problems of impeachment, opens his attack on judicial usurpation tellingly titled, *Government by Judiciary,* with the matter-of-fact observation that

> The Fourteenth Amendment is the case study par excellence of what Justice Harlan described as the Supreme Court's "exercise of the amending power," *its continuing revision of the Constitution under the guise of interpretation.*[4] [Emphasis added]

And he closes his study with the peroration that the nation "should not tolerate the spectacle of a Court that pretends to apply constitutional mandates while in fact revising them in accord with the preference of a majority of the Justices who seek to impose *their* will on the nation."[5] Striking the same theme, Erwin Griswold, former dean of the Harvard Law School, commented in 1976:

> Some Supreme Court Justices employ the ruse of saying, "What we are doing is interpreting the Constitution," when what the Court is doing is deciding what is good for the country.[6]

THE WORKS OF THE JUDICIAL RULERS

I am somewhat embarrassed to take the reader's time with the foregoing comments, so commonplace has their thesis become. But old biases die hard, and some may never quite fade away. As children we learned in civics class that the United States—the States United, i.e., the nation's Federal Government—was the creation of practical political philosophers who profoundly distrusted the centralization of power. Having had their fill of King George, they determined that never again would Americans suffer the rule of royalty who were unelected officials with lifetime tenure. We learned, further, that "separation of powers" meant that the Federal Government was divided into three distinct and *equal* "Branches"—Legislative, Executive, and Judicial—and that each had its own particular functions, that of the Judicial being to interpret the laws and, on rare occasion, clarify what the unchanging Constitution meant. With the naive gullibility of children we also took it for granted that the national legislature made the laws, and that "We the People" would never be required to do something we did not like, unless that something had the approval of a majority of our elected representatives. We did not learn much about the Supreme Court, except some thoughts out of *Marbury* v. *Madison,* of which all we could remember as adults were that somehow the Supreme Court has "the power of judicial review," which meant that when necessity called, the Justices would "lay the statute next to the Constitution" to see if it "fit" and, if not, like a tailor altering a baggy suit, they would order that the offensive segment be cut out ("declared unconstitutional"). The purpose of this complicated, tripartite government, we understood, was "checks and balances":[7] because, as Lord Acton was to put it later, "Power tends to corrupt and absolute power corrupts absolutely." Consequently, each

Branch had to "check and balance" the others.

But, reminiscent of Orwell's remark in *Animal Farm* that "All animals are equal, but some animals are more equal than others," one of the "co-equal" three Branches—the Supreme Court—has taken it upon itself to "check and balance" the other two Branches far more aggressively than they have checked it. A brief and partial list of judicial policymaking should remind us how extraordinary has been the revolution the Court has achieved before our very noses: It has been a veritable *coup.*

Thus, since 1960, the Supreme Court has:

1. Restructured state and local government through its reappointment rulings;[8]

2. Radically transformed state criminal procedures;[9]

3. Substantially restricted States from using the Death Penalty;[10]

4. Written a national regulatory code permitting abortion-on-demand despite popular plebiscites on the issue in such States as Michigan and Nebraska voting abortion restrictions consonant with over 100 years of American history;[11]

5. Invented a constitutional "right of privacy" without a majority even agreeing on the constitutional text on which to base this new right;[12]

6. Approved and even required the use of compulsory cross-district busing to achieve racial balance in public schools;[13]

7. Come within an inch of legalizing "hard core" pornography and prevented any state control of offensive sexual material that is not quite "hard core";[14]

8. Expelled prayer and Bible-reading from the public schools, making the public schools institutionally Secular Humanist;[15]

9. Virtually destroyed congressional attempts to protect the Nation's internal security;[16]

10. Destroyed almost all State efforts to provide some financial relief to the parents of children in private schools.[17]

This *partial* enumeration is extraordinary. Over the years, the Supreme Court has variously replaced State legislatures . . . hospital governing boards . . . public school boards and thousands of parents . . . state censorship authorities . . . the U.S. Congress itself. Over the years its nine unelected officials with lifetime tenure have claimed an expertise superior to that of the American People, their elected representatives in state legislatures, and the U.S. Congress itself, in such wildly diverse matters as: political districting; balancing the rights of defendants and victims; deciding how frequently and if at all legislatures may protect the people by imposing death for heinous crimes; deciding when life begins (the Court says *it* cannot, but it did not quote *any* modern gynecologists or fetologists, who *have* been able to decide since at least 1857); protecting public morality or encouraging religion in schools. And at this writing the Court has pending a case wherein a three-judge District Court in 1980 held unconstitutional the draft registration requirement imposed on men but not on women,[18] saying that *these judges* may tell the U.S. Congress and the Defense Department who may be drafted and how the Nation *must* compose an effective fighting force (despite two hundred years of contrary history, the fact that the 14th Amendment "equal protection clause" dealt with race and not sex, and the text of the Constitution itself).[19]

With such an Imperial Judiciary, surely one has warrant to recall and slightly paraphrase the remark by Cassius to Marcus Brutus:

Now, in the names of all the gods at once,
Upon what meat do these our Caesars feed
that they are grown so great?[20]

OF GOOD ENDS AND QUESTIONABLE MEANS

Like Caesar, our judicial rulers are not without their virtues. A fairminded critic should admit that sometimes they have indeed done justice. Indeed, it is frequently observed that the Court has to take on the role of policeman/conscience—or, in the idealistic eyes of some, schoolmaster—for the rest of us; it is said that where a manifest wrong exists and neither Congress nor "the People" will correct it, the Supreme Court must act. A bit profanely, this may be called "the Lifeguard Theory of Judicial Activism": Some person or group is thrashing around helplessly in the pounding legislative surf; the many political onlookers stand on shore passive and impassive; only the Lifeguard has the courage to plunge into the water to the rescue.

The usual example of the Judicial Lifeguard theory is *Brown* v. *Board of Education,* which held that law-imposed school segregation is unconstitutional.[21] I happen to believe *Brown* was an absolutely correct decision, though weak in its theoretical rationale. A second example sometimes given is the first reappointment case, *Baker* v. *Carr,*[22] though here the Court departed from its custom of judicial restraint in matters characterized as a "political question." The Court obtained "good results," it will be said; and consequently we should not be overly concerned about how it got them. The Court discerns "emerging social values" and, because no other institution has the will to act, must drag the legislatures and the People, kicking and screaming perhaps, into conformity with those values. What the Court's *Brown* decision did in the area of racial segregation in the schools, at last grudgingly admitted to be right by all factions of society except the most extreme, the Court can do in any other area, whether it be the role of religion, the rules on abortion, or the running of the Army.

The thesis that results are more important than process, that ends are more important than means—or, that good results validate bad process even as, in some ethical codes, good ends justify bad means, is a thesis that should be strange and uncomfortable on the lips of lawyers. For the history of Anglo-American law is to a large degree the history of "due process," the gradual development of standards of procedure the integrity of which is even more important, over the long haul, than getting the "right result" in a given case by bending the rules a little or a lot. Similarly, the thesis that some appointed group of Guardians has, like the mystic oracles of ancient Rome, a deeper insight into life's true meaning, and has powers of prophecy not bestowed on us ordinary citizens, is also a thesis that should make lawyers uncomfortable. Whence does the

Court derive this power to "discern emerging social values"? How does the Court know which values are "emerging"? How can it tell when the values have "emerged" far enough to warrant discovery in—i.e., writing into—the Constitution? During the last few years, for instance, was it possible to discern whether Jerry Falwell's or Hugh Hefner's values were emerging faster? What is it about the process of fact-finding used by courts that gives judges a more accurate intuitive "feel" for emerging values than the perceptions of, say, State legislatures or of the Congress? Often defenders of "judicial activism" boast that the courts are "above the political process" as though that asserted insulation gave them as much wisdom as it gives them independence. Really, however, they are in a dilemma: Either the Supreme Court, and to a considerable degree the "activist" Federal Courts following the Supreme Court's lead, are indeed "political" bodies—"They read the election returns"—in which case we should drop the pretense of detachment and dispassionate objectivity . . . or they are truly "above" the earthy world of political compromise and maneuver—in which case, being truly out of touch, they can hardly have any more grasp of sociomoral trends than a monk in a Trappist monastery, and surely have far less grasp than elected members of legislatures.

But the problem is deeper than mere result-oriented jurisprudence more interested in ends than means. The problem is also one of implausible rationales for decisions, which rationales later break loose from their factual moorings and drift, like some errant hot-air balloon, into foreign fields where they do not belong. I will demonstrate this point with some examples below; but here the serious reader might undertake a preliminary intellectual exercise: He should ask himself to what extent the American people would accept the Supreme Court's social rulings if the Court lacked the *power* to insist on enforcement and had to rely, instead, solely on the *intrinsic persuasiveness* of its reasoning. Put another way: If the Supreme Court had only an advisory role, in which it would "declare" an act of Congress "unconstitutional" but could not invalidate that act unless Congress itself chose to accept the Court's position and vote to repeal the act, then the Court would indeed be the conscience to, but not a substitute for, the other Branches of Government. But it would be a conscience whose claims to guide Congress, President, and People would rest solely on its moral authority, the clarity of its analysis, the accuracy of its historical research, the logic of its ratiocination, the power of its thought. I do not say that this *should* be the Court's only role. I do say that many times the Congress and the People have acquiesced in the Court's decisions—"The Supreme Court has spoken"—because they believed there was nothing else they could do, *not* because the Court in any way convinced them that its directives were compelled by the Constitution. If the Court had to rely on persuasion alone and not on power, one suspects that it would venture more cautiously into fewer areas of controversy, and when it did it would compose opinions of such unchallengeable good sense that scarcely anyone would disagree.

To return to the problem of implausible rationales which break loose from their factual moorings: In *Griswold* v. *Connecticut*[23] the majority on the Court groped for a coherent reason to find unconstitutional Connecticut's laws making it a misdemeanor to counsel or assist in the using of contraceptives. A plurality, led by Justice Douglas, discovered "that specific guarantees in the Bill of Rights have penumbras, formed by emanations from those guarantees that help give them life and substance." He argued that "various guarantees create zones of privacy" and concluded with a powerful encomium to marriage as a relationship having "a right to privacy older than the Bill of Rights" even. Other Justices found the basis for the "right of privacy" in the Ninth Amendment, and others in the Fourteenth Amendment's "due process clause," into which the Court had long felt authorized to read substantive rights (even though the text and history make it plain that only procedural rights were intended). But whatever the rationale, when the Court's ink dried on *Griswold,* the "right of marital privacy" was written into the Constitution.

Confined to the institution of marriage, the new "right of privacy" might not have done much mischief. But at virtually the first chance to hack away the mooring ropes, the Supreme Court cut out the very basis for the right—the marriage relationship—and applied it to strike down a law prohibiting the *distribution* of contraceptives to an *unmarried* person. Thus in *Eisenstadt* v. *Baird*[24] Mr. Justice Brennan denied the distinctiveness of the marriage relation: "If the right of privacy means anything, it is the right of the *individual,* married or single, to be free from unwarranted governmental intrusion into matters so fundamentally

affecting a person as the decision whether to bear or beget a child."
The Court's philosophical legerdemain has evoked considerable
comment. Thus, Professor Gerald Gunther, author of one of the
most widely adopted constitutional law texts, remarked:

> What is clear in Griswold is that all of the Justices in the majority
> found some ordering of constitutional values justified: some "funda-
> mental values" deserve special protection. That consensus poses a
> question common to all of the modern substantive due process cases:
> How does the Court determine the proper place of a particular right
> on the hierarchy of values? . . . What *are* the proper sources of
> "fundamental values" in constitutional adjudication?[25]

Eisenstadt conveniently set the stage for *Roe* v. *Wade,* which
legalized, for all practical purposes, abortion-on-demand. The
Court through Mr. Justice Blackmun explained that "This right of
privacy, [wherever in the Constitution it be found] is broad enough
to encompass a woman's decision whether or not to terminate her
pregnancy." Later he stated that Texas may not, "by adopting one
theory of life, . . . override the rights of the pregnant woman that
are at stake." On this passage Professor Gunther asks the rhetorical questions:

> Why should not that lack of consensus lead the Court to defer to,
> rather than invalidate, the State's judgment? Can the Court's judg-
> ment be supported by anything other than a judicial authority to
> infuse a particular set of moral values into the Constitution?[26]

However one answers these questions, he must surely pause when
he sees the next field into which the winds of ideology will blow the
unmoored right of privacy. In a 5 to 4 decision, in *Planned Parenthood of Missouri* v. *Danforth*[27] the Court invalidated a provision
requiring an unmarried woman under 18 to obtain the consent of
a parent or a person *in loco parentis* as a prerequisite to obtaining
an abortion in most circumstances. In passing Justice Blackmun
articulated a statist philosophy of rights: "The State does not have
the constitutional authority to give to a third party an absolute
. . . veto over the decision of the physician and his patient to
terminate the patient's pregnancy." So in a mere ten years, we
jump from the constitutional right of married adults to obtain

contraceptives to the constitutional right of unmarried minors to procure an abortion. Quite a leap.

In other areas as well, the Courts indulge in their process of discovering a right in particular facts, expanding it beyond those facts to other areas increasingly remote, and then dropping all pretense at using analogy or precedent by applying the new right to a completely different situation, one where it would never have dared to discern it *de novo*. Thus, after the *Brown* case in 1954 the Court naturally wanted to strike down racial segregation in the public schools of the District of Columbia.[28] I have no quarrel with the result; I agree with Justice Warren's observation, "In view of our decision that the Constitution prohibits the states from maintaining racially segregated public schools, it would be unthinkable that the same Constitution would impose a lesser duty on the Federal Government." But to get this good result the Court played that old sleight of hand trick again: it held that segregated D.C. public schools violated the due process clause of the Fifth Amendment!—more precisely, that they violated the equal protection component of this clause. But the difficulty with this view is fundamental: The due process clause of the Fifth Amendment deals, as the context makes clear, with criminal procedure—and, in any event, it simply does not *have* an "equal protection component"! The Court got a good result by reading a new phrase into the Constitution—amending it—and then interpreting the phrase which it had just inserted into the document. Many years later, the Court's invention, like the Frankenstein monster which broke loose from the laboratory table and lurched out to terrorize the townsfolk, came back to haunt it: In *Fullilove* v. *Klutznick*,[29] the question was whether Congress could so structure a spending program that 10 percent of federal funds granted for local public works projects must be used by the state or local grantee to procure services or supplies from "minority" enterprises. This "affirmative action" type of program was attacked as "reverse discrimination." In upholding the plan the Court found it had to circumvent its own creation; in the words of Chief Justice Burger, writing for himself and two other Justices, ". . . we must go on to decide whether the limited use of racial and ethnic criteria . . . is a constitutionally permissible *means* for achieving the congressional objectives and does not violate the equal protection component of the Due Process Clause of the Fifth Amendment."

That the Court decided to uphold the instant program probably does not trouble most people. Indeed, probably not one person in one hundred ever heard of the program or the case. But there are other areas where the Court's floating jurisprudence is immensely troubling. Perhaps the most obvious area is that of compulsory busing of grammar and high school students to achieve racial balance. This is perhaps the classic instance of theory run amuck.[30] In a nutshell: The Court started with a good principle, namely, that assignment of students to schools on the basis of race violates the Equal Protection Clause of the Fourteenth Amendment. This is the core holding of *Brown.* At that time the Court focused on the process of assignment and not the results. At the time of *Brown* and shortly after, courts could state that the Constitution "does not require integration. It merely forbids segregation." But in a case in 1968, *Green* v. *County School Board,*[31] the Court focused on the effects rather than on the purpose and good faith of desegregation efforts and held that a unified or "racially nondiscriminatory (in fact) school system" must be effectuated. The Court then approved even cross-district busing in *Swann* (1971),[32] giving the green light to activist Federal District Judges to push for virtual, if not actual, racial quotas, and to achieve them by, of all things, *assignment of students to schools on the basis of race*—the very principle the Justices had struck down in *Brown!*

I will not tarry here to note the utter lack of popular support for the massive busing judges have ordered. Nor will I take the reader's time discussing the uselessness of it all from an educational standpoint. Nor will I more than mention that massive busing has contributed to "white flight" and thus harmed the cause of racial harmony and integration. Rather, I will mention only the jurisprudential fact: Too often the Court's opinions lack coherent principle and too often the Court takes what principle it does have and, in its eagerness to remake society along its own ideas of what is right, misapplies it out of context. The result is that in many controversial areas the Court's opinions simply do not persuade. One gets the feeling that the opinions are afterthoughts tacked onto a ruling, to give the impression of reasoning from accepted premises to necessary conclusion, whereas in reality they are no more than fancy clothes in which to garb royal edicts.

KEEPING THE REPUBLIC: EVERY
CITIZEN'S DUTY

As he left the Constitutional Convention, the story goes, Benjamin Franklin met a passerby who asked him, "What form of government did the delegates give us?" To which Franklin is said to have replied: "A Republic—if you can keep it."

When asked to contribute an essay to this book, I found myself feeling some misgivings about the title. For it seems to me that the problem of Judicial Supremacy completely transcends the categories of "New Right" or "New Left" or whatever. I do not care to demean the discussion by flippant use of convenient slogans or groupings. The problem I have tried to sketch is the *central problem of our political society*. The problem is no less than how to answer the question, "Who shall govern?" Who shall make the rules for all of us? Our Founding Fathers had a very clear answer to this question: Our elected representatives shall govern. For a considerable period in the second third of this century the Court has been preventing our elected representatives from governing in sociomoral matters the way they want. I would think that both Right and Left would see how deep lies the difficulty and would set aside their rhetoric of anathema and distrust to make common cause in seeking a remedy. For pendulums do swing. Though it is largely the Conservatives who today decry the courts' usurpations, with the appointment by a new President of a few conservative Justices, it may well be the Liberals who tomorrow decry the courts' usurpations. Important as are many of the substantive issues that this paper has used to illustrate the activity of the Imperial Judiciary, they pale into insignificance when the full enormity of our situation comes home: *An ostensible Republic, with the forms of democratic institutions, is in most important matters governed by unelected judges with life-time tenure.* The Revolutionary War was fought to achieve self-government. Unbridled Judicial Review claims the power to take it away. (It is ironic that the Warren Court's insistence on the "one-man–one-vote" rule of districting in the reapportionment cases came from the same Court which felt no inhibition in striking down, wholesale, the enactments of legislatures and Congress whenever those "ones" put representatives in who did not share the Court's social philosophy.) One begins to wonder what use elections are, if courts can so freely set aside the laws the elected officials seek to enact. Professor Graglia has noted the problem quite trenchantly:[33]

> Under the unique system of American government . . . a victory at the polls remains a victory only so long as it is not disapproved by the courts—a function performed in some other systems by the military.

So I urge my colleagues, friends, and fellow lawyers on both Left and Right to set aside denominational feuding on this issue. Procedure *is* important. Persuasive rationales for decisions *are* necessary. We are talking about the governance of a free, literate, and fairly sophisticated adult people—not a kindergarten. We must find ways to ensure that the courts are responsive to the People, for it is "We, the People" who have formed this Government and it is we to whom the Constitution entrusts the power to amend.

I believe that whatever one's political philosophy, Left or Right, he should be able to agree that the courts have taken over legislative powers through three steps: (1) the creation of the power of *unrestricted* "judicial review"; (2) the facile *claim* that a vague constitutional clause written decades ago —"due process," "equal protection"—not only prevents Congress or a State from doing X but sometimes even mandates that it do Y; (3) reliance on the mystic prestige of the Supreme Court, on Americans' traditional respect for law, plus the fact that Congress has not yet limited in any serious way the power of judicial review.

The reasons Congress has not acted include these: (1) myopia: Congress and affected groups do not fully realize this is a radical *structural* flaw in our entire system of republican government; (2) some "solutions" are too extreme, e.g., impeaching a given Judge; (3) resistance to judicial imperialism has been aimed at specific isolated issues—e.g., school prayer, racial busing—and necessary coalitions have not been built; (4) there has been no schematized scholarly source of principled analysis of the generic problem along with a comprehensive spectrum of practical proposals for reform.[34]

Were they with us today, some of the nation's greatest presidents, such as Jefferson, Jackson, and Lincoln, would certainly join in the effort to devise institutional limitations on the Court's power. For the record, I offer some of their remarks, which commonly appear in law school casebooks:

> But the opinion which gives to the judges the right to decide what laws are constitutional, and what not, not only for themselves in their own sphere of action, but for the legislature and executive also, in their spheres, would make the judiciary a despotic branch.
>
> Thomas Jefferson, letter to Abigail Adams, September 11, 1804 (VIII *The Writings of Thomas Jefferson,* Ford ed. 1897, p. 310).
>
> You seem to consider the judges as the ultimate arbiters of all constitutional questions; a very dangerous doctrine indeed, and one which would place us under the despotism of an oligarchy. [The] Constitution has erected no such single tribunal, knowing that to whatever hands confided, with the corruptions of time and party, its members would become despots. It has more wisely made all the departments co-equal and co-sovereign within themselves.
>
> Thomas Jefferson, letter to William C. Jarvis, September 28, 1820 (X *The Writings of Thomas Jefferson,* Ford ed. 1899, p. 160).
>
> The opinion of the judges has no more authority over Congress than the opinion of Congress has over the judges, and on that point the President is independent of both. The authority of the Supreme Court must not, therefore, be permitted to control the Congress or the Executive when acting in their legislative capacities, but to have only such influence as the force of the reasoning may deserve.
>
> Andrew Jackson: Veto Message (on Bill to recharter the Bank of the United States), July 10, 1832 (II *Messages on Papers of the Presidents,* Richardson ed. 1896, pp. 576, 581–83).

I did not forget the position assumed by some that constitutional questions are to be decided by the Supreme Court, nor do I deny that such decisions must be binding in any case upon the parties to a suit as to the object of that suit, while they are also entitled to very high respect and consideration in all parallel cases by all other departments of the Government. And while it is obviously possible that such decision may be erroneous in any given case, still the evil effect following it, being limited to that particular case, with the chance that it may be overruled and never become a precedent for other cases, can better be borne than could the evils of a different practice. At the same time, the candid citizen must confess that if the policy of the Government upon vital questions affecting the whole people is to be irrevocably fixed by the decisions of the Supreme Court, the instant they are made in ordinary litigation between parties in personal actions the people *will have ceased to be their own rulers,* having to that extent resigned their Government into the hands of that eminent tribunal.

Abraham Lincoln, First Inaugural Address, March 4, 1861 (VI *Messages and Papers of the Presidents,* Richardson ed. 1897, pp. 5, 9–10). (Emphasis added.)

THE LIMITS OF JUDICIAL REVIEW

In *Federalist* 78, Alexander Hamilton attempts a principled justification of judicial review. He urges that "the judiciary from the nature of its functions, will always be the least dangerous to the political right of the Constitution; because it will be least in a capacity to annoy or injury them." He states that unlike the Executive, who "holds the sword of the community," and the legislature which controls the purse and makes the rules, the Courts do not have "FORCE nor WILL, but merely judgment . . ." Later he makes his "fundamental law" argument: The Constitution is "fundamental" and all laws (ordinary legislative acts) which conflict with it are void. This means that "whenever a particular statute contravenes the Constitution, it will be the duty of the judicial tribunals to adhere to the latter and disregard the former." For, "the Constitution ought to be preferred to the statute, the intention of the people to the intention of their agents."

Later in his essay Hamilton grapples with the problem of possible unconstitutional acts by the judiciary itself. He seems to realize that if Congress and the President are creatures of the Constitution, so is the Court—but if we give the Court the power to declare what the Constitution means, we give the Court the power to be judge in its own case, to create itself, as it were. The question then becomes, what limits do we put on the Court, even as *it* puts limits on the other two Branches? *Quis custodiet ipsos custodes?*

The Court, Hamilton tells us, may nullify acts of Congress when the latter violates specific constitutional prohibitions—e.g., passes an ex post facto law or bill of attainder—or where it passes acts "contrary to the manifest tenor of the Constitution." *Manifest* must mean obvious, clear, undisputed. Again, Hamilton remarks that in ascertaining the meaning of the Constitution, as a fundamental law, the judges must ascertain the meaning of any particular act proceeding from the legislature. "If there should happen to be an irreconcilable variance between the two," the Constitution is to be preferred. *Irreconcilable* suggests only those cases where no reasonable man could find a way to reconcile the statute and the Constitution; otherwise, an ordinary variance, one that can be harmonized by skillful interpretation of either statute or Constitution, would not warrant striking down a Congressional act. And finally, Hamilton urges that the Judges "should be bound down by strict rules and precedents, which serve to define and point out their duty in every particular case that comes before them." It should be apparent that if the judges follow *strict* rules and precedents, they will not come up with bizarre interpretations of vague phrases or reverse meanings in their own prior decisions.[35]

There is considerable question, however, whether even this version of highly self-restrained and limited judicial review reflected the desires of the rest of the Founding Fathers. Hamilton was eager to see the new Republic adopt an aristocratic form of government; his plan, which he presented to the Philadelphia Convention, provided for a president elected for life, for senators with life terms, for the reduction of the states to mere administrative arms of the national government by having the president appoint state governors for life and give them power to veto any act of the state legislatures even if unanimously passed.[36] This extraordinary centralization was designed to defend the interests of the propertied, financial, commercial classes. It was an "aristocratic republic" as opposed to a "democratic republic." Obviously, it was more a monarchy than a republic. As such, it received short shrift from the other Founders. This rejection forced Hamilton to seek to provide the judiciary the powers that the other Founders would not grant the other branches; and yet he had to do it, in *Federalist* 78, with enough qualifications—manifest tenor, irreconcilable variance, strict rules and precedents—as to make its power seem innocuous.

The actual architect of the Constitution was James Madison. Madison was the philosopher-statesman who guided the Convention. He believed in legislative supremacy, but felt that there needed to be some way to protect the judiciary from legislative excesses. In the debates over the Council of Revision, Madison observed that:

It would be useful to the judiciary department by giving it an additional opportunity of defending itself against legislative encroachments. . . . Experience in all the states had evinced a powerful tendency in the legislature to absorb all power into its vortex. This was the real source of danger to the American constitutions; and suggested the necessity of giving every defensive authority to the other departments that was consistent with republican principles.[37]

Later Madison enunciated words the thrust of which would later be expressed by Jefferson, Jackson, and Lincoln:

But the great objection . . . is that the legislature itself has no right to expound the Constitution; that wherever its meaning is doubtful, you must leave it to take its course, until the judiciary is called upon to declare its meaning . . . but I beg to know upon what principle it can be contended that any one department draws from the Constitution greater powers than another, in marking out the limits of the powers of the several departments. . . . The Constitution is the charter of the people in the Government; it specifies certain great powers as absolutely granted, and marks out the departments to exercise them. If the constitutional boundary of either be brought into question, I do not see that any one of these independent departments has more right than another to declare their sentiments on that point.[38]

But whether one takes Hamilton's view that self-restrained judicial review was granted in the Constitution, or Madison's view that judicial review does not reach acts of the co-equal Branches but operates only defensively, to permit the Court to construe the Constitutional meaning as applied to itself and cases before it, we come to the same conclusion: Since the U.S. Supreme Court and the other Federal Courts do not even show the self-restraint that their own philosophical defender, Hamilton, would require of them, it is time for the Nation to find a way to return to the original purposes of the Founding Fathers, and create an *institutional* check on the unbridled power of the Courts.

PRACTICAL STEPS TOWARD REFORM

Just as people do not attend to police or fire protection very much until a wave of arson or burglaries breaks out in the neighborhood, so also most Americans don't spend much time on political theory. Life fumbles along fairly satisfactorily; most of us do not think about theory and attend to such questions as separation of powers or the federalist system. This disinterest may suggest how far afield from the point of view of the Founding Fathers we have traveled. Nonetheless, the burden of this essay is that political theory—correct political theory—is vitally important. But not only the theory, which, abstractly speaking, Americans do somewhat understand even if they do not spend much time thinking about it. Equally important is the political practice.

As the quote from Abraham Lincoln noted: "If the policy of the government, upon vital questions affecting the whole people, is to be irrevocably fixed by decisions of the Supreme Court, the instant they are made, in ordinary litigation between parties in personal actions, the people will have ceased to be their own rulers . . . ." This is the situation in which we find ourselves today. And it does not matter whether sometimes the Supreme Court's decisions are correct. The issue is not so much the goodness or badness of a policy decision as *how it is made.* The Founders meant this country to be a republic; in practice it is rapidly becoming an aristocratic dictatorship. The Founders meant this country to rely in its governance on representative democracy; in practice it is relying more and more on a judicial policymaking branch. The Founders meant for the various factions and parties in the political arena to contend and struggle through debate and compromise to achieve legislative policies, which often could be revised by further coalitions and voting patterns in future legislative sessions; when a court or a set of courts such as the District Courts and then the Courts of Appeal and the U.S. Supreme Court, absorb to themselves the policymaking power, that action of theirs denies all the utility to the long legislative and political efforts that so many people, parties, and factions entered into. It renders their activity in the electoral process nugatory, useless. Legislators are open to public comment, suggestion and advice; one can write to one's Congressman and visit him; one can organize groups to support or challenge him in the next election, which invariably will occur in a short period of time. The Supreme Court, on the contrary, is not amenable to such popular commentary. Indeed many people feel it would be improper to write to a member of the Supreme Court about one's feelings on an issue, certainly if such an issue were before the Court in litigation. Furthermore there is grave doubt whether members of the Court would read and seriously ponder any sizable amount of mail. Therefore the members of the Court are completely insulated both institutionally and psychologically from popular comment on their actions. Surely this reminds us of the kings and their courts in the Middle Ages: a royal elite wearing special robes and sometimes speaking a different language from the ordinary people in the fields and villages, making rule by edict, declaring and insisting and imposing and demanding, but never responding.

It cannot be stressed enough that this was not the way the Founders meant it to be. Nor can it be stressed enough that this system will not work well over a long period of time. A "bevy of Platonic Guardians" simply lacks the wisdom to rule a nation of over 230 million people. However one might support the Supreme Court's decisions in such extraordinary cases as *Brown* v. *Board of Education,* we must face up to the fact that the price of such decisions, if it be unrestricted judicial review rummaging and pillaging through historical precedent and common sense in a will-o'-the-wisp pursuit of the perfect society, is too high to pay. To restore a balance to our system there simply *has* to be a method of institutionally checking the Supreme Court.

Institutional "checks and balances" are the method the Founding Fathers hit upon to deal with human nature and political reality as they are. The Founders carefully limited both the legislature and the presidency by numerous means too well known to need recounting here. They also intended to check the potentially arrogant power of the national government by delegating to it only limited authority and reserving to the States or the people the remaining and sizable amount of authority for daily legislative activity. Perhaps because they felt the Supreme Court was indeed the "least dangerous branch" they did not carefully provide for institutional limits on that Court, although it is obvious from the Constitution that they felt the judges could be impeached or that their jurisdiction could be removed. Indeed Article III of the Constitution, Section 2, Paragraph 2 states in part: ". . . the supreme Court shall have appellate Jurisdiction, both as to Law and Fact, with such Exceptions, and under such Regulations as the Congress shall make." In any event, whether the Founders thought that impeachment or removal of jurisdiction of the Supreme Court would be used frequently or rarely, the question for us moderns—as those who support judicial activism often tell us—is how to bring the Constitution up to date: that is, how to develop constitutional principles appropriate for our modern society. I suggest *the most important constitutional principle which we must develop is a practical institutional method to control the excesses of judicial imperialism.*[39] This means putting unrestrained judicial review on a leash. Unless we take steps to create an institutional means that is firm and solid to control judicial review, all the legislative struggles of various competing factions, organizations, and groups in our society can well come to naught. For all that is required to overturn years of political labor is a five-man majority on the Supreme Court reading the opaque tea leaves of such general phrases as "due process" or "equal protection" to strike down statutes which it took a decade or more to enact.

Moreover what many people do not realize is that the Supreme Court is not the only source of the problem. Rather, the problem strongly emerges from the lower federal courts where a single federal district judge, giving way to his social reformist desires and taking his lead from some comment by the Supreme Court, will strike out into the political thicket to cut his own path of reform regardless of having any warrant in the Constitution or for that matter even in an actual Supreme Court decision. Because the time, the cost, and the distraction of energies best spent on other matters are so great in an effort to overturn on appeal the ruling of a federal district judge, many times school boards, prison authorities, community housing groups, and state legislatures throw up their hands in disgust and frustration and yield to the edict of a single unelected, life-tenured federal judge, rather than expend the resources to try to challenge him in a higher court. Thus what has happened is to some extent the very thing which Hamilton recommended: that the states be ruled by appointed officials themselves receiving their authority from the central government. Although Hamilton had in mind the state governors, it appears that the federal district judges in the states have taken on much the role Hamilton envisioned.

Now I realize there are those who will read these remarks and say that, although they may be interesting, they are quite beside the point. They will say that the Supreme Court's right to pass on the validity of legislation is now too much part of our constitutional system to be brought into question. They may agree that it was historical accident or bad logic that explained the inception of judicial review, but they will say that over 170 years have gone by with this system in force and it is now too late to change. This is a "conservative" viewpoint in the worst possible meaning of that word. It should never be too late for a free people to change a system which they have found has departed from their original purpose or no longer works. We changed the system of slavery, although it took the price of a civil war; we withdrew from Vietnam, although we had already committed an enormous amount of treasure to the task of staying there. We are constantly changing the racial makeup of our public school assignments even though in most cases they grow out of residential patterns that were created over a hundred-year period. To say that we must continue to do a thing the wrong way because we have always done it that way is the essence of the reactionary conservatism that enlightened people have always rejected. Rather, what we must restore is the proper balance among the three branches of government and between the federal and state governments; this one might call a revolutionary conservatism, not unlike the efforts of the Founding Fathers to break us loose from England in 1776 and restore to the Colonists the "rights of Englishmen" which they had enjoyed before the depredations of King George and his henchmen. What I suggest we need, therefore, is a "conservative revolution," which will re-establish the proper balance among our governmental branches and thereby restore the power of self-governance to the American people.

There are a variety of practical recommendations that various parties have made or that one can readily imagine. I will list some of them here with comments.

(1) Congress could define the grounds for impeachment of a federal judge to include such decisions as ordering expenditures from the United States Treasury or from the State or local Treasury for a specific purpose without the Congress or State legislature or local unit authorizing and appropriating funds for such a purpose. This is the thrust of HR 4200 introduced in May of 1979, in the 96th Congress, in an attempt to deal with the directive of U.S. District Judge John F. Dooling, Jr., who ordered the federal government to pay for Medicaid abortions. The constitutional warrant for such an approach is found in Article 1, Section 9, Clause 7 of the Constitution, stating: "no Money shall be drawn from the Treasury, but in consequence of appropriations made by Law." My own belief is that impeachment of a judge for whatever cause is an

extraordinary remedy and as a practical matter would not, and perhaps should not, be used frequently enough to deal with the broad problem of the usurpations by the federal judiciary.

(2) It has been suggested that Congress could pass a law which provided that any federal or state law which is declared unconstitutional by the Supreme Court under the appellate jurisdiction of the Court (over which the Congress has full authority) may be overturned by a two-thirds vote in each House of Congress within one year after the decision of the Court. This is the thrust of HR 4111, which was introduced in May of 1979 in the 96th Congress. I would observe that passage of such law could well trigger a constitutional crisis—which may be a good idea, so that all the cards are on the table—because the Supreme Court might assert that reversal of a finding of a constitutional "right" in a case before the court is itself unconstitutional. However, if the thrust of this bill were stated in a constitutional amendment which the Congress had properly passed and submitted to the States, and which in turn was ratified by the requisite member of States, then the people, by ratifying the amendment, would have transferred from the Supreme Court to the Congress the power to make legislative public policy.

(3) Another Bill introduced in May of 1979 in the *ninety-sixth* Congress provides that any Federal or State law declared unconstitutional by the Supreme Court, and which falls under the appellate jurisdiction of the Court, shall require the concurrence of at least seven Justices. The thrust here is to require a "super majority" so that one or another "swing man" on the Court could not impose his will on the people without developing a substantial consensus on the Court itself. While the requirement of roughly three-fourths to enact a constitutional change is laudable and consonant with the rules on constitutional amendments, this recommendation does not get to the essence of the problem: A judicial oligarchy usurping legislative prerogatives is still an oligarchy, whether it is constituted by five men or seven. However the enactment of such a requirement will probably diminish the current mischief.

(4) Another suggestion, commonly made since the time of the reapportionment and school prayer cases, has been the removal by Congress of controversial political and social questions from the appellate jurisdiction of the Supreme Court. Indeed Congress could go so far as to remove such decisionmaking from all federal courts and leave it in the hands of state courts. In my judgment this is a

good, but partial, answer to the problem. It is likely that the Congress would not exercise this power very often, and even when it does it is possible that the Supreme Court may attempt to subvert the congressional power to control jurisdiction. By holding that it does not have that power where "constitutional rights" are involved, the Court will itself then declare those rights, another boot strap operation not unlike the exercise that occurred in *Marbury v. Madison.*

(5) Some people suggest a constitutional amendment abrogating lifetime tenure of federal judges and limiting them to a specified term of office. This term could be, of course, seven or nine years. This will require reappointment of Supreme Court Justices, perhaps for only one additional seven-year term. This too is a good idea insofar as it provides for "new blood" to be transfused into the Federal Judiciary; but once again it does not get to the essence of the problem. The problem is not so much not having enough new judges but having unrestrained power in the hands of judges whether they be old or new.

(6) One could envision a method, enacted by constitutional amendment, that abrogated the power of judicial supremacy. This device could enable the Congress to overrule a Supreme Court decision or a Federal District decision by, say, a two-thirds vote; or a Federal District Court decision by, say, a majority vote by both Houses, as noted above. Or as to the question whether a given case such as on reapportionment, school prayer, abortion, or possibly drafting women into combat service in the Armed Forces, was rightly decided, it could put that case up to the people for a plebiscite in the next national election. Such a means might be cumbersome, but it would have the advantage of allowing the people to officially inform the Supreme Court that the Court was wrong.

CONCLUSION

The Latin *"Quis custodiet ipsos custodes?"* asks the ultimate question: "Who will watch the guards themselves?" If the Supreme Court Justices are the "guardians of the Constitution," we must quickly find an institutional way to watch the guardians themselves. Otherwise they will be a "Bevy of Platonic Guardians," responsive to no one—*outside* the law—*above* the Constitution.

ENDNOTES

1. Adolph A. Berle, *The Three Faces of Power* (1967), p. 3.
2. Louis Lusky, *By What Right?* (1975), p. 14.
3. *Ibid,* @ 19. The "seven men" are the majority in *Roe* v. *Wade,* the seminal abortion-on-demand case.
4. Raoul Berger, *Government by Judiciary* (1975), p.1. Emphasis added.
5. *Ibid,* @ 417.
6. Quoted in Philip B. Kurland, *Government by Judiciary, Modern Age* (Fall, 1976) 358, @ 365.
7. This virtual truism scarcely needs citation. Cf., e.g., Charles G. Haines, *The Role of the Supreme Court in American Government and Politics* (1960) p. 132. See also James Madison, *Federalist* 51: "In republican government, the legislative authority necessarily predominates . . . usurpations are guarded against by a division of the government into district and separate departments."
8. *Baker* v. *Carr,* 369 U.S. 186 (1962); *Reynolds* v. *Sims,* 377 U.S. 533 (1964); *Lucas* v. *Forty-Fourth Gen. Assembly* 377 U.S. 713 (1964), and others. In *Lucas* the voters of Colorado had approved the districting by a referendum and rejected a plan to apportion both state houses on the basis of population. Justice Harlan's dissent thoroughly exposes the shallow political philosophy the majority embraced, as they imposed *their* will on the people of Colorado.
9. E.g., *Mapp* v. *Ohio,* 367 U.S. 643 (1961); *Miranda* v. *Arizona,* 384 U.S. 436 (1966, and others. The former, *Mapp,* imposed the "exclusionary rule" on the States, requiring the "exclusion" from a criminal trial of reliable and probative evidence often because the "constable blundered" technically in obtaining it. The Rule violates common sense and does not exist in Canada or England; see Chief Justice Burger's critique in his dissent in *Bivens* v. *Six Unknown Named Agents,* 403 U.S. 388 (1971). For telling critiques of the rule, see, e.g., Dallin Oaks, *Studying the Exclusionary Rule in Search and Seizure, 37 U. Chicago L. Rev.* 665 (1970); and Steven R. Schlesinger, *Exclusionary Injustice* (Marcel Dekker, New York, (1977).
10. *Furman* v. *Georgia,* 40 8 U.S. 238 (1972), a case that produced nine opinions!
11. *Roe* v. *Wade, Doe* v. *Bolton,* 410 U.S. 113, 179 (1973), in which Mr. Justice White declared, in dissent, "I find nothing in the language or history of the Constitution to support the Court's judgment . . . I find no constitutional warrant for imposing such an order of priorities on the people and legislatives of the States"; and Mr. Justice Rehnquist in dissent called the decision one that uses "the conscious weighing of competing factors, [an approach] far more appropriate than to a judicial one."
12. *Griswold* v. *Connecticut,* 381 U.S. 479 (1965), in which Mr. Justice Black, in dissent, urged the Court was "exalting a phrase . . . used in discussing grounds for tort relief, to the level of a constitutional rule which prevents state legislatures from passing any law deemed by this Court to interfere with 'privacy.' " And Mr. Justice Stewart asked in dissent—and the majority did not really answer—"What provision of the Constitution, then, does make this state law invalid?"
13. *Green* v. *County School Board,* 391 U.S. 430 (1968); *Swann* v. *Charlotte-Mecklenburg Board of Education,* 402 U.S. 1 (1971); *Keys* v. *School District No. 1, Denver, Colorado,* 413 U.S. 189 (1973), and other cases.
14. *Miller* v. *California,* 413 U.S. 15 (1973), a case which nonetheless was an *improvement,* from the public decency perspective, over the reversal-of-convic-

tions-without-reasons approach begun in *Redrup* v. *New York*, 386 U.S. 767 (1967).

15. *Engel* v. *Vitale*, 370 U.S. 421 (1962); *Abington School District* v. *Schempp*, 374 U.S. 203 (1963).

16. E.g., *U.S.* v. *Robel*, 389 U.S. 258 (1967), invalidating a Federal Act's section making it a crime for a member of a Communist-action organization to work in defense plants.

17. E.g., *Lemon* v. *Kurtzman*, 403 U.S. 602 (1971); *Comm. for Public Ed.* v. *Nyquist*, 413 U.S. 756 (1973); *Meek* v. *Pittenger*, 421 U.S. 349 (1975); but for a more tolerant approach see *Comm. for Public Ed. & Rel. Lib.* v. *Regan*, 100 S. Ct. 840 (1980).

18. Justice Brennan stayed the lower court's injuction pending appeal. *Rostker* v. *Goldberg*, 49 U.S.L.W. 3013 (1980).

19. The Constitution clearly and unambiguously confers *plenary* power over the Armed Forces upon the Congress and the President. E.g., Article I, Section 1 vests *"All* legislative Powers" in Congress; Article I, Section 8: "The Congress shall have Power . . . to provide for the common Defense. . . . To declare War . . . . To raise and support Armies . . . . To provide and maintain a Navy. . . . To make Rules for the Government and Regulation of the land and naval Forces." Certainly these sections leave no doubt that Congress and Congress alone, under our Constitution, may create the Armed Forces and decide their general composition.

The *running* of the Army the Constitution confers solely upon the President (and his delegates), subject of course to Congressional lawmaking and appropriations powers. Article II, Section 1 vests "the executive power" in the President, and Article II, Section 2, begins by stating: "The President shall be Commander in Chief of the Army and Navy of the United States . . ."

Article III, which creates the Judicial Power, is *utterly silent* about providing for or running the Armed Forces.

That Judges have *no competence* and *no authority* to decide who, what type of, or how many men or women might be required to register, be drafted, or—by the same logic—be assigned to combat, is a proposition so self-evident that no *serious* student of American history, the words of the Constitutional text, the Founders' intent, the functional purpose of military forces, or the near-unanimous desires of the American people could possibly argue otherwise. I am confident that the Supreme Court will realize these elemental truths.

However, the very *fact* that *three* unelected Federal Judges would dare to tell 100 elected Senators, 435 elected Representatives, and the elected President whom to register for the draft shows how far down the path toward judicial oligarchy we have drifted.

20. William Shakespeare, *Julius Caesar,* Act I, Scene 2.

21. *Brown* v. *Board of Education,* 347 U.S. 483 (1954).

22. *Supra,* N. 8.

23. *Supra,* N. 12.

24. *Eisenstadt* v. *Baird,* 405 U.S. 438 (1972).

25. Gerald Gunther, *Cases and Materials on Constitutional Law* (Foundation Press, 10th Ed., 1980) p. 589–590.

26. *Ibid.,* p. 602–603.

27. *Planned Parenthood of Missouri* v. *Danforth,* 428 U.S. 52 (1976).

28. *Bolling* v. *Sharpe,* 347 U.S. 497 (1954).

29. *Fullilove* v. *Klutznick,* 448 U.S. (1980).

30.   See the brilliant exposition and dissection of the entire series of court rulings in Lino A. Graglia, *Disaster by Decree: The Supreme Court Decisions on Race and the Schools* (Cornell University Press, 1976).

31.   *Green* v. *County School Board,* 391 U.S. 430 (1968).

32.   *Swann* v. *Charlotte–Mecklenburg Board of Education,* 402 U.S. 1 (1971).

33.   Graglia, *supra,* N. 30, @ 164.

34.   A step toward such a publication, excellent on analysis if somewhat cursory in recommendations, is: Hon. Robert K. Dornan, M.C. and Csaba Vedlik, Jr., *Judicial Supremacy: The Supreme Court on Trial* (Nordland, 1980).

35.   This analysis is based on George W. Carey, "The Supreme Court, Judicial Review, and Federalist Seventy-Eight," *Modern Age* (Fall, 1974) 356.

36.   See Dornan and Vedlick, *supra,* N. 34.

37.   Arthur Taylor Prescott, ed., *Drafting the Federal Constitution* (Louisiana State Univ. Press, 1941), quoted in Dornan and Vedlik, *supra,* N. 34, p. 66.

38.   Jonathan Elliot, ed., *The Debates in the Several State Conventions on the Adoption of the Federal Constitution* (N.Y., 1888) Vol. I., p. 382, quoted in Dornan and Vedlik, *supra,* N. 34, p. 69.

39.   The phrase is Nathan Glazer's: "Towards an Imperial Judiciary," *The Public Interest* (Fall, 1975) p. 104.

Robert W. Whitaker

SOCIETAL PROPERTY RIGHTS

In a true free market economic theory, there must be a place for all who make production possible—including those who form the society in which production takes place. President Reagan's flirtation with opening America's borders to Mexico is not only bad politics, but bad economics as well.

W hy is it that labor is worth so much more on one side of a border than on the other? This is a question basic to immigration policy. Is it merely the irrational greed of American workers which keeps our borders closed to the tens of millions of people from poor countries who would be willing to come here and work for less?

As a matter of fact, liberals, libertarians, and big businesses are in implicit agreement on this point. Liberals are generally opposed to enforcement of our immigration laws. Big business sees a great prospect for profit as represented by large-scale immigration of cheap labor. Libertarians believe in equal pay for equal work everywhere on earth. They believe that all labor of the same quality should be paid the same, so restricting the movement of labor between nations is immoral.

This reasoning can go pretty far. Some time back, a conservative magazine contained an article protesting the lax enforcement of U.S. immigration laws on the Rio Grande. A flood of letters poured in, most of them with a single theme: A border to keep people *out* of the United States is as immoral as the Berlin Wall, which keeps people *in* East Germany.

To equate the Berlin Wall with American immigration laws is to say that the rest of the world has as much right to settle in the United States as East Germans have to emigrate. The point libertarians lose sight of is that immigration laws mean that we have something other people want. There are things in America, the product of Americans, which others would like to share. Some of these things are noneconomic, such as freedom. But we cannot share freedom by letting everybody on earth come here. Few free market economists would disagree with that statement. Yet our economic benefits are also the product of Americans, and free market economists quite seriously maintain that we have no right to keep them to ourselves.

Libertarians and free market economists generally believe that one obtains the highest level of production by following, insofar as possible, two principles. The first is that distribution of goods and services should be done by the market place, through supply and demand. Production, on the other side, is maximized by paying each person according to his contribution to production. But they restrict the definition of "contribution to production" to the three classical factors of production: land (including resources), labor (including skilled labor and management), and capital. If labor of the same quality is paid more in one place than in another, it represents an economic distortion.

According to pure free market economics, if wages for the same work are low in Calcutta, true economic theory requires that labor should be allowed to go elsewhere, until there is everywhere equal pay for equal work. Therefore, if Japanese workers are receiving more than Indian workers, they are getting the extra pay because they are exploiting somebody.

But whom? Whom is the Japanese worker exploiting? Is it capital? If Japan's investors were paid too little, the immense flow of capital into Japan from all over the world—including India— would stop. Is the Japanese worker exploiting management? There are firms all over the world who would like to have some Japanese managerial talent, and that managerial talent is perfectly free to leave. If it is exploited, why doesn't it go elsewhere? The reason is that, far from being exploited, managers in Japan do extremely well. Is it resources, then? Is Japan so rich in resources that the extra pay for workers there exploits vast mineral wealth for its benefits? Hardly. Japan does not have a tenth the resources per capita that India does.

Japanese workers receive more for their work because Japan is a productive society. Those who advocate unlimited immigration assume that all societies are equally productive, so the fact that Japan has a high living standard is a happenstance. If we assume the higher wage in a productive society is coincidental, then certainly an Indian has as much right to it as does a Japanese.

Free market economics, in other words, does not take into account contributions of the members of a society, not only as workers and savers, but as citizens.

Societal productivity requires, among other things, a resistance to demagoguery. There is real economic value in having a population in which those unemployed do not try to seize all property. But docility is not necessarily more desirable than constant rebelliousness. The enforced docility of the Franco government for its first two decades in Spain was almost as anti-Capitalist as it was anti-Communist, producing a suffocating system which resisted economic change and growth. Saudi Arabia, even if it were perfectly safe from a Communist take-over, would not be a place for the building of an industrial society, despite popular docility. Popular docility breeds stagnation, and an industrial society requires steady change. The balance of change and political stability, an accomplishment of tremendous size, is something Western market economists take for granted. They assign productivity to what they call the factors of production, and see the environment for such productivity as a given.

Libertarians say that capital produces wealth, and therefore the capitalist has the right to the rewards. They say that labor produces wealth, and therefore labor as a right to the rewards. The Japanese society and body politic produce wealth, but libertarians insist that that wealth belongs to the world. Otherwise, they would have to admit that immigration restrictions are not mere "economic distortions," but a means of protecting a property right as valid as that of Mitsubishi stockholders.

The difference between wages paid in Calcutta and those paid in Tokyo is the result of something as real as interest rates, and as palpable as a blast furnace. Higher wages are not produced by a people as a result of their performance as laborers only or as investors only, but by their performance as voters and citizens. The societal performance of the people of Japan produces wealth, and the right to that wealth therefore accrues to the people of Japan.

If oil is discovered in Mexico, free market economists will differ with Marxists and liberals about which Mexicans have a right to that oil. Marxists will say that the oil belongs to the people of Mexico, free market economists will say it belongs to the owners of the land on which it was found, and liberals will say it belongs partly to the land owners, and partly to the Mexican people. But all agree on one point: Oil found in Mexico belongs to somebody in Mexico.

One may argue whether the productivity of Japan belongs more to the capitalists of Japan or to the Japanese workers. But by argument analogous to that on oil, it should belong to somebody in Japan. Yet free immigration libertarians are in the ridiculous position of saying that a people has a right to oil which happens to be discovered beneath their soil, but not to the productive environment they produce.

If an Indian laborer is able to make more by moving to Japan, it is because he is able to share the productivity of Japanese society and Japanese politics. By the same token, Mexicans can make more money in America because they are able to share the productivity provided by American society and American politics. Immigration restrictions reward a people for their performance as voters and citizens, a reward which is not only moral, but which makes good economic sense.

The reason for rewarding members of a productive society is the same as for rewarding any other productive activity. Workers acquire skills because skilled labor is paid more than unskilled. Rich people are rewarded for saving instead of spending, not because they deserve the rewards on some abstract moral plane, but because their savings buy capital with which we produce more wealth. For the same reason, the welfare check of a citizen of Dallas, Texas allows him to buy more than a full-time laborer in Tijuana, Mexico can earn. He is being paid for being a part of a productive society. A full-time laborer in Dallas earns several times what a full-time laborer, doing the same work, in Tijuana earns. He is benefiting by what his society has accomplished, while his Mexican counterpart is paying for the fact that his society has a record of three centuries of demagogues and instability.

This disparity is often unfair. But the conservative economist has little to complain about. It is not fair for many wealthy people to receive the benefit of the fact that their ancestors saved money and worked hard. But every conservative economist will tell you very quickly how essential it is that we pay the dividends of those who inherited stock. He will explain that we must respect property rights, because, even if a particular person doesn't deserve them, it is dangerous to society to deprive him of those benefits. The present generation would see no need to save for their children if property rights are likely to be violated. Further, the expropriation of inherited property implies a threat to the security of all property.

But these same conservative economists never even consider that citizens of a productive body politic should be similarly rewarded.

The cost of ignoring societal property rights is the same as the cost of ignoring any other real property rights. To leave any factor of production out of economic theory is to court disaster. By preaching that only labor produces value, and therefore that interest on investments was evil, the London School of Economics (LSE) guaranteed poverty for most of the Third World for generations to come. India, desperately in need of capital, had leaders who, taught by LSE, refused to bring in that capital by simply allowing it to make money in India, instead devoting themselves to various socialist schemes to provide capital through the state. If societal property rights are left out of economic theory, underdeveloped countries miss a vital point: If they wish to succeed, they must copy not only the technical, but the societal and political methods of successful countries.

A refusal to recognize societal property rights can be equally destructive for a developed economy. If one wishes to stop all investment, one outlaws interest payments. If one wishes to destroy productive societal attitudes, one removes all the benefits provided by societal property rights. It is no accident that even the poorest Americans refuse to vote Communist or Socialist. Part of the reason is that every American shares to some extent in the benefits of American capitalism. These are not the terms in which such voters think. Rather, they are aware that even poor Americans are better off than they would be in other countries, and therefore choose to resist the appeal of radicals.

Clearly, politics is part of economics; society a factor of production. Workers in richer countries are being paid for the politics their country chooses to follow. Economists then have two alternatives. First, they can follow their present course, and wish away this uncomfortable fact of life. Second, they may simply consider politics, and the societal attitudes which produce those politics, another real factor of production, which must be paid for like any other factor of production.

If one considers politics to be something to be wished away by economic theory, all welfare payments are inexcusable. But if one believes that real-world economics must face real-world facts, one must notice that productive societies all make welfare payments to the poor. Such minimum public assistance and relatively high wages are simply part of the price of maintaining a stable body politic today. Given this reality, the completely anti-welfare libertarian degenerates to the level of a liberal moralist: It is a fact, he admits, but it shouldn't be. Anyone who considers himself a realist, and who insists welfare is unnecessary in today's world, must first find a wealthy country where this payment is not required.

I wish, along with libertarians, that the political systems where I am willing to invest my money would stop making me pay taxes for welfare to some of the people who make up those countries. I wish, again with libertarians, that I could have the profits of Indian cheap labor and the safety for my investment provided by a Swiss political system. I wish, with liberals, that oil companies would give me oil free, and that new sources of oil would find and develop themselves while I am enjoying free oil. I wish I had a herd of shmoos. As bases for logical economic thought, all these wishes are precisely equal.

A free market economist I know was very impatient with an Indian socialist, and for good reason. The socialist was saying that, if he believed in the profit motive, he was justifying price-fixers and monopolist exploiters. To justify profits, the socialist said loudly, was to say that those who worked and exploited children in nineteenth century sweatshops were right to do so. My free market acquaintance tried to explain to the shouting ideologue that free market economics only justified some profits, and condemned outright price-fixers as completely as did any socialist. But the socialist ideologue was shouting, and would not listen.

A few days later, this same free market economist was shouting. He said, in effect, that my argument about societal property rights would justify the British welfare state. He said I was trying to stop the free movement of labor all over the world, and, in effect, blamed my kind of thinking for the Berlin Wall. I tried to explain to him that the concept of societal property rights only justifies *some* welfare, and *some* immigration restrictions, and that it condemns a runaway welfare state as completely as does any other free market approach. But he was shouting, and would not listen.

The free market will take care of the British welfare state. Britain is in desperate straits because its political system is simply asking a higher price than the market will bear. Many people would like to invest money in Britain, but the cost, in taxes and economic restrictions, is too high, so they are going elsewhere. British talent is leaving the United Kingdom to go where their talents receive a due reward. The result is an increasing poverty, which results in the British electorate moving away from the stagnant policies of the past. The British political system, in short, is being forced, by competition, to become more competitive.

If Britain had the only society in the world, it could raise its taxes even higher, just as the only steel company in the world could charge almost anything it chose. The British Labour Party acts as if this were the case, and that taxes can be as high as Britons choose without driving talent and capital away and leaving the country impoverished. This is not true, and Britons are being forced to lower taxes and economic restrictions because there are other societies competing for the same talent and resources.

But there are British libertarians who apply an equally illogical assumption: that Britain should have no taxes, and no welfare. They are saying, in other words, that the United Kingdom should provide its productive environment free of charge. Germans, through taxes and high wages, charge money for investment in Germany. France charges money for investment there. Americans will not be surprised to learn that the Internal Revenue Service is still in action. But, say libertarians, Britain should ignore its competitors, and give investors a free lunch. Yet libertarians are also the people who wear buttons saying TANSTAAFL—"There ain't no such thing as a free lunch."

A steel mill can charge only what the market will bear. If there were an infinite number of steel mills, and a finite number of users of steel, the price of the metal would be almost zero, because every mill would rather get something, however little, than nothing.

Likewise, the United Kingdom cannot name its own price, because it is not the only productive location on earth. But it is equally absurd to ask that it charge nothing, because its competition is not infinite.

As a result, the principle of equal work for equal pay everywhere makes no sense at all, because work is not all there is to the person who produces it. However matter-of-fact it may be for a skilled worker in Italy to belong to a union dominated by Communists, that fact drives out investors and lowers the value of his work. If he were made aware of this fact, he would take a new look at this matter, and whether it should continue to be a fact. But so long as even conservative economists insist that politics has nothing to do with economics, and join with Marxists in insisting that unequal pay for equal work is the result of a plot, poor countries will concentrate, not on becoming productive, but on looking for the plot.

It might be added that no libertarian will put his money where his mouth is. I once asked a libertarian who was upset at the idea that labor should be worth more in El Paso than in Tijuana about where he would put his money. Not surprisingly, it turned out that he would never consider investing his money in Tijuana at the same rate of interest he would receive in El Paso. Capital, it turns out, is very different if it is invested in Mexico than when it is invested in Texas. There is nothing artificial about a national border when a libertarian's own capital crosses it.

Libertarian and "free market" theories imply the ideal of a single, free market world, in which the artificial restrictions imposed by separate political units are removed. I see such a unitary body politic as a monopoly, demanding what its captive market will bear. Every libertarian expects the exclusive owner of any product to demand as much as he can for his product, without regard to the fact that, in the long run, his greed may reduce everybody's standard of living, including his own. A world state could set taxes at ninety percent or more, because the only choice any firm might have would be to pay the taxes or go out of business. But the libertarian/old rightist assumes that his world state would not act like the monopoly it is.

Marxists ignored competition. They therefore concluded that a single state-owned company would be the most productive, since it would provide the maximum economy of scale. Libertarian economics is based on a similar error. Ignoring competition between states, he concludes that a world state will provide minimum taxation and maximum competition. He scorns the socialist, who says that competition is not necessary to force companies to do their best, but he assumes that a single, world-wide electorate would not, sooner or later, behave like the societal monopoly it is.

In the real world, political separation limits the power of any one state over the free market within its borders. If taxes or wages rise too high, investors may choose to go elsewhere. Each society thereby receives the rewards its performance earns.

Against this competitive function, there is the argument that political separation leads to war. That is the thesis behind the United Nations. But the fact is that, throughout the twentieth century, no two democratic states have been at war with each other, though the League of Nations and the United Nations both presided over a world in which war was commonplace. It is not in artificial political unity, but in a movement against totalitarianism and authoritarianism, that the road to peace lies. In such a movement, neither the League nor the UN has ever pretended to take part. Popular rule and national sovereignty are the directions in which the world must move, in order to secure peace to the full extent that the limitations of human nature make it possible.

The New Right, therefore, is not only politically practical, but economically sound, in demanding the enforcement of immigration restrictions. By the same token, we do not advocate an end to welfare, though we do feel, as witness the competitive economic condition of the United States, that it has gone too far. We have no use for the United Nations as the way to peace, because it quite clearly has nothing to do with addressing the causes of war. All these policies dovetail into a rational, and a truly free market, political economy.

Thomas Fleming

OLD RIGHTS AND THE NEW RIGHT

One aspect of the New Right which has received wide, if distorted, attention has been its emphasis on a return to basic American values. One major intellectual source of those values, Southern traditionalism, has received little consideration. It is discussed here by Dr. Thomas Fleming, who is editor of the Southern Partisan, *a quarterly journal representing the Southern intellectual traditionalist viewpoint.*

"The South . . . the great conservative power, which prevents other portions, less fortunately constituted, from rushing into conflict. In this tendency to conflict in the North between labor and capital, which is constantly on the increase, the weight of the South has and will ever be found on the Conservative side; against the aggression of one or the other side, which ever may tend to disturb the equilibrium of our political system."

John C. Calhoun in 1838

N ow that the Republican majority has finally emerged, the masters of the news media have conceived a sudden interest in the doings of *conservative man.* Reports from Heritage Foundation are front-page news and the opinions of Mr. Paul Weyrich are eagerly solicited by CBS with the kind of persistence they used to reserve for George Meany.

Many people who describe themselves as "conservative" are happy for the first time since Barry Goldwater urged on his cavalry of Y.A.F. and Goldwater Girls to the Little Bighorn. There are a few dissonant voices in the right-wing halleluiahs, but in general, we seem to have entered a bipartisan era of good feeling. The greatest problem we have to face is a basic—and I believe irreconcilable—difference between two groups of conservatives. The first group is familiar to everyone as the dedicated right wing of the Republican Party. They may no longer assert that what's good for General Motors is good for America, but their conservatism still boils down to free enterprise. For convenience's sake, let us call

them capitalists. The other group is as much concerned with the
social and moral issues which Phyllis Schlafly and Dr. Falwell have
done so much to popularize. We may call them traditionalists or
social conservatives. The New Right, which is largely a coalition of
such socially conservative forces, actually represents a much older
conservative tradition than the so-called old right.

Even before Mr. Reagan was elected, cracks in the conservative alliance began to show up, as free enterprise conservatives
began to worry about the "fanatics" in the Moral Majority. The
New Right groups are under attack for several reasons: Many of
their followers are blue-collar workers—even union members—
whose devotion to the principles of Adam Smith is suspect. Their
out-and-out opposition to the ERA, busing, pornography, abortion,
—even the teaching of evolution—brings back memories of the
Scopes Trial. They are tagged as racists, sexists, and religious
fanatics.

It is not surprising that the strongest support for social conservatism is still in the South, or that Southern senators, like
Helms, Thurmond and the newly-elected John East, are the leading traditionalists in the Congress. Indeed, this struggle between
economic and social conservatives has often been portrayed as a
sectional conflict between North and South.

The struggle for power, then, is not a bilateral conflict between
"liberals" like Ted Kennedy and conservatives like Ronald Reagan.
It is a trilateral (pardon the expression) war going on among three
groups—first, those who call themselves liberals, but whose doctrines and policies are nearly pure socialism; second, free enterprise conservatives, whose doctrines are unadulterated liberalism;
and the traditionalists, social conservatives, whose leadership and
support is typically—but by no means exclusively—Southern. The
one issue on which the three groups most sharply disagree is the
old question of the Rights of Man—rights which the South is supposed to have denied her people for the basest of reasons.

Hostility toward the South—especially from conservatives—is
an old, perplexing story. By conventional standards, the South is
the most conservative part of the nation. If we can trust surveys,
Southerners go to church more often, drink less (or like to think
they do), defend their honor—both personal and national—with
greater zeal, and maintain closer family ties than do the people of
other sections. Southern workers have even resisted the blandish-

ments offered by union leaders and there are still some Southern ladies who believe that a woman's place is in the home. Our oldest caricature of a conservative is the bombastic Southern senator in linen suit and planter's hat. This stereotype is older than the War Between the States, a struggle that Europeans viewed as a final conflict between liberal and conservative principles. On the one side were ranged all the noisy forces of progress—industrialism, capitalism, and unitarianism—and on the other stood the hopelessly outnumbered planters and farmers who clung to the old time religion.

On the surface the problem comes down to race. Southerners, at least a small percentage of them, once owned Black slaves, while the cannier Yankees managed to get rich by buying and selling them. At the time when wealthy Southerners were sending Blacks out to labor in the fields, wealthy Northerners were sending the poor Whites—the Irish in great numbers—men, women, and children, into mines and factories under conditions that filled Southern slaveholders with moral outrage. Blacks have been lynched in the South, but their treatment in New York during its draft riots and in Chicago during its race wars might better be described as massacre. When it comes to economic and racial oppression, no section of our country has clean hands, but the North continues to perpetuate the myth of the Southern heritage of guilt. In all other areas of life, they have managed to forget the doctrine of Original Sin and that quaint old Biblical idea that a father's sins are visited upon his children. Even if the progeny of slaveholders deserved punishment, relatively few people in the modern South are much tainted with the blood of Masters, and it has been four generations since Mr. Lincoln freed the slaves. But the Southerner's guilt is a peculiar one. It may be the only example of a people condemned merely for their geographical location—unless we want to revive the Puritan's fancy that America is the Devil's province and the Indians his special children.

Complaints against the South's racism cannot be taken seriously. They do, however, point to the real source of contention between true and false conservatives. The typical Northern capitalist (as glimpsed at Republican Conventions and suburban cocktail parties) is a strong defender of what he likes to call Free Enterprise, by which he too often means a government-encouraged monopoly or oligopoly of business interests. He stands up for Amer-

ica against the menace of Soviet Communism (the Soviets believe
in redistributing the wealth), although he is not averse to turning
a profit from trading with countries "behind the Iron Curtain." He
deplores all forms of social welfare (except those that benefit his
own class) as paternalism, thereby managing to forget that it was
his ancestors' greed and rapacity that forced this country to turn
socialist. Religion, he is heard to argue, is a very good thing, so long
as it is not contaminated by fanaticism (his ancestors would have
called it *enthusiasm*), the besetting sin of Southern Baptists and
traditional Roman Catholics up North.

It is obvious to anyone that many capitalist "conservatives"
are nothing better than nineteenth century liberals with a hang-
over. Their libertarian ideas of freedom, expressed almost always
in economic terms, are tempered only by the recognition that it
takes force to keep the discontented masses in their place. However, when a Southerner calls himself a conservative, he is usually
thinking of a way of life, of a social and moral order for which the
people of the 1860s went to war. He is more disturbed by the
disintegration of the family than by rising interest rates. He believes in Free Enterprise and might even be happy to go to war to
resist Soviet aggression, but he is not so delighted with the mobility
and tawdriness of modern life, with the fast food and fast buck
artists who seem intent on turning the New South into a suburb
of Chicago. He does not like to see family farms swallowed up by
Agribusiness in the interest of profit and productivity. Above all,
he knows the value of stability and the price of progress.

One of the most perplexing things about most Southern conservatives is their continued loyalty to the Democratic Party. Most
Southerners still think of themselves as Democrats, even at the
moment they are pulling the lever for Richard Nixon or Ronald
Reagan. Part of their loyalty is an inheritance from the past. Some
Southerners remember that the GOP began as a sectional party,
whose leaders—Fremont, Sumner, Lincoln—were bent on destroying the political influence of the South. Not forgotten either are the
aggressive war ruthlessly waged by Sherman and Grant against
the whole Southern people and the succeeding regional exploitation from whose effects the South is escaping only in our own
generation. This allegiance to the party of their fathers is often
ridiculed as the sentimentality that is to be expected from an igno-
rant and rustic population, despite the fact that the South is ra-

pidly becoming far more suburban than rural. But sentimental
loyalty to the past is the only secure bedrock of conservative opinions. For the very reason that they are conservative, most Southerners are unwilling to desert the party of Thomas Jefferson, John
C. Calhoun, and Jefferson Davis or to join the party of Lincoln,
Grant, and Hoover. Of course, some Republicans do remember
their roots. When liberal Republicans like George Gilder (now reformed) were founding a progressive movement in the Republican
Party, they called it the Ripon Society, after Ripon, Wisconsin,
where the party was founded, as if to remind Republicans of their
traditional commitments to social progress, liberal construction of
the Constitution, and the destruction of the conservative South.

No one is going to argue that the Mason-Dixon Line forms a
natural barrier between true and false conservatism. For several
decades, the banner of principled conservatism has been upheld by
the sage of Mecosta (Michigan), Mr. Russell Kirk. Even so, the
South remains the nation's greatest reservoir of native conservative opinions.

The real complaint against the South is that it is genuinely
conservative—an intolerable situation. Consider the differences between Northern and Southern literature in our century. Works of
fiction—novels and poetry—can mean more to a people than all the
political manifestoes and reports from all the think tanks and
foundations ever established by misguided philanthropy. A people's character, at its best and worst, can be read from its novels.
The modern South lives in characters like Faulkner's rustic gentle-
men Buck and Buddy McCaslin, in the tainted heroism of Willie
Stark *(All the King's Men),* and in the gentlemanly despair of Will
Barrett *(The Last Gentleman)* in whom Walker Percy has traced
the lineaments of our modern failure of nerve—the quandary of a
decent man sorting things out in a society that has rejected God.
As for the serious literature of the rest of the country, I shrink from
measuring a people's character by the standard of Alex Portnoy or
Myra Breckenridge or from deducing any moral significance from
the works of Norman Mailer and E.L. Doctorow. If there is anywhere a vision of America where tradition and principle are at
least taken seriously, it is in the best of Faulkner, Miss Flannery
O'Connor and those Southern Agrarians who, in their lives and
works, represented the only conservative intellectual movement
taken seriously in America.

Northern capitalists are apt to answer all this with a preemptory wave of the hand. "It is all," they say, *"Gone With the Wind* —a sentimental myth." It never occurs to them that political man lives by myths. What else but myth is the divine right of kings for which so many conservatives have spilled their blood, or the Glorious Revolution (so dear to Whigs and Capitalists) with James II's Catholic heir smuggled in on a warming pan? Or the myth of Class Struggle with students at the barricades and Joe Hill facing the firing squad? Or best of all, the courageous newspaper reporters, risking the perils of wealth and fame to unmask the conspiracies of the evil Pentagon and the tyrannical Nixon? We have lost nearly all of our conservative myths—the benevolence of kings, the valor of soldiers, the piety of priests. The only really conservative myth left to Americans is the South. It is a fairy tale place, of strong, courageous men and gentle but determined ladies, where the land and the family are loved more than money and productivity, where the Constitution is respected more than progress, where there are still a few churches in which the idols of Mammon are not worshiped and the social gospel not preached.

"All this is very well," our Northern brothers will say, "but such rhetorical display on the topics of chivalry and tradition belong to the novels of William Gilmore Simms, not to the New South. You people said the same things before the Civil War—and look where it got you. What you mean by tradition is your history of repression against the rights of Blacks and women. You revere the Constitution only as a barrier against wholesome social improvements like integration and equal rights for women. More of you may go to church, but only to hear superstitious tirades against knowledge and progress. The South's conservatism—like South Africa's—is nothing more lofty than the denial of human rights."

When people as different as President Carter and Mr. Buckley agree to speak of "human rights," it indicates a kind of American consensus on the subject. To the extent that capitalists and socialists share a common vision of America, it is a land of equal opportunity for all, a place where our human rights are protected. As futile as it is to dissent from this overwhelming consensus, for the life of me, I do not even begin to know what they are talking about. In the free enterprise world of nature, the only right would seem to be: *Prey or be preyed upon.* From a naturalist's perspective, the whole duty of man is summed up in the proverb, "Root, hog, or die." Any

notion of rights other than those defined by law is essentially mystical and totally incompatible with the scepticism and atheism
which characterize liberal thought. Even men of faith, whose belief
in a purposeful creator gives them some basis for talking about
rights, are on shaky ground when they attempt to endow civil
liberties with supernatural grace. The Scriptures are remarkably
reluctant to recommend any one form of government, and obedience to the imperial authority was enjoined in the days of Tiberius
and Nero, rulers whom it would be hard to cast in a republican
mold. Kingship—however much as *faute de mieux*—was granted
by God to the people of Israel for their correction. Finally, while
free speech and representative government are not included in the
Ten Commandments—or on the golden tablets which the angel
Moroni brought to Joseph Smith—St. Paul never abandoned his
attempt to instill a sense of obedience—to government, to husbands, even to masters. When we examine human rights with any
attention, they will change, before our very eyes, into Natural
Rights, according to which I am entitled to everything I can lay my
hands upon.

Even though the doctrine of human rights has been the ignis
fatuus—the will o' the wisp leading good men astray in the swamps
of political abstraction—good Christian men reared in the traditions of the West may reasonably expect to retain those privileges
which their ancestors labored to acquire and enjoy. These *Civil
Rights*—the privileges of citizens—fall conveniently under the
headings of life, liberty, and property—John Locke's liberal trinity
—insofar as they concern the individual. But inasmuch as society
is composed not of individuals, but families, a second set of rights,
guaranteeing the existence, integrity, and property of the family,
must be devised.

In defining each of these three classes of rights, capitalists,
socialists, and conservatives disagree seriously. Conservatives
speak of preserving specific rights secured by their ancestors,
rights which are defined, at least in part, by the circumstances that
produced them. On the other hand, liberals—capitalists and socialists—prefer to speak abstractly. They discuss rights in general with
as much windy metaphysics as Tom Paine or Anacharsis Cloots. On
the question of capital punishment, liberals speak of a generalized
human right that is subject to no restriction. However, conservatives know that no civil right is absolute. Society has always been

free to take life itself from those who forfeit it by committing murder, rape, treason, or armed robbery. It is a right defined and restricted by various historical circumstances, for example, by an Englishman's right to trial by jury, the principle of *habeas corpus,* the traditional distinctions between civil and military jurisdiction and between burglary and highway robbery.

It is a mistake to label liberal opponents of capital punishment as "bleeding hearts." Virtues like mercy have no place in the mouths of capitalists or socialists. In their vocabulary charity is replaced by utility and progress (in the case of the capitalists) and social justice (in the case of socialists). Opposition to capital punishment, although it is partly rooted in the obsessive fear that it could happen to *me,* is justified intellectually on the grounds of the individual's absolute right that the State cannot take away what it never gave—a deduction that only holds true for Adam and anarchists. Leave aside the question of the State and try to imagine a modern American surviving very long without the protection offered by society in the form of the Armed Forces, police, production and trade of goods. Socrates recognized that his city had a right to take the life it had given him, even when their decision was manifestly unjust.

Socialists like the Kennedys—and those happily former senators Bayh, McGovern et al.—are particularly unwilling to admit any historical constraints on our rights. What is the purpose of the Supreme Court, if not to override the provisions of our archaic Constitution? Even so, they do introduce qualifications derived not from that faith in the past we call history, but from faith in the future—speculative theories of economics and political science. They imagine how wonderful our world could be, if only man were not so human. On the right to live, socialists (and even some capitalists) allow their hallucinations of the future to obscure their vision of the present. In the socialist gospel, the Future will be a perfect world. Non-violent perfect specimens will enjoy an abundance of physical and aesthetic blessings without the dreadful liabilities of Christian superstition. Men and women, put in full possession of their equal rights, will respect each other "as individuals" rather than as stereotypes of male and female. One has only to read books like *Walden II* to get the impression—graceful androgynous robots in white gowns enjoying their equal rights on the rolling green lawns in front of a Doric temple. Most liberal utopias turn out to be an ill-starred cross between the alien planet with higher life forms and an expensive lunatic asylum.

It seems absurd, but socialists are able to draw very definite conclusions from their fantasies. Since it is impossible to establish the Future in the crowded streets of New Delhi or New York, it is nothing short of criminal to bring so many unwanted children into the world. Not only does this superfluous population not enjoy their lives, they prevent us from enjoying ours. There is no place for the mentally or physically deformed or for the unwanted offspring of rape, incest or teenage pregnancy. One prominent abortionist recently predicted that the time is coming when society would recognize that girls under the age of sixteen did not possess the *right* to bear children. Dr. Mengele could not have expressed it more precisely.

If a fragile human life manages to run the gantlet of the feminists and abortionists, the Right to Death crowd is waiting for him, at the end, to show signs of senility, unbearable pain, or a diminished "quality of life." The disabled elderly, sent to rest homes and "hospices," are to be popped full of Valium and gin, shot up with heroin, then gently pressured into doing the right thing—dying with dignity—anything to avoid becoming a burden.

Most capitalists, it must be said, do not favor abortion or euthanasia. But their insistence on social utility and economic growth makes them feeble advocates for life. Some of them worry that the poor, especially the black and brown poor, are overpopulating the world and need to be restrained, somehow. They too, as much as the socialists, confuse material well-being with happiness, quality of life with virtue. Even when they hold the reins of power, capitalists have shown themselves unable to stem the tide of "progress."

It is in property rights that conservatives most sharply disagree with their opponents. True conservatives maintain that a family's right to hold and dispose of property is among the privileges of a free people. In times of war, extraordinary taxes have been levied on property, soldiers quartered in the home, land confiscated, without compromising the basic notion of property rights. False conservatives of the Free Enterprise school (as well as their socialist heirs) have introduced a number of qualifications which have tended to destroy this most precious of our civil rights. Capitalists, with their eyes fixed on profit and progress, always favor construction of highways, dams, even sports arenas at the expense of local property owners who may have been in possession for generations. That sense of continuity provided by "the old family place" has been the center of European family life from the very beginning. When the Federal Government first began to show its canine teeth, proponents of schemes for building roads and canals used the power to regulate as the constitutional peg to hang their legislation on. John Randolph, a Virginian, warned that such a liberal construction of the Constitution would lead to a time when the government could "say to every wagoner in North Carolina, you shall not carry any commerce across the Virginia line . . . because I have some other object to answer by a suppression of that trade. . . ." The TVA in Tennessee and the Santee-Cooper in South Carolina were fine, liberal conceptions that flooded whole communities including graveyards, churches, and historic sites, and uprooted the lives of countless families—all to provide power for factories in distant cities and sport fishing for the city dwellers.

The socialists, picking up where the capitalists leave off, regard property itself as something near criminal and certainly of less importance than social justice. They are willing, through fair housing laws, to instruct a man to whom and under what circumstances he may rent or sell his property. As Randolph warned, this tyranny is justified by the Congress's power to regulate commerce.

The South, whatever its failings, has usually opposed such invasions of property rights. It is after all difficult to distinguish between our right to property and our right to liberty. A racist ideologue is still a man and a citizen. If he is told that he may not consult his prejudices, when he rents or sells his property, then his liberty of conscience is as much affected as his right to hold property. Senator Sam Ervin used to say that "the Constitution gives a man the right to make a fool of himself." Ervin not only opposed fair housing laws, he also stood firmly against Mr. Nixon's ill-advised experiments in thought control. What surprises most socialists is the conservative Ervin's resistance to the Nixon administration's crime bills. This "conservative" legislation included provisions for no-knock entry into suspects' homes and preventive detention. It clearly tampered with our civil and constitutional protection against illegal search and seizure—not to mention the presumption of innocence. Ervin observed that "the supreme value of a civilization is the freedom of the individual, which is simply the right . . . to be free of governmental tyranny."

Southerners like Ervin and all true conservatives believe that a man's home is his castle, where "the poorest man may in his cottage bid defiance to the Crown." If we cannot keep the government out of our homes and out of our families, then freedom will cease to exist. I do not mean the paltry right to vote of which we are so proud. In a society like our own, suffrage is only the right to collaborate with our captors. It is the high privilege of stool pigeons and prison trusties. Real freedom is the right to think our own thoughts, lead our own lives, and rear our own children. Most men are only really free when they are with their families. Chesterton, who called the home "the one anarchist institution," admonished reformers that "the state has no tool delicate enough to deracinate the rooted habits and tangled affections of the family. . . . The truth is, that to a moderately poor man, the home is the only place of liberty. It is the only spot on the earth where a man may alter arrangements suddenly, make an experiment, indulge in a whim."

It is the family to which we owe our life, our nurture, our education (the part of it that matters most) into the secrets of society. Participation in the family is the source of all our civil rights and liberties—not in theory, in fact. Before anything like the state had been created, the family was and after the family, the clan and all the brotherhoods of community life—guilds and unions, churches and colleges. Sir Henry Sumner Maine, in his *Ancient Law,* made the invaluable point that all law is in origin a kind of international law designed to regulate affairs between families. Within the family circle, the government was without authority. So great was the early Roman father's authority—his *patria potestas*—that, as Livy tells us, the Senate was unable to condemn the wives and children of men who had been convicted of taking part in forbidden religious ceremonies. It had to turn them over to their own families—who dutifully condemned them to death.

We have come a long way, in the name of progress, from the Roman father's free exercise of the *patria potestas.* Most of these changes, up to the nineteenth century, provided important guarantees of individual rights. Neither the family nor its head (since the time of Cicero and Caesar) may deprive one of its members of life, liberty, or property without arousing the state's interest. Of course, women and children did not possess the *same* rights to liberty and property as grown men; nonetheless, murder, mutilation, starvation, and theft have been punished as crimes, even when they were committed by the head of a family against his wife and children. So much state intervention may have been wholesome, even necessary. But in the past one hundred and fifty years, the State has attempted to bypass the family entirely and to deal with everyone as individuals. The effect of this atomization is a kind of social starvation. It is as if a hungry man were fed a diet of carbon, hydrogen, and oxygen atoms, instead of molecules of sugar, water, and the complex proteins of even more complex foods. Our poor, starved American society is forced to sustain itself not on the nourishment of corporate life—the churches and guilds that are made up in turn of families—but on the elemental fare of individuals. Worse than starved, we are being poisoned by the raw chemicals of individual rights.

The destruction of the family began long ago in the apparently innocent decision of state and local governments to provide for schools. Public education, the proudest boast of democratic America, has turned out to be the principal weapon used by the enemies of the family. Compulsory attendance laws require children to be sent to *a* school. High taxes—federal, state, and local—combined with the high tuition of most private schools ensure that most children will be sent to public schools where they will be taught how to become good Americans. Parents acquiesced in the school's experiments in social engineering so long as lip service was paid to the values of most Americans—respect for God and country, simple morality and common decency. As we all know, the disciples of John Dewey have used the schools for laboratories, our children for rats. They have played with sex education, pornography, values clarification while at the same time attacking religion—especially the Christian faith.

Protests against pornographic text books in West Virginia and against sex education in California are only the early symptoms of a revolt against the tyranny of the Education Establishment. It is only a question of time before parents, on a wide scale, begin to rebel against abortion counseling given to junior high school girls and the "simulated" homosexual acts required in at least one California guidance class. Of course, the busing of children to achieve some vision of social harmony simply adds fuel to the flames of rebellion. And yet, it is clear that most parents refuse to acknowledge that the greatest mistake lay in allowing government, even local government, to assume authority over the rearing of children.

Now that the socialist planners, through their efforts of indoctrination (thirty hours a week, nine months a year, for ten to twenty years) have brought the family to bay, they are resolved to go in directly for the kill. They have devised and supported Head Start programs, federally funded day care centers, and a myriad other programs to make sure that they can begin the propaganda at an earlier age, when children's characters are more supple. Most recently, they have begun proposing legislation—much of it inspired by the Year of the Child—which enables the government to intervene in families where the child's physical, social, or emotional well-being might be threatened by the parents. North Carolina's Child Health Care Plan provided for "aggressive outreach and even government intervention . . . to safeguard the child's well-being." Included in the child's well-being are his right to pregnancy testing, sex education, and contraceptives. Concern was also expressed over the ill effects of religious bigotry. Baptists and Catholics, presumably, will not be allowed to teach their churches' peculiar doctrines or even the common beliefs of all Christians, summed up in the Nicene Creed.

The socialists would like to destroy the ailing family and to put in its place the authority of government. It is a great deal like urban renewal. We systematically demolish dilapidated single-family dwellings to erect row after row of uniform, standard public housing. We can imagine the workers' paradise to be something like the People's Republic of China, where a large proportion of the children are "raised" in public day care centers. Foreign observers and even some Chinese have remarked upon the disquieting docility of these children: toilet-trained at twelve months, passive and obedient at two years, these products of an ideal day care program betray few signs of their human origin. Laughter and tears, desire and hate—all appear alien to them. They will pose no threat to the People's Republic's ambitious plans for social reformation. They are too well broken. We have seen the Future and it works—alas, too well.

Socialists and conservatives, therefore, take opposite sides in this question of governmental interference in the family. But what of those we have termed false conservatives—the free enterprise liberals and capitalists? These people argue, quite sincerely, that

they too believe in the family and that they oppose the government's intrusion except in cases of wife-beating and child abuse.
They are against Federal day care centers as a violation of the
spirit of Free Enterprise. And yet, policies and ideas accepted by
many (if not most) of these "conservatives" have, generation by
generation, brought us closer to the China Syndrome.

The capitalists are tripped up by their belief in liberty and
equality. When they get into an argument with their socialist
friends, most free enterprise liberals fall back on equal opportunity
as their first line of defense: "We believe in equality of opportunity,
which is fair, democratic, and practical, while you *radicals* advocate equality of condition, which unfairly sacrifices the interests of
the many to aid the few and which requires more governmental
control than is safe for a free society." It seems no one, not even
those who call themselves conservatives, has the temerity to declare against equal rights. Recently, a highly respected intellectual
historian, Stephen J. Tonsor, asked in *Modern Age*, "Would any
state based upon the principle of inequality . . . be functional in our
present day world?" With full knowledge that any criticism of
equal rights will get a writer branded as a racist, a sexist, and a
Southerner, let us examine the text of this received doctrine.

Equal opportunity means that everyone, rich or poor, man or
woman, Christian, Jew, Moslem, or Atheist, should have roughly
the same chances in life. In order to equalize economic opportunity
between rich and poor, we pass ruthlessly exorbitant inheritance
taxes that put estate-building out of the reach of all but the weal-
thiest plutocrats. This Marxist system of taxation—along with progressive income taxes—is aimed directly at the family. The inevitable effect is to reduce a family to one generation of greedy
individualists, each pursuing his own selfish interest. It used to be
common to find families of three and four generations all living
together—not always in harmony. But now we give as little
thought to our children and grandchildren as we do to the parents
and grandparents whom we willingly consign to rest homes, nursing homes, and hospices. It is the State's responsibility to see that
our children are able to take care of themselves when they are
grown, and it is up to some institution to take care of our parents,
when they have worn out. Five years of day care, twenty years of
schooling, ten to fifteen years of retirement cities, the time will

come when a man who lives to be eighty will have spent half his life under the care of institutions.

It is *not* wrong for a man to work hard to ensure that his children will possess greater advantages than the children of less industrious or less fortunate men. We shall soon be approving Horace's cynical admonition:

> Feast then thy heart, for what thy heart has had
> The fingers of no heir will ever hold.

This advice was addressed to a generation of Romans that had so abandoned the family that the Emperor Augustus felt it necessary to pass legislation practically compelling the well-to-do to marry and rear children.

The worst effect of the craze for equal opportunity lies in the curious phenomenon of women's rights. Leaving aside the whole question of inequality of ability, let us consider equal opportunity's effect on the family, when a mother decides that the family income and her own "self-fulfillment" take precedence over her maternal duties. Whatever a woman's reason for going to work—economic necessity, greed, selfishness—the law guarantees her an opportunity for employment equal to that of any male, head of the house. The unfairness of an ordinary father with a wife and two children to support having to compete in the job market with, say, a physician's wife who *elects* to enter the work force, is obvious to anyone. But the hardship worked upon men is the slightest of the problems.

When men and women are free to choose their own "life styles," and to decide what image of humanity they wish to represent, their children must be left increasingly to the protection of the State, which either operates or oversees the schools, children's homes, and day care centers that are replacing the family. Such matters as abortion counseling, contraception, spanking, and choice of schools are no longer, in many places, within the parent's control. A recent ACLU study, "The Rights of Parents" by Sussman and Guggenheim, contains the chilling statement that "State involvement in the raising [sic] of our children is a fact of life." The high divorce rate spawned by a permissive society is among the contributing factors.

It seems obvious that divorce is a kind of invitation to the State to involve itself in the family. After all, a father and mother who decide that their own pleasure or happiness is more important than their children have declared their parental incompetence to the world. Most decent free enterprise liberals deplore the dissolution of the family. Many of them, their eyes opened by the social and moral decay of modern America, are becoming genuine conservatives—a process that is easy for people who already describe themselves as conservative. Such converts realize that the power residing in freedom of choice is only a power of repulsion within the family. It can only cause family members to fly apart, to dissociate. It cannot attract or hold them together.

Most capitalists do *not* see the need to regulate marriage and divorce. Such interference in private affairs is inconsistent with personal freedom. Divorce is, they say, a matter of contract and personal preference, an aspect of life where the State has no business. Women should not be compelled to remain married to a man they no longer love nor should married men and women be any more constrained in their choice of mates than bachelors and spinsters.

Divorce is certainly a device for equalizing opportunity, but it is a matter more complicated than the exercise of free choice. In the case of a traditional church marriage, where the couple has exchanged the usual vows "for richer for poorer, in sickness and in health, till death us do part," there is no reason why they should not be held to their contract. But society may claim to have an interest even in civil marriages. John Locke, one of the authors of the natural rights craze, conceded that "this conjunction betwixt male and female ought to last, even after procreation, so long as is necessary to the nourishment and support of the young ones, who are to be sustained by those that got them till they are able to shift and provide for themselves." But, Locke added, once these claims of nature were satisfied, "there is no impediment in nature to their separation." Of course there is no impediment in *nature*. Nature does not even insist that a male human animal remain with his mate long enough to see his children born. Only maternity is entirely natural. The sense of paternal responsibility is an acquired habit that may be lost in a society that puts no prize on stability, honor, and fidelity. Every time a couple is divorced, society is saying, "Go, thou, and do likewise."

The strains imposed on the family by equal opportunity are

enormous—husbands competing with their own wives, men and women entering into marriage "so long as love shall last," mothers feeling compelled to abandon their families for a career or to satisfy their sexual appetites. The real effect of this collective delusion of women's rights is only to reduce the once sovereign family to a support system for various governmental agencies.

Properly considered, the whole idea of equal *opportunity* is only a pretense. There is no way to equalize opportunity so long as the clever and energetic accumulate more wealth and power than the dull-witted and lazy, so long as the handsome and wealthy are able to pick beautiful mates, so long as . . . men are men and women are women. Equal opportunity is one of those democratic ideas whose only effect is to widen the gap between men. Almost a century ago, W.H. Mallock showed us conclusively that all the apparatus of democratic process—universal suffrage, trade unions, etc. —creates new classes of privilege. The only remedy for the inequalities inevitably produced by our pursuit of equal opportunity is the socialist solution—equality of condition. It does not matter that such equality is impossible, since in our efforts to secure it we shall concentrate still more power in the socialist state. That is the meaning of affirmative action, busing, and child care laws, whose ultimate cause is nothing more sinister than the equality of opportunity for which, we are told, so many of the world's poor have come to the United States.

The whole notion of rights—of liberty and equality—is, after all, a capitalist conception. If man is, by nature, endowed with certain assets—rights, if you will—special status that is based on blood, religion, or race is an unnatural infringement upon these rights which belong to all of us simply by being born human. It follows that man should be free to work at any trade (guilds and unions are unnatural), to make as much money as he can, and to take whatever place in society he has earned by the fruits of his labor. Inequity will only result from some men's superior ability at getting and keeping money. It is a truism that liberal democracy turns very quickly into plutocracy, a society based on wealth. George Fitzhugh, a Virginian, sounded the warning in the 1850s:

Free competition is but another name for liberty and equality . . . The war of the wits, of the mind, which free competition or liberty and equality beget and encourage is quite as oppressive, cruel, and exterminating as the war of the sword, of theft, robbery, and murder. [In such a society] virtue, if virtue there be, loses all her loveliness, because of her selfish aims. Selfishness is almost the only motive of human conduct with good and bad in free society, where every man is taught that he may change and better his condition . . . where men of strong minds, of strong wills, and of great self-control, come into free competition with the weak and improvident, the latter soon become the inmates of jails and penitentiaries. . . .

Fitzhugh was not alone in his warning; his *Sociology for the South* is simply the most mature expression of the Southern doctrine. Though the liberal principle of inalienable rights was enshrined in the Declaration of Independence, the product of a wayward Southerner's perfervid brain, even during the American Revolution, South Carolinians like William Henry Drayton, Henry Laurens, and John Rutledge were much more concerned to justify their rebellion on the grounds of their legal rights as Englishmen. The abstract talk about human rights made them manifestly uncomfortable. The Southern doctrine first assumed a partisan shape in the speeches of John Randolph of Roanoke, whose aristocratic manner ("I am an aristocrat. I love liberty; I hate equality") did not blind him to the evils of plutocracy ("England is Elysium for the rich; Tartarus for the poor"). His most brilliant jeremiads were reserved for "the fanatical and preposterous theories about the rights of man." It may be easy to dismiss some Southern opponents to natural rights as apologists for slavery, but Randolph, the grandfather of the movement, had little affection for the "peculiar institution."

Opposition to the rights of man reached its climax in the decades leading up to the Civil War. John C. Calhoun, whom we have quoted at the beginning of this essay, saw the traditional, agrarian South as the only effective counterpoise to the radicalism of socialism *and* the radicalism of capitalism. Governor James Hammond, another South Carolinian, rejected out of hand the whole idea of rights: "Individual rights, no, individual pretensions, passions, and desires, mistaken for rights—are just what governments are instituted to control and regulate." To the Yankee critics of the Southern system, Hammond pointed out that the North's economic system was an infinitely more ruthless form of slavery and exploitation than anything that existed in the South—a point on which the Marxist historian of slavery, Eugene Genovese *(Roll,*

Jordan, Roll) seems to agree. In his "Mudsill Speech," Hammond replied to the charge that the whole world had done away with slavery, "Aye, the *name,* but not the *thing."* He warned the North that their slaves could vote and vote socialist:

> If they knew the tremendous secret, that the ballot-box is stronger than 'an army with banners' and could combine, where would you be? Your society would be reconstructed, your government over-thrown, your property divided, not as they have mistakenly attempted to initiate such proceedings by meeting in parks with arms, but by the quiet process of the ballot-box.

Hammond's predictions were fulfilled by Franklin Roosevelt, John Kennedy, and Lyndon Johnson, whose administrations were made inevitable by the behavior of nineteenth century capitalists and industrialists, once they had freed themselves from the restraints imposed by the Southern leadership.

Our capitalist friends have made an idol of freedom and have invoked its aid to solve every social ill that man is heir to. But freedom is not a god; it is not even something precious like gold, an entity like the church, or a condition like goodness. It is just an abstraction—and a negative one at that. If we had any clear idea of freedom, we would not hear definitions like, "Freedom is the recognition of necessity", much less "Freedom's just another word for nothing left to lose". Why such a frenzy over the absence of restraint? If we are learned in logic, we will not put freedom among the predicates of substance, e.g. being, or quality, e.g. whiteness, but of relation, e.g. doubleness, since there can be no *absolute* freedom. A republican's freedom is an anarchist's slavery. Whenever we turn an abstraction, a word into a living force, we create an idol.

The ill effects of our idolatry are felt throughout our lives. We are forced to endure the pornography supplied to our children in movies, magazines and TV, the dissolution of families, the murder of unborn children—all in the name of freedom. Still worse, our worship of the idol of freedom has destroyed the real thing, by forcing us to surrender our civil and constitutional rights to the government that enslaves us all.

Like it or not, our rights—our property, our liberty, our life itself—are not safe in the hands of any mere men, much less men whose infatuation with "human rights"—with liberty and equality

—has made them deaf to the appeals of law and tradition. We have let them have their way—these economists and political scientists —for over one hundred years, tinkering, fiddling, and fine-tuning our Constitution until they have spoiled it. They have been prodigal—not with their own goods—but with ours, and it is time that we called them to account. It is conventional to say that socialists like President Carter and the Kennedys are essentially decent and compassionate men, whose only fault is their desire to do better by the human race than our species can endure. We poor creatures cannot live up to the lofty standard they have set for us. Such a concession from conservatives is misplaced generosity. The enemies of order and tradition are the witting or unwitting agents of social movements whose end result can only be the destruction of human society (not merely civilization) as we have known it upon earth.

Mr. Reagan's election and the emergence of the New Right give us an unprecedented opportunity to reexamine our commitments as a people. Free enterprise, the best of all economic systems, is not a way of life and it will not save us from the moral anarchy and governmental despotism that has overtaken us. Our social vision, fortunately, is not limited to a choice between economic theories of political life—capitalism and socialism—both reflexes of the same degraded, aluminum coin, both sound as the paper dollar. Traditional conservatism—not so much a theory as an attitude and a way of doing things—is still waiting to be tried. The hardest task for conservatives will be to convince our capitalist allies that the common rights of humanity, as embodied in the family, and our civil rights as Englishmen and Americans take precedence over our desire for profits and productivity. Southerners—with a little help from up North—have been arguing for years that the land, the home, and the church—not the marketplace— are the only proper foundations for a healthy society. The revival of social conservatism among the American working people gives us all the first hope since 1865 that we can turn back the clock and renew the conservative struggle in the North and South. This second "civil war," without the issue of race to divide us, promises to be more exciting than the first. And this time, we are fighting on the same side.

Robert Emmet Moffit

SOVIET-AMERICAN RELATIONS IN THE 1980s– Taking "Peaceful Coexistence" Seriously

Conservative foreign policy is still frozen in the mold of the late 1940s. We defend Europe and Japan as if they were still prostrate from World War II, and police nearly alone the resources upon which the entire industrial world depends. The old right concentrates almost exclusively on the expansion of American military power for the containment of Communist military power as the keystone of our foreign policy.

Our long-term international strategy must concentrate more on our own needs, and take account of more than military factors. It is from this point of view that Dr. Moffit, a founding director of the Washington-based Council for Interamerican Security and a former Senior Legislative Assistant for Foreign Affairs, recommends a more modern and better-targeted approach to dealing with the Soviet Union.

> *"The Internationalist Policy conducted by the socialist countries with respect to the national liberation movements is just in its aims and lawful in its methods. Whoever is defending a just cause has no need to violate the principles of peaceful coexistence."*
>
> *From* Problems of War and Peace, *Moscow: Progress Publishers*

T he American Republic has entered one of the most dangerous decades of its national life. In an era of revolutionary change, America's political leadership has been presented with unprecedented military, economic, and diplomatic challenges. To accept these challenges and to transform them into opportunities, will require of American leaders a political imagination of a very high order. A unique combination of boldness and prudence, rare in the history of any nation, is essential to the safety and prosperity of the Republic.

THE SEARCH FOR A POLICY

In spite of the vast and continuing changes that have taken place within the international system since the beginning of the Cold War—the growth in the number of new states, the expansion of sophisticated systems of mass communications, a rapid rate of

technological innovation, an accelerated growth in world population, and the rise of new regional and economic power blocs—the
central issue of American foreign policy remains the uneasy relationship between Washington and Moscow.

Reflecting upon the face of global change, it is often fashionable for students of international politics to call attention to the
emergence of a new international system, in which the principal
issues are those between the industrialized and the nonindustrialized nations of the world. New divisions between the North and the
South are said to be supplanting the ideological, political, military
and economic competition between East and West. The more fashionable tendency to address global issues from the North-South
perspective is rooted, of course, in a fundamental truth concerning
a real and growing relationship of dependence of the major bloc of
industrial consumers of raw materials—the United States, Western Europe and Japan—on the nonindustrial, developing producers of critical raw materials in the post-colonial era. While the
crucial importance of these relationships should not be ignored or
de-emphasized—indeed the burden of this essay suggests otherwise
—the fact remains that the preponderance of the world's military
and economic power is divided between the American Republic and
the Soviet Empire, and among the allies that cluster around one
or the other. The fact also remains that, on an international scale,
the express geopolitical interests of the American Republic and the
Soviet Empire are diametrically opposed; and the nature of that
opposition is not merely political or economic, but philosophical
and basically irreconcilable. Professor Hans Morgenthau has suggested that the inclination to reframe our conceptions of global
issues in terms of a "North-South" context is understandable not
only because it suggests the possibility of a "new beginning" or new
possibilities for cordial and cooperative relations with new, developing nation states, but also because such a focus allows an emotional and psychological retreat from the hard and less tractable
and unpleasant reality of the continuing and increasingly dangerous East-West conflict.[1] This reality has become increasingly unpleasant because of the dramatic growth in Soviet strategic military power since the 1962 Cuban Missile Crisis, complementing the
Soviet superiority in conventional military forces. Along with this
unprecedented growth of both strategic and conventional military
power, the Soviet Empire has also developed an impressive capabil-

ity to project that power both directly, through a large modern naval force, and indirectly through foreign proxy forces to the remote but critical natural resource bases of the less developed countries of the world.

The central and unavoidable issue of the 1980s will remain: How should the leaders of the American Republic deal with the rulers of the Soviet Empire? Like the Kremlin's leaders, the policy-makers in Washington must learn to adjust and readjust strategy and tactics to new and rapidly changing global conditions. The formulas of the past—the conventional anti-communism of "containment" formulated by George Kennan, the process of *"détente"* promoted by Henry Kissinger, and the "liberal internationalism" of the Carter Administration—can serve as no sure guide for the future.

Conventional anti-communism as embodied in the "Containment Policy" guided American foreign policy throughout the early years of the Cold War and overlapped the short reign of *"détente,"* a set of policies aggressively pursued by Secretary of State Henry Kissinger. First articulated by Dr. George Kennan in 1947,[2] the theoretical foundations of the Containment Policy were simple and compelling. A combination of intense Soviet ideological hostility and an ingrained Russian messianic tradition encouraged the Kremlin's leadership to look outward and pursue an expansionist foreign policy. The objectives of this expansionist foreign policy would normally be realized through the aggression of pro-Soviet or Soviet-backed forces in various areas of perceived opportunity. If these Communist forces were left unchecked, the non-Communist world would be besieged by Soviet-inspired revolutionary war, as well as the malignant growth of a dangerous and unacceptable Soviet military power. The failure of a containment of Communist forces would end in the global hegemony of the Soviet Empire. By stopping Soviet expansion through effective defensive measures, according to proponents of containment, the Kremlin's leadership would be forced to turn inward and address itself to ever more pressing domestic and economic concerns, eventually "mellow," and become a "status quo" rather than an "imperialistic" state within the international system. As an operational principle of American foreign policy, the "containment of Communism" served as the successful basis of the Truman Doctrine (the aid to anti-Communist forces in Greece and Turkey in 1947–48), undergirded

Dulles's threats of "massive retaliation" with nuclear weapons in response to potential Soviet aggression in Europe, and provided justification for direct U.S. military intervention in Korea, the Dominican Republic and Vietnam. For all practical purposes, the containment policy died with the psychological and military collapse of the American effort in Southeast Asia in 1975.

Containment served its immediate purposes throughout the early years of the Cold War, most importantly preserving a recuperating Western Europe from falling under Soviet domination or influence. But with the passage of time, the deficiencies of the "containment" policy became increasingly apparent. First, with the exception of the allied country on whose territory a military response to Communist aggression was required, the American Republic was forced to assume a disproportionate burden of the military responsibility, and hence the casualties, in defense of the non-Communist world. Second, in practice, the policy of containment left the initiative solely to the Kremlin and its allies, forcing the American Republic either to react to Communist thrusts, including the employment of American troops, at a time and place of the Communists' choosing, or to lose its credibility in its expressed commitment to thwart the Communist advance. As a result, the vaunted credibility of the "containment" policy became more important than the question as to whether or not any particular political, economic or military commitment best served the real interests of the Republic. Finally, and most importantly, the natural assumption of a defensive posture only served to reduce Western "victories" to mere "repulsions" of continuing, and apparently unending, Soviet-backed incursions into territories outside of the Soviet sphere of influence or control.[3]

In the wake of the final collapse of the containment policy in Southeast Asia and new Soviet-backed thrusts in Africa, particularly in Angola, American will to resist Soviet initiatives seemed paralyzed.

American foreign policy received a new, if short lived and confused, direction under the Carter Administration. In his first major address on foreign policy at Notre Dame University in 1977, President Carter set the tone of the nation's foreign policy when he decried the "inordinate fear of Communism," expressing an idea long dominant within the liberal intellectual community, a view particularly popular in the aftermath of the Vietnam tragedy. The

Carter Administration's essential pronouncements thus signalled the triumph of modern liberal internationalism, an American stance in world affairs markedly different from the Cold War internationalism of the 1950s and 1960s.

Rather than a systematic theory or coherent strategy of international politics, modern liberal internationalism represents a generally optimistic approach to international political problems. This approach is characterized by an emphasis on the unity of the human race, a stress on the need to address common human concerns on a rapidly shrinking planet, and an intense interest in the status of human rights, particularly in certain non-Communist states. The long-term security of American interests requires bold diplomatic overtures to Third World States and sympathy with their pressing economic concerns. Liberal internationalists are, more often than not, motivated by a belief in human progress and an abiding faith in a secular, rational approach to resolving the many outstanding and complex problems that burden the international system. Expanded communications are seen as a means of offering unprecedented opportunities for the growth of mutual understanding among peoples with differing social, economic and political systems.

Liberal internationalists often perceive the Soviet Union as an essentially status quo state: a large, militaristic, bureaucratic society that has long since losts its revolutionary *élan*. Russian wants and needs cannot be radically different from those that prevail in the West; and the most important of these is preventing war. It is in the vital interest of the Soviet leaders, as much as in the interest of the American people and humanity in general, to put an end to the senseless and costly and dangerous arms race and normalize relations with the American Republic and other nations of the West. American demonstrations of good will and restraint are essential to this process.

It is not surprising that liberal internationalists put strong emphasis on the efficacy of international organizations and conferences, and stress international cooperation on a great variety of social, economic, and cultural projects. Increased international communication and cooperation, the multiplication of person to person contacts, is undertaken with a view toward establishing the foundation for more far-reaching agreements on higher diplomatic levels, particularly in the critical areas of disarmament and the legal and peaceful resolution of international conflicts.

Viewing the international political system in evolutionary terms, some liberal internationalists have gone so far as to predict the convergence of ideologically opposed political and economic orders, including that of the American Republic and the Soviet Empire. Such a convergence will be facilitated through the growing economic interdependence of states, the process of continued industrialization and the development of a common, technologically advanced global civilization. Parochial ideological and nationalistic interests will be reduced to irrelevance by virtue of the imperious advance of new economic, technological forces, altering the social conditions and giving rise to new needs that the traditional political and economic structures of the nation-state cannot or will not satisfy.

The vices of liberal internationalism are rooted in its virtues. The central vice of liberal internationalism, particularly in the formulation of foreign policy, rests in its exaggerated expectations of a flowering of virtue. Conflicts of interest, say between the American Republic and the Soviet Empire, are held to be really rooted in ignorance and distrust, misunderstandings of the mutual interests, in residual parochial norms and outdated perspectives, or even irrational (or "inordinate") fears. None of these obstacles are insurmountable through bold or innovative diplomatic initiatives; perhaps another international conference, another round of negotiations, another arms control agreement, yet another unilateral demonstration of sincerity or good will. Underlying this approach is a residual Enlightenment Faith in the progressive evolution of political society from "traditional" to more "rational" structures of social and political order with a corresponding evolution of "parochial" notions into more "modern" patterns of political thought. The men of the Kremlin inhabit the same, small, shrinking planet. Given their need to "modernize" and "rationalize" their economic order and devote more of their resources to the betterment of their people, they must realize the essential absurdity of the wasteful and ultimately irrational stockpiling of unproductive weapons of mass terror and destruction. Given their "rationalist" perspective, then, liberal internationalists often tend to "mirror image" the Soviet leaders, and, in effect, suggest that "they" are "just like us" in the essential features of their international needs and interests.

The logical consequence of such a view, of course, is that official Soviet ideological commitments to a radically different view of the world, extolling conflict rather than harmony, is either ignored or downgraded. It is often suggested that the Soviet leadership is not really committed to its avowed revolutionary mission to destroy the capitalist system and to establish a global "socialist" order in accordance with the canons of Marxism-Leninism. Soviet doctrine on the meaning and destiny of the Communist revolution, war and the historical role of the Soviet State, is largely dismissed as either a mere rationalization of Soviet power, rhetorical bombast for domestic consumption, or cultic trappings left over from a bygone era of revolutionary enthusiasm.

This dismissal of the importance or even the relevance of ideology in assessing Soviet conduct or intentions is reinforced by two other intellectual tendencies pervasive within the Western liberal intellectual community: *pragmatism* and *relativism*.

Institutions, social structures, or even ideas are "rational," in the pragmatist view, if they are functionally efficient or "workable." It can be pursuasively argued that the Soviets are in a certain sense pragmatic, indeed ruthlessly pragmatic. But they are apparently not pragmatic outside of the ideological or political confines of their system. If the Soviets were pragmatic in the Western sense, one has difficulty explaining their official maintenance of the clearly inefficient "socialist" system of collective farming, for it is an organization of agricultural resources that regularly guarantees food shortages. On an international level, pragmatism would seem to dictate genuine accommodation and cooperation with the West.

Obviously, a revolutionary commitment to the total destruction of another's social, cultural and political order, given the development and deployment of weapons of mass destruction and the clear need to resolve outstanding global problems, is essentially irrational. To ascribe ideological sincerity to the Soviets is, therefore, to ascribe to them a pathological irrationality; to ascribe to them such an irrationality is to reject the bounteous political potential inherent in extended "rational" discussion with them on matters of "common interest," even at the very highest diplomatic levels. Obviously, the premises underlying the liberal vision of a potentially cooperative and harmonious global order, if not the tenets of the liberal faith itself, are called into question. Tending to the sacred fires of the old faith, amidst periodic torrential storms of Soviet misbehavior, is an exacting obligation, sometimes requiring superhuman intellectual ingenuity.

The pervasive influence of doctrinal relativism, or the notion that truth varies with time, circumstance, or condition, on modern foreign policy is worthy of extended investigation. Needless to say, American policymakers should be sensitive to the provincial character of their own modernity, especially in dealing with devout representatives of Islamic states, for example, who wholly reject Western-style relativism on religious grounds, and its social and political implications.

In an odd sort of way, relativism represents an intellectual commitment against commitment. In the final analysis, it is the belief that no idea, particularly a political or moral or religious idea, can really, in and of itself, be objectively true, so that, logically, one should not, in the final analysis, take it or any other idea seriously. Ideas are mere matters of subjective opinion, and one notion is as serviceable as another, depending upon the peculiar circumstances of the moment. Thus, the independent role of ideas in politics is denied, and ideas, ideologies, or belief systems are categorized as mere abstractions, or as rationalizations for actions or institutions, the froth on the beer, or as Marxists would say, the epiphenomenal "superstructure" of the underlying "substructure" of "class interests" and the relations of production.

Modern Western liberals, imbued with relativism, tend to judge their own domestic institutions in trendy terms, or in terms of their "functional efficiency," rather than view such institutions as the embodiment of ideas that are or could be objectively true. Reverence for tradition or ancient visages of institutions is quaint, but little more than a sentimental indulgence. The seemingly inevitable process of industrialization, modernization, technological innovation and bureaucratization will tend to "rationalize" decision making, even in the Soviet Union, and encourage modern, secular modes of thought incompatible with the parochial rigidities of outdated ideologies or belief systems. Progressive social and economic change will alter the grounds of "ideological" rationalization, and more and more, the Soviet elite will progress and eventually come to think, speak and act like pragmatic men of the modern secular society of the West.

The peculiarity of this point of view is that it imputes an

intellectual dishonesty to the Communist leadership that is rarely, if ever, imputed to ourselves. The elaborate Communist ideology is casually dismissed as an old, withered faith that cannot be taken seriously by the sophisticated elite that governs a modern, industrial superstate. But in the American experience, we are directly familiar with talented individuals who hold positions of authority, in both the public and the private sector, who espouse beliefs that are, at bottom, strange, superstitious, or just plain bizarre.

Consider the large number of Americans from all walks of life who indulge the daily claims of astrologers. Or consider even the "orthodox" belief systems prevalent within our own society, or Western societies in general. Western men adhere to religious values that, from the vantage point of hardened, materialistic, Soviet rulers, must appear thoroughly incredible or fantastic. How does a Communist evaluate the mystical claims of Christianity? On the level of political theory, very few of the greatest teachers of the political arts and sciences can be found who express unreserved sympathy with the idea that the common man should be entrusted with a "high degree of control" over his political leaders or the destiny of the state. And yet, across the length and breadth of Europe and America, a firm and sincere belief in the goodness, the wisdom and the practicality of a democratic form of government flourishes. Democrats take democracy seriously; Christians take Christianity seriously; liberals take liberalism seriously, more or less. Each one of these belief systems the rulers of the Kremlin formally consider merely absurd or the remnants of an antiquated, moribund social system.

The fact remains that the people of the pluralistic West do indeed take their own ideas seriously, even ideas that have cosmic significance concerning the nature of man and the universe. This is a fact verified by direct experience. It is only a rare occasion when a democrat utters an opinion about the need to democratize this or that social or political institution that a political opponent will rise and question the sincerity of his commitment to democracy; indeed the extremity of a democrat's commitment to democracy is enough to set the few remaining aristocrats in desperate motion to curb assaults on the few remaining outposts of privilege.

The great challenge to liberal internationalists, particularly in the formulation of foreign policy, is to take the Communists seriously. To keep one's mind open to all intellectual possibilities, as the mark of the true liberal, should mean being open to the terrible possibility that the men in the Kremlin, and their Communist allies, do indeed mean exactly what they say.

Diverse elements of conventional anti-communism, or "containment," and liberal internationalism are woven into the mosaic of *détente*. As policy, *détente* was initially developed by former Secretary of State Henry Kissinger. The centerpiece of *détente* was the so-called SALT process.

In ordinary Western usage, *détente* had a distinctly pleasant connotation. It was a "relaxation of tensions" between previously antagonistic states. As envisaged by Kissinger, *détente* was also a comprehensive *process* enabling Soviet and American policymakers to build a new "structure of peace" by concluding a series of scientific, cultural, economic, and technical disarmament agreements between the American Republic and the Soviet Empire.

It was widely believed by proponents of *détente* that a multiplicity of such agreements would not only prove economically and militarily beneficial to the signatories, but would also give the Soviet leadership a "vested interest" in the maintenance and continued progress of conventional commercial, economic, and diplomatic processes. By being carefully co-opted, so to speak, into an attractive set of commercial, economic and military agreements and conventions, Soviet revolutionary zeal would inevitably erode; for the deliberate destabilization of the new and prosperous global order arising out of the *détente* relationship would be perceived by the Soviets as too costly in both material and psychological terms. The Kremlin, then, would be less likely to pursue aggressive policies that would derail the progress of even warmer East-West relations.

Détente withered like a delicate flower in the Russian winter. While Washington policymakers looked hopefully toward a new and lasting era of relaxed tensions, precedent to even broader international cooperation, the Soviet elite saw *détente* as a reflection of relative American military weakness vis-à-vis the Soviet Empire and a time to consolidate and expand the international gains made by the "Socialist camp," as well as to assist the ubiquitous, anticapitalist forces of "national liberation" on a global scale. Soviet leaders viewed Washington's enunciation of *détente* not merely as a desire to avoid general conflict or build a "new structure of peace," but rather as a historically significant renunciation of the Cold War policy of dealing with the Soviet Empire from a "position of military strength." Given the new "correlation of forces" in the 1970s and '80s, the military, economic, diplomatic and psychological tides of modern history—the capitalist "ruling circles" of the West could no longer exercise decisive military options against the militarily powerful Soviet Empire. According to the "objective conditions" of modern history, in the official Soviet view, the American Republic had no historical choice but to accept "peaceful coexistence," the Soviet term for what in the West is called *détente*. On the precise meaning of "peaceful coexistence," the Soviet leadership has never deviated since its definitive postwar enunciation at the 20th Soviet Party Congress on 1956: It is the continuation of the international class struggle, in all of its ideological, economic, and political dimensions, by any and all means, short of general nuclear war. Of course, the renunciation of general war with the imperialistic West as a matter of policy did not (and does not) entail the renunciation of support for "just wars" of "national liberation" on the part of "struggling peace loving peoples" against the imperialistic aggressors.

In accordance with formal Soviet doctrinal declarations, Soviet international behavior during the era of *détente* was hardly an improvement over Soviet international behavior during the Cold War. One major difference was that during the height of the Cold War era in the 1950s, Soviet policy was constrained by Soviet military weakness and by the threat of massive nuclear retaliation by the United States and so focused instead on the consolidation of post-war gains in the Eastern Bloc Empire.

During the era of *détente*—the "End of the Cold War"—Soviet foreign policy took on a decidedly more aggressive character: full-scale support of the North Vietnamese takeover of South Vietnam and Laos and continued support for the North Vietnamese invasion and occupation of Cambodia: the encouragement of the Arab oil embargo of 1973 and the continuous attempts to sabotage the delicate peace negotiations in the Middle East; the encouragement and material support of heavy Cuban military intervention in Africa with the assistance of East German and Bulgarian advisors; the maintenance of a full combat brigade in Cuba and the introduction of nuclear-capable MIG 23 aircraft in Cuba: an open and contemptuous dismissal of the human rights provisions of the 1976

Helsinki Accords and a continued and relentless persecution of
Christian and Jewish minorities in the USSR and the Eastern bloc;
the penetration and subversion of Iran and the broadcast of viru-
lent anti-American propaganda into Iran during the "hostage crisis"; the acceleration of a massive strategic and conventional military build-up; and the seizure of each and every opportunity to
capitalize upon American and Western misfortunes or to destabil-
ize states outside of the Soviet-Cuban Axis. The invasion and brutal
occupation of neutral Afghanistan was, of course, the death of
détente. With the end of the Era of *Détente,* a sophisticated Soviet
military machine occupied a mountainous South Asian country
just 350 miles from the strategically crucial Straits of Hormuz, the
oil "spigot" of the Western World.

One of the ripening fruits of *détente* was a rapid increase in
East-West trade, including the transfer of sophisticated, even militarily sensitive modern technology to the Soviet Empire. There was
a certain surrealistic quality to business negotiations between
Western representatives of "free enterprise" and the hardened
representatives of a Communist elite that has vowed to destroy
them. There may have been practical men of business in the West,
gifted with a deeper sense of history and acutely aware of the
ideological cleavage between East and West, who concluded agreements with the Soviets but chose to put the eventual consequences
of their transactions temporarily out of mind. To borrow an analogy from moral theology, they behaved as fallen Christians, su-
premely conscious that the wages of sin is death, but ready to
surrender to immediate temptations with the view that the ultimate pains of hell were still a long way off.

The creation of a "new structure of peace," the abstract object
of Kissinger's *détente* policy, presupposed a Soviet adaptation to
the conventional politics of the nation state system and a sincere
appreciation of the need and desirability of a community of international interests. In effect, the success of *détente* depended upon
nothing less than a radical revision or renunciation of Soviet perceptions and policies. That success presumed something akin to a
Soviet acceptance of the norms of the European state system. But
the European state system, particularly in the nineteenth century,
was graced with a consensus on moral, cultural and political
norms, and (with the notable exception of Hitler's Germany) a well
understood and commonly accepted sense of restraint on the exer-

cise of the power of the nation state. Perhaps, from the perspective of the post-*détente* era, the very least that can be said is that proponents of *détente* may have erred in their premature importation of civilized expectations, reminiscent of nineteenth century continental diplomacy, into a twentieth century reality of ideological divisions and totalitarian ambitions.

THE SOVIET IMPERIUM

Because the Soviet rulers wish to overthrow the international status quo, and seek a new distribution of world political, economic and military power, they are, in the terms of Professor Hans Morgenthau, the strategists of an imperial power.[4] They are imperialists whose geopolitical ambitions clearly exceed the dreams of Peter the Great and their objectives transcend the traditional continental interests of the Russian Czars. To be sure, the occupation of Eastern Europe, the maintenance of pressures on Finland and Iran, the Dardanelles and the Balkans[5] can easily be ascribed to traditional, and largely defensive, Russian national interests. But the diplomatic, economic and military penetration into Africa, Southeast Asia and Latin America, the employment of an elaborate global propaganda and espionage apparatus, the annual investment of millions of rubles into an economic disaster such as Cuba in return for Cuban military participation in revolutionary wars on other continents suggests a broader world view. Czarist ambitions did not include the maintenance of warm water ports in, say, the Caribbean or East Africa.

The broader world view is rooted in a sense of ideological mission that sharply and uniquely characterizes Soviet geopolitical thought and action.

History is the God of the Kremlin. The future of humanity is closed; the outcome of the world-historical process is inevitable. Those who understand that process can lay claim to the future. Those who cannot or will not grasp the truth of that historical process—the inevitable destruction of "capitalism" and the ultimate victory of "communism"—are condemned to either deliberate destruction or the nether world of historical insignificance. In the final analysis, there are only two rivals in the world historical struggle, the decadent "bourgeois" and the revolutionary "proletariat," the children of light and the children of darkness, "peace loving peoples" and "imperialistic wrongdoers," the progressive camp of the "socialist states" and the regressive camp of the "imperialist states." This polarized world view is the ideological and cultural framework within which Soviet policy is formulated and applied.

In the Marxist-Leninist analysis, world history is propelled by increasingly intense class conflicts, rooted in its advanced states, in the "monopoly capitalist" control of the means of production and distribution on an international scale. The global expansion of the economic order "monopoly capitalism" is ultimately responsible for all social injustices, political upheavals and international conflicts. According to V.I. Lenin, the father of Soviet Communism, the Western capitalist system has been transformed into a global system of class exploitation, grounded in the search for new markets, cheap labor and raw materials in the nonindustrialized nations of the world. This global expansion of Western capitalism is not a matter of individual or collective national will, but is an inevitable, impersonal historical process. The internationalization of the capitalist system and its attendant evils serves to internationalize the class struggle, and thus the seeds of the destruction of the capitalist order are sown in the process of its own growth. The class struggles between bourgeoisie and the proletariat, those who *own* as opposed to those who *work* the means of production, are thus no longer self-contained social phenomena within the industrialized economies of the Western capitalist economies; but, as a result of the transformation of the capitalist system from a merely regional into a global economic order, penetrating deep into remote areas of the globe, these struggles against capitalism become struggles against economic imperialism, or "national liberation struggles" against foreign capitalistic influences. Because capitalism had become an international phenomenon, Lenin declared, the struggle against capitalism, or "capitalist exploitation" must likewise become an international phenomenon. In this respect, there is not now, and never was, an "international Communist conspiracy"; for there was never anything secretive or conspiratorial about the international character of the class warfare that the Soviet leadership praised or promoted. International class warfare was an objective law of history, in the official Soviet view, and it will only end with the elimination of classes or the victory of a classless society.

Soviet ideology not only sets forth an elaborate theory of conflict, but an internally logical theory of peace. The elimination of wars, social injustice, and international conflicts will only come with the elimination of capitalism itself. The struggle for "peace" then, is integral to the continuation of the international class struggle. The advance of "scientific socialism" on the national and international level is thus the precondition for the progress of justice and international tranquility. The well-publicized peaceful declarations of Soviet leaders are not, if properly understood, merely transparent attempts at deception, or doubletalk, but rather a true reflection of a coherent, dynamic and apparently sincere world view. It is a world view that has been instilled in Soviet leaders since creation of the Soviet State in 1917.

Though the course of world history is seen as moving inexorably onward and upward toward the climactic victory of "socialism," Soviet rulers are not locked into anything like a political or diplomatic rigidity. Those who ascribe rigidity to the Marxist-Leninist outlook misunderstand the essentially dynamic quality of the Communist perspective. Because the *objective* factors of history are undergoing constant change, Soviet foreign policy must, if it is true to the Marxist-Leninist doctrine, be infinitely flexible. What applies in one historical condition does not apply in another historical condition; the transformation of the economic and class conditions that account for social and political reality necessitates constant analysis and tactical readjustments in order to seize historical opportunities. But the destruction of the "class enemy," the capitalist order, remains the *constant* object of a dynamic policy. Clausewitz's doctrine that war is a continuation of politics by violent means is accepted as the correct interpretation of international conflict, but it is also true that politics is a continuation of war by non-violent means. In terms of a clear understanding of final ends, as well as the application of historically relevant revolutionary means, Marxism-Leninism serves as the invariable theoretical framework, the "philosophical" point of reference, animating Soviet policymakers.

Of course, in the final analysis, it is impossible to know for certain to what degree individual members of the Soviet hierarchy are motivated by a sense of ideological mission, the more mundane yearnings for political power, or the greater glory of a Russian dominated miltaristic state. Even among high level Soviet defectors, who have held exalted positions within the Soviet political and scientific community, there is disagreement over the basic motivations of the tiny class of men who rule the Kremlin and shape the foreign policy of the Soviet Empire. It is impossible to know with absolute certainty, at any given moment, whether a particular initiative in foreign policy is directly rooted in the tenets of Marxism-Leninism or the exigencies of power politics. The attempt to make a definitive determination in any particular case is a fruitless enterprise. Aside from particular individuals or particular national policies, however, one can say with a great deal of assurance that the doctrines of Marxism-Leninism contain the justification for the powers and prerogatives of the Soviet state; they provide the peculiar ideological framework within which general Soviet geopolitical analyses of the external world are made, and through which most, if not all, specific policies are defined.

Given the polarized *Weltanschauung* of the Sovet elite, the Soviet state plays two special and historically decisive roles. First, the Soviet state exists to protect the "evolving domestic socialist system," and the "socialist systems" of its allies in the "socialist camp," from inveterately hostile capitalist and imperialist forces. Second, the Soviet State exists to champion the cause of world historical revolution, and to assist the inevitable growth of anti-capitalist forces of "national liberation" on a global scale. The role of the State is at once defensive and offensive; the international reality of an inherently hostile and irreformable capitalism permits no other alternative. Viewed from this grim perspective, the conflict with the American Republic, the bastion of western imperialism, is an objectively necessary struggle.[6] It is, in the final analysis, a mortal struggle. As expressed in recent Soviet statements and declarations, it is only the progressively changing "correlation of forces," most importantly the growing military might of the USSR, that deters the irretrievably malevolent "imperialist" forces of the West from unleashing a new world war.[7]

The congruence between Soviet imperial behavior and Marxist-Leninist theory can be found not only in the growth and specific deployment of Soviet strategic military forces, but also in the boldness of new Soviet foreign and military policy initiatives, particularly as they apply to the so-called Third World.

After the humiliating Cuban Missile Crisis of 1962, the Kremlin's leadership embarked upon the most ambitious military program of modern peacetime history, paralleling similar and sustained efforts undertaken by Hitler's Germany.[8] In virtually every sphere of modern weaponry, the Soviet Empire has made impressive gains. Complementing the conventional superiority of Soviet forces, particularly in Eastern Europe, the Soviet high command has exerted a tremendous effort in increasing and modernizing its nuclear strategic forces. Clearly, the greatest concentration of Soviet effort has been manifest in the increase and the upgrading of Soviet strategic missile forces. The once enormous American lead in sophisticated military technologies, particularly in the modern missile systems, has largely disappeared. The latest generation of "heavy" Soviet missiles, particularly the fearsome SS-18s, combine massive destructive power with far greater degrees of accuracy. With the addition of on-board computerization, the ability to add multiple warheads to each ICBM, and sharp improvements in accuracy, the once-inferior, relatively inaccurate and slow-to-launch Soviet ICBM force has become the greatest single strategic threat to the smaller force of American land-based Minuteman and Titan missiles.[9] The large and formidable Soviet ICBM force now accounts for approximately 70 percent of all Soviet strategic nuclear forces.

The sustained increase and progressive sophistication of the Soviet ICBM force has been complemented by quantitative and qualitative improvements in Soviet air and sea power. Traditionally, heavy bombers have not played a significant role in overall Soviet strategic forces, and still account for no more than 5 percent of all Soviet nuclear forces. But in a historically significant attempt to counter American air superiority, the rulers of the Soviet Empire are developing and deploying a new generation of advanced, supersonic, long-range bombers. The most formidable new addition to the Soviet air fleet is the Backfire bomber, a fast and powerful supersonic aircraft with an estimated range of 5000 nautical miles. With each aircraft capable of flying at more than twice the speed of sound, the fleet of over 130 Backfire bombers presents American defense planners with a new level of difficulties, a set of strategic problems aggravated by the relative inferiority of American air defense. The increasing deployment of the Backfire gives the Soviet Empire not only new capabilities to project airpower over the vital sealanes, compounding the maritime threat already posed by an enormous fleet of Soviet submarines, but also enables the Soviet high command to increase and diversify Soviet strategic striking power against military and civilian targets within the continental United States. For all official Soviet declarations of the Backfire being an intermediate range or theater bomber, Soviet defense planners have, in point of fact, developed the Backfire as a weapon against the United States.[10]

The accelerated deployment of nuclear missiles and submarines has been completed with an unprecedented growth in Soviet naval power, enabling the once exclusively land-based Eurasian military power to project its military presence abroad through what is now the second most powerful naval force in the world. Through the sustained efforts and the brilliant leadership of the Kremlin's premier naval strategist, Admiral Sergei Gorshkov, the Soviet Navy has grown from little more than a strategically inconsequential coastal defense force into a large and sophisticated "blue water" force. Soviet naval power presents new and unprecedented threats to the vital sea lanes of the Indian Ocean and the South Atlantic, the great trade routes for the enormous quantities of imported oil and raw materials that fuel the industrial economies of the American Republic, Western Europe and Japan. Of particular importance in this respect is the large and formidable Soviet nuclear submarine force, a force that is constantly being increased and modernized to cope with maritime and intercontinental strategic missions.[11]

This amassing of conventional, naval and overall strategic military power does not necessarily imply a Soviet determination to initiate a general war with the American Republic and its Western European Allies. For all of the emphasis on international class conflict, the inevitability of violent and revolutionary change in the world historical transformation from "capitalism" to "socialism," the Soviet leadership entertains no casual or cavalier attitude toward war in general or nuclear war in particular. The use of military force is legitimate only to the extent to which its application accords with a "scientific analysis" of the historical conditions, that is, the "objective factors" of the international system. Moreover, even among a leadership hardened to an unsentimental application of force and violence—the most outstanding achievement of the Soviet system—memories of the horror and great suffering that accompanied the Great Patriotic War against Nazi Germany, the loss of more than 20 million men, women and children, are still fresh. A close reading of Soviet official literature on the subject clearly reveals a revulsion at the prospect of a thermonuclear exchange with the American Republic, the awesome destruction and the tremendous loss of human life. Granting this, the official understanding of both the nature and the consequences of war, even a general nuclear war, remains markedly different from the view that prevails among the political leadership of the West.

In the official Soviet view, war is not simply armed conflict between two opposing nation states, the devastating interaction of modern military technology on an unprecedented scale; but in accordance with the canons of Marxist-Leninist teaching, a general East-West war would be a continuation of the class struggle in the form of a violent clash of opposed social systems. Following the maxims of Karl von Clausewitz, the theoretician of war *par excellence,* the Soviets hold that all war is a continuation of politics, the politics of the class struggle; just as politics itself is understood as a form of domestic and international social war, the continuing and inevitable war of class struggle. No war is, or can be, devoid of its political or class conflict; no explanation of war is valid that ignores its political or class content.[12] While the massive strategic arsenal of missiles, bombers and submarines directly serves the function of deterrence, the deterring of an increasingly desperate ruling class of the capitalist imperialist West from unleashing a thermonuclear attack against the "socialist Motherland" is not the only purpose of Soviet strategic or conventional military forces. The primary function of Soviet strategic forces is to be able to fight, survive and win a war against the West, even a nuclear war.[13] Victory over the international class enemy is seen not only as the possible or likely result of a new international armed conflict, but the inevitable consequence of a titanic armed clash of opposed social systems.[14]

Once again, one can discern a unity between Soviet theory and practice. Soviet strategic force configurations are apparently congruent with the doctrinal "war fighting" requirements, particularly the heavy concentration of fast and increasingly powerful ICBMs, enabling quick and devastating counterforce strikes into the enemy's heartland. Soviet military doctrine stresses the superiority of the offensive; the outcome of a future war will be determined by the success of offensive actions within what the Soviets call the "initial phase" of general combat. The destruction of the opponent's military and industrial capabilities and the devastation of his communications and transportation systems will paralyze his will to resist and hasten a victorious conclusion to general hostilities. However, being able to fight an offensive action is not enough; one must be able to survive the enemy's retaliatory assaults. In accordance with Soviet military requirements, the Soviet Empire has deployed a massive and increasingly sophisticated air defense system to protect military and civilian targets from strategic penetration. And, in violation of the Western prescription that nuclear war is an unthinkable option, the Soviets also possess a vigorous, costly and expanding civil defense program designed to shield their political leadership and their industrial population, as far as is possible, from the devastating impact of thermonuclear strikes.[15] Even though such preparations must appear absurd to a certain school of Western defense analysts, the fact remains that the Soviets are indeed pursuing such a program and such a program is congruent with their own doctrinal declarations concerning the survivability and winnability of a nuclear war.

While the Soviet strategic build-up may not indeed be a deliberate preparation for the final onslaught against the capitalist West, the possession of such a vast arsenal of military power would serve to enhance Soviet diplomatic and psychological pressures in localized confrontations with the American Republic or its Western allies in a crisis situation. In a crisis situation located in geographical proximity to the Soviet Empire itself, the newly acquired nuclear power may serve as the strategic umbrella for the possible or limited employment of Soviet conventional forces to secure a limited, though strategically important, Soviet objective. In effect this has already happened with the invasion and occupation of Afghanistan. Future possibilities for similar limited actions might include tempting targets such as Pakistan or West Berlin.

Soviet conventional superiority, the achievement of strategic parity with the American Republic, a weak and vacillating American leadership, the American preoccupation with a series of unsettling events in Iran, were surely factors contributing to the 1979 Soviet decision to invade and occupy Afghanistan with 80,000 troops.

The significance of the Soviet invasion of Afghanistan cannot be underestimated. Among a certain class of progressive literati within the comfortable setting of a Georgetown salon, it may be fashionable to view the Soviet invasion of Afghanistan as basically a "defensive" move, a reflection of Soviet domestic frustrations, another abysmal loss in the great arena of "world public opinion." Needless to say, such sophisticated evaluations are quite lost on the embattled Afghans. Of course, Soviet domestic frustrations, particularly with the economy, are real enough; but it is difficult to see how such frustrations can be effectively relieved through a relatively expensive military adventure into a neutral Southern Asian state that is mountainous, rebellious and difficult to govern. And "world public opinion," whatever it is or however it is to be gauged, has proven to be a very mild restraint on the immoderate appetites of the Kremlin. A more suitable explanation may be found in the political and strategic exhaustion of previous policies toward the Soviet Empire and the military and ideological dynamics of Soviet expansionism.

The Soviet invasion of Afghanistan sealed the fate of the short-lived and long-dying policy of *détente*. The invasion was also a memorial to the utter collapse of the older containment policy, for the Soviet takeover of Afghanistan constituted the first Soviet military occupation of a territory outside of the Eastern Bloc since 1946. The relentless drive to consolidate Soviet power in Afghanistan through the employment of an utterly ruthless "scorched earth" policy, the terror bombing of villages and the killing of civilians on a mass scale, cannot be understood apart from broader Soviet geopolitical objectives.

In his classic work, *Imperialism: The Last and Highest State of Capitalism*, a work that still remains the theoretical foundation of Soviet foreign policy, Lenin taught that the less developed nations of the world were pregnant with revolutionary possibilities and would eventually prove to be the soft underbelly of advanced industrial capitalism. And while the theoretical details of Lenin's doctrine are never neatly congruent with the modern circumstances, there remains a strong Soviet focus on exploiting Third World fears, anxieties, and ethnic and cultural divisions. The most significant Soviet effort, of course, is the alignment of Soviet power, overtly or covertly, with like-minded Marxist-Leninist revolutionary elites in the Third World who pursue the strategy of "national liberation," that is, employing the powerful rhetoric of a virile nationalism in order to establish a centralized and ultimately repressive Marxist-Leninist state. Of course, the achievement of "national liberation" is little more than crude and unsophisticated bourgeois "idealism" if it is not connected with broader historical forces, most importantly economic forces, the "objective factors" that finally determine the course of national and international politics.

The "objective factors" of contemporary international politics consist in the increased economic dependence of the American Republic and its Western allies and Japan on the minerals and oil resources of the less developed, nonindustrialized nations of the Third World in the post-colonial era and an overall change in the balance of East-West military power unfavorable to the West.

Given these objective factors, it appears that the Soviet invasion of Afghanistan is elemental to a comprehensive, indirect, geopolitical assault against the Western world: the control of the access to critical raw materials, oil and minerals, in strategically vulnerable regions of the Third World. Afghanistan is not being invaded because the Soviets have a peculiar lust for domination over unruly, fiercely independent Afghan tribesmen. Afghanistan is being occupied because of the strategic location of its territory, a territory that can serve as a base of subversive operations and from which Soviet fighter bombers could, if it were deemed necessary, strike targets in the oil-rich Persian Gulf. The particularly brutal subjugation of Afghanistan is only the most recent phase in a campaign to expand Soviet influence.

An ever larger vise of political and military pressure around the Gulf states has been tightened. Indeed, the collision of Western economic and political interests and the Soviet geopolitical ambitions is nowhere more dangerous than in the strategically critical, oil-rich Persian Gulf.

Ever since the 1968 British withdrawal west of Suez, a steady Soviet diplomatic and political attempt to penetrate into the Middle East, South Central Asia and the Indian Ocean has been a regular feature of Kremlin policy. Soviet influence grew in Iraq, Syria and Yemen. With the outbreak of the Iran-Iraq War, the Soviets supplied arms and material to both sides of the conflict, a policy which served to reduce the flow of vital Persian Gulf oil to the industrial nations of Western Europe and Japan and to promote further divisions within the regionally powerful but politically fragmented Islamic camp. With the assistance of thousands of Cuban ground forces, along with Soviet, Bulgarian and East German advisors, Ethiopia defeated pro-Western Eritrean secessionist forces and Soviet influence in Ethiopia has been consolidated. The Soviet-backed Ethiopian regime threatens Somalia, the current residence of a pitiful multitude of starving refugees, and increases pressure on the strategically critical Horn of Africa.

In view of its geopolitical importance, Soviet denial or control of the flow of oil from the politically unstable Middle East–Persian Gulf region and the denial or control of Western access to the vast mineral resources of Subsaharan Africa would surely undermine Western economies and divide the Western Alliance. The tightening Soviet grip on Afghanistan and the intensified Soviet-Cuban effort to establish and maintain pro-Soviet regimes in Africa, particularly in Angola and Mozambique, astride the great Indian Ocean and South Atlantic sea lanes, is fully in accord with a long-term policy of striking at the soft underbelly of the Western industrialized world. Whether or not this Soviet policy of penetration and consolidation of influence will be successful depends upon a number of factors, including the effectiveness of the Black nationalist resistance to Soviet-Cuban incursions into Africa, the quality of Western military and economic assistance to friendly Middle Eastern and African states, the diplomatic role of Western allied states as stabilizing elements in Africa and the Persian Gulf, and the extent to which the utterly foreign Northern Russians can continue to promote their identification with the sentiments, aspirations and national interests of Black Africa and certain Islamic states.

If Soviet policy in Africa should fail it will not fail for a lack of concentrated effort. State Department assessments indicate that total Communist technical and military personnel in Subsaharan Africa amounted to almost 80,000 by 1978. Below the embattled Horn of Africa, thousands of Cuban proxy forces have been employed in waging "revolutionary wars" in defense of Communist rule in Angola and Cabinda. Cuban military advisors have assisted left wing or pro-Soviet regimes in Mozambique, Benin, Guinea Bissau, Zambia and Equatorial Guinea. Cuban and Eastern Bloc forces have also supported guerrilla bands such as the Polisario Front against Morocco, SWAPO in Namibia, and the unsuccessful guerrilla thrust into Shaba Province in Zaire. Thus far, the greatest continental achievement of the Soviet-Cuban Axis has been the establishment of the Marxist-Leninist Angolan regime astride the South Atlantic and the presence of an avowedly pro-Soviet regime

in Mozambique on the coast of East Africa. Soviet political fortunes
in Subsaharan Africa have also been enhanced by the election of
a self-styled Marxist-Leninist, Robert Mugabe, in Zimbabwe. A
combination of diplomatic failures, Western vacillation, or a failure of nerve on the part of Western political leadership could set
the stage for a "final showdown" in Southern Africa, probably
culminating in an accelerated guerrilla war against the Republic
of South Africa.

Given the nature and intensity of the Soviet-Cuban offensive
in the Third World, the American Republic must of necessity
strengthen its relations with those Third World states that are
favorably disposed towards the West. Beyond that essential level
of cooperation and friendship, American diplomacy must attempt
to forge new cooperative relations and institutions among members of the Western Alliance and Japan in order to address the
profound challenges that confront Allied interests in the Persian
Gulf and Subsaharan Africa. The interests of the Allied states
transcend the regional affiliations formalized in NATO and the
European Economic Community, and the recognition of the danger
to these interests in the Gulf and Subsaharan Africa should entail
a recognition of new diplomatic and military obligations.

The Middle-Eastern/Persian Gulf region and Subsaharan
Africa are thus the two main pressure points in the global struggle
for oil and raw materials.[16] The conservative Islamic states of
Saudi Arabia, Kuwait, Qatar, Oman and the United Arab Emirates
justly fear the grave political, economic and military consequences
of the intense antagonism of the radical Arab states and the gradual Soviet encirclement of their rich oil field through the conquest
or political domination of neighboring territories. Soviet control of
Afghanistan, a successful Soviet penetration into Iran, combined
with Soviet alliance with South Yemen highlight the anxieties of
the conservative Islamic states.

The encircling pressures on Saudi Arabia and the conservative
Persian Gulf States are mirrored by increased external as well as
internal pressures on the strategically valuable Republic of South
Africa, the dominant military, technological and economic power
of Subsaharan Africa and itself a virtual "treasure trove" of mineral resources, particularly rich deposits of gold, diamonds, copper
and iron ore. Just as the narrow Persian Gulf serves as the most
concentrated oil distribution center of the world, the oil "spigot,"

the Cape of Good Hope in South Africa serves as the focal point of the heavy East-West maritime traffic, the world's commerical "throat," connecting the South Atlantic–Indian Ocean sea lanes. Approximately 90 percent of European oil imports and 70 percent of all other strategically critical raw materials for the NATO alliance are shipped around the Cape.

In the event of East-West hostilities, the long and exposed lines of Western economic dependence would enable the Soviets or their allies to apply direct military pressure, simultaneously or alternately, at the Persian Gulf "wellhead," at various Eastern or Western African points along the South Atlantic and Indian Ocean sea lanes, or given the tremendous concentration of tonnage routinely rounding South Africa, at the vulnerable Cape of Good Hope. A prolonged disruption of oil or mineral lifelines would surely result in severe Western economic crisis with attendant social and political upheavals. In Western European capitals, the domestic dislocations resulting from such a disruption would likely induce some form of "neutralism," pacifism, or a desire to accommodate new Soviet initiatives.

A NEW ANTI-IMPERIALIST POLICY

In fashioning foreign policy toward the Soviet Union, it is not enough to assume that the Soviet State is an imperial power in Professor Morgenthau's sense of seeking a favorable global redistribution of political, economic and military power. In assessing the goals and intentions of the Soviet Empire, it is sometimes suggested that the Soviet foreign policies are motivated more by a traditional state's desire for power and influence than a new ideological mission. The central problem is that the Soviet state is not a traditional state; it is officially designated as an engine of international revolution and historical transformation on a global scale. And it acts accordingly.

The relationship between power and ideology is not mutually exclusive, but dialectical: The power of the Soviet state is justified in terms of its ideological mission and the ideological mission of the Soviet state is realized in and through the power of the state. Given the basic ideological supposition of Soviet foreign policy, the existence of an inevitable and comprehensive conflict between competing and fundamentally irreconcilable social systems, the peculiar imperialist ambitions of the Kremlin are sanctified by inexorable forces of history, the final judge of all dominions and powers. In that respect, Soviet-imperialist ambitions are limited only by the final destruction of the capitalist system on an international scale and the creation of a new world order of fraternal "socialist" states.

As Professor Morgenthau, among others, has properly warned, an "imperialist" policy cannot be successfully countered by a status quo policy, or treating the imperialist power as if it were merely another actor within the international system whose commitments or objectives were realizable within the confines of extant power relationships. One cannot treat an imperialist state as if it were not an imperialist state without courting disaster, that is, allowing the so-called "correlation of forces," to use a Soviet term, to shift decisively from the nonimperialist to the imperialist state. To permit such a shift is to reduce one's political options to an impotent accommodation of war, and very possibly a war devoid of the likelihood of victory or even survival.

The nature of the challenge determines the nature of the response. The American Republic must confront the Soviet Empire as it is, not as its political leaders hope or wish it to be. The growth of Soviet military power virtually eliminates the initiation of a direct challenge to the Soviet Empire on military terms. Even if a decisive advantage were somehow secured, there are ample moral and political restraints, deeply and firmly rooted in Western thought, that would preclude the initiation of a general conflict with nuclear weapons. At the same time, there is and can be no successful strategic retreat from the grim reality of Soviet expansion, nor comfortable isolation from the consequences of its relentless continuation in virtually every area of opportunity on the globe. There is and can be, under the circumstances, no return to an isolationist past, a reactive containment, or some new version of *détente*.

In the face of the geopolitical realities, the American Republic must adopt a "counterimperialist" policy. The immediate goal of such policy should be nothing less than the neutralization of Soviet power and influence beyond its traditional sphere of influence in Eastern Europe. The secondary goal of such a policy should be the weakening of Soviet power and influence behind Soviet-controlled borders, striving for the self-determination of nation states currently under the direct domination of the Soviet Empire. The final and most important goal should be the compelling of the Soviet elite to abandon global imperial ambitions.

It will be objected that such a policy is nothing more than a return to the Cold War. Of course, such an objection begs the question as to when the Cold War, in point of fact, ever ceased. In any event, such a policy would not constitute a return to the Cold War in a fashion in which Americans are used to waging a Cold War. A new counterimperialist policy must prudently employ a combination of economic, political, military and psychological measures with a view toward waging the same kind of "protracted conflict" that the Soviet Empire has adopted as its official policy toward the American Republic and the West. The American Republic, in short, must adopt its own policy of "peaceful coexistence."

In the Soviet understanding of the term, it will be recalled, "peaceful coexistence" is nothing less than a continuation of the "class struggle" on an international scale short of general war between the chief antagonists. In the West, in certain liberal circles, Soviet official declarations of a commitment to "peaceful coexistence" were greeted with enthusiasm, were seen as an indication that the Soviets were finally "mellowing," and provided an invitation to Soviet-American cooperation on a wide variety of mutual concerns. An official American commitment to "peaceful coexistence" policies would establish a level of "mutual understanding" between the rulers of the Soviet Empire and the leaders of the American Republic rarely demonstrated during the darker days of the old Cold War.

An American commitment to a policy of "peaceful coexistence" would also constitute a new international politics of reciprocity. The principle of reciprocity is an equitable principle. If it is legitimate for the Kremlin to launch massive and vituperative propaganda campaigns against the American Republic and its allies, roundly condemning the "evils" of capitalism, and to use venomous language in describing Western leaders as "exploiters," "racists," "imperialists," and "warmongers," then it is perfectly legitimate for the American Republic to exploit, through the airwaves or through whatever media are available, the glaring ideological inconsistencies, economic weaknesses, and routine injustices of the Soviet Union and its Eastern bloc satellites. Inasmuch as the Soviet Empire is continually trying to sow divisions among non-communist states, the American Republic is under no moral compulsion to refrain from driving diplomatic or economic wedges between or among states of the Soviet Bloc, widening the fissures wherever possible, and sowing discord where unity might otherwise prevail. If the rulers of the Soviet Empire feel compelled to sign a multiplicity of friendship and cooperation treaties with leftist Third World states in order to isolate the American Republic, there is no reason why the American Republic should not increase its presence in strategically critical, less developed areas of the world by signing anti-Soviet friendship and cooperation treaties with moderate and rightist Third World states.

Where indirect conflict is intensified, there are ample opportunities for the leaders of the American Republic to seize the initiative. The strength of Soviet foreign policy is that it is a flexible policy geared toward the offensive; the weakness of American foreign policy is that it has been too long frozen in the defensive. If the Soviets wish to arm or support Communist "national liberation" movements in the Third World, there is no reason why the American Republic should refrain from supporting or arming pro-Western nationalist forces in order to extend its geopolitical influence. Soviet support for guerrillas in Central America, the SWAPO forces in Namibia, the Polisario Front in Morocco is integral to Soviet interpretations of "peaceful coexistence" for these are "just wars" of national liberation. The resistance of Black nationalist forces in Angola, the secessionist Eritrean forces fighting for self-determination in the Horn of Africa, and the National Islamic Front for Afghanistan are likewise causes worthy of American support, overt or covert, direct or indirect. It is time to seize the initiative, put the Soviets on the defensive, and reap the psychological and political rewards of Soviet opposition to "national liberation" forces fighting weak or repressive Marxist-Leninist client states in areas remote from the centers of Soviet military and political power.

The "correlation of forces" does not have to run against the American Republic and the West. The Soviet Empire suffers from grave and exploitable weaknesses. While the Soviet state enjoys a great military power and an abundance of natural resources, the Soviet system labors under inefficiencies in production and distribution inherent in its economic organization. Beyond these deepening economic problems, the Empire faces long-term demographic difficulties and potential tensions arising from the presence of a multiplicity of Soviet ethnic and linguistic groups and a great Russian population in relative decline. Domestic cultural and economic problems are compounded by sterility of Soviet ideological appeals in Soviet-dominated peoples in Eastern European states. While Soviet ideology is the ground of Soviet legitimacy, the Empire seems unable to maintain the legitimacy of its imperial hegemony in Eastern Europe without the use or threat of military force. Soviet ideology may very well serve the Soviet elite as a fighting faith in an international struggle with the diabolical monopolists, but its hollow prescriptions cannot satisfy the spiritual yearnings or the material expectations of the great mass of the Soviet and Eastern European peoples. Soviet Communism holds forth little hope for delivering on its basic promise: a better life for the "masses."

Both in formal characterizations of its chief adversary and in regular propaganda broadcasts and publications, Soviet leaders carefully distinguish between the morally bankrupt and guilty "ruling classes" and the morally pure and innocent "oppressed masses" of the West. This is an excellent tactic in the psychological warfare between East and West; for it enables the Soviet leadership to appeal directly to the citizenry of the Western democracies, over the heads, so to speak, of the political adversaries with whom they are regularly engaged in political or diplomatic combat. A Soviet specialist in the Department of Defense may casually dismiss the latest Soviet call for "peaceful coexistence" or the latest Soviet "peace offensive," for what it is, another propaganda effort to further Soviet geopolitical aims, and yet many otherwise intelligent individuals may take Soviet formal declarations at face value, without comprehending their deeper ideological import or specific meaning in the Communist lexicon.

This attempt to separate, or divide, the Western leadership from the mass of Western citizens has been, occasionally, successful. Soviet sponsored cultural exchanges, sports events, scientific meetings, and the like, are often subtly politicized, consciously designed to demonstrate the alleged superiority of the Soviet system. This formalized distinction between the rulers and the ruled, the elite and the masses, is ready made for Western success. Its singular beauty is that no society is more rigidly stratified, shot through with elite privileges, than Soviet society. No one seriously doubts the rigid formal division between the tiny, self-perpetuating ruling Soviet elite and the great mass of the Soviet citizenry, least of all the Soviet citizens themselves. There is nothing theoretically inconsistent in pursuing hard-nosed, Soviet-style diplomatic initiatives on the one hand, and promoting increased tourism, social science and cultural exchanges on the other. In a psychological sense, the greatest single asset of the American Republic is simple truth concerning the material abundance of Western society and the equally undeniable and widespread freedom of speech, thought, press, conscience and religion. It is on this level of personal experience that the abstract promises of Soviet ideology are unable to compete. The case in Poland is instructive.

Official American policy should always be grounded in the true distinction between the Communist elite and the masses it governs. American policymakers must attempt to ingratiate themselves with the Soviet and Eastern European peoples, potentially the West's greatest allies in a sustained propaganda contest with the Kremlin. No policy should be pursued which would directly injure the Soviet population while leaving the Soviet political leadership unscathed. Likewise, no economic or trade policy, such as the transfer of high-level or sophisticated technology, should be pursued which benefits the Kremlin leadership and which does not benefit, or positively injures, the mass of the Soviet population. Crafting such a policy of distinctions will be a delicate undertaking, but it holds out the possibility of reaping significant psychological and political rewards. If this be characterized as a form of subversion, then we should make the most of it.

Is the pursuit of such a policy toward the Soviet Empire realistic? Such a policy toward the Kremlin is no more or less realistic than the current policy of the Kremlin toward the American Republic and other states of the West. It correctly recognizes the global character of Soviet-American competition. It encompasses a studious avoidance of direct confrontation, as opposed to indirect confrontation. It prescribes an avoidance of general, and even limited, war between the two principal adversaries. It prescribes the seizure of geopolitical opportunities, the maximization of one's strengths and the exploitation of the adversary's weaknesses.

Such an American policy of reciprocity toward the Kremlin would be far more modest indeed than the oft-proclaimed Soviet objective of creating a new world order in accordance with the scriptural pronouncements of Marx, Engels and Lenin. The American Republic may indeed have a providential mission to promote personal and political liberty on a global scale, but the policy outlined here is not to be understood as an instrument for ushering in the Millennium. Under the proper political conditions, such a mission may one day be commenced. But for the immediate future, American objectives must be more modest, more tangible, and more boldly self-interested; for it appears that America's survival as a strong, free, prosperous and independent nation state is at issue.

The idea of an American mission in the world is a recurrent theme of American history. But American idealism has been chastened by harsh experience, especially in the wake of the Vietnam tragedy. Altogether too many noble articles of democratic faith have been dashed on the hard rocks of international politics in the post-war era. The hope once prevalent among the intellectual and political leadership of the Western democracies of converting the multitudes of the Third World to democratic principles, political equality, popular sovereignty and majority rule has waned. Civil liberties, personal and political and economic freedom are becoming precious.

The modesty of our post-war achievement in promoting personal and political freedom should not surprise or even depress us. Aristotle wisely taught us in the childhood of our own civilization that unique historical, social, economic and cultural factors condition the character and prosperity of political regimes and establish the parameters of reform and even the success of revolutions, including democratic revolutions. Though America may not be able to export her values and institutions, and though large doses of personal and political freedom may not be digestible on a global scale, Americans still have the wherewithal to protect themselves and those who identify with her. For ourselves and for those nations deemed worthy of our alliance and commitment, the success of a counter-imperialist policy is an imperative. The clearly articulated policies of America's adversaries leave little room for discretion. If indeed the totalitarian threat were effectively neutralized, America would not only ensure its own national security but would also become the main force for stability in the world. Such stability would nurture international trade and economic

growth, raise the global standard of living and promote real progress in human rights. But the success of such a policy will depend
upon the prudent and careful employment of our abundant economic, technological, military, psychological, and spiritual resources.

ENDNOTES

Throughout the text, the author has chosen to employ the terms "American
Republic" and "Soviet Empire" in order to distinguish, even more clearly, the
nature of Soviet-American difference on the theoretical level. The United States
is the preeminent "republic" of the West; that is, political authority is held as a
public trust and is to be exercised over the *res publica,* rather than the *res privata,*
within the constitutionally defined institutions of the federal political order. The
critical distinction between public and private spheres of life is the distinction
which makes personal and political liberty possible. In the Soviet Union, political
authority rests in the hands of a self-perpetuating elite that imposes a centralized
rule over a multiplicity of nationalities through a centralizing organization of the
Communist Party. Even if the Soviet Union were to abandon all claims to military, political or economic domination of other states beyond its borders it would
still remain as one of the world's great imperial powers.

1.   See Professor Morgenthau's remarks during a discussion at the Center for
American Foreign Policy, "Morgenthau on Foreign Policy: A Center Dialogue,"
as part of a compilation of essays in *What Should Be The Future Foreign Policy
of the United States,* Congressional Research Service, Library of Congress (Washington, D.C.: U.S. Government Printing Office, 1979), p. 11; reprinted from *World
Issues,* V, 2, December 1977–January 1978.

2.   See George Kennan (Mr. "X"), "Sources of Soviet Conduct," *Foreign Affairs,*
Vol. 25, No. 4, pp. 566–582 (July 1947).

3.   The most penetrating analytical presentation of this critique remains
Robert Strasz-Hupe, *et al., Protracted Conflict* (New York: Harper Colophon
Books, 1963).

4.   Hans Morgenthau, *Politics Among Nations: The Struggle for Power and
Peace* (New York: Alfred Knopf, 1968), pp. 37–38.

5.   Morgenthau, *Politics Among Nations,* p. 54.

6.   The demonic role of the United States is a recurrent theme in the historical
drama, running through much of the theoretical literature of the Party and the
Soviet Armed Forces. The following statement is representative: "The reactionary
imperialist order headed by the U.S. monopolists do all they can to hold back the
inexorable course of history. They are willing to commit the most hideous crimes
against humanity; even to resort to nuclear war in the attempt to resolve the basic
contradictions of today—the contradictions between socialism and capitalism."
Col. B. Byely et al., *Marxism-Leninism on War and The Army* (Moscow: Progress
Publishers, 1972), p. 9.

7.   The change in the military relations between the USSR and the Western
powers heralds a historically significant growth in the momentum of the change

or transformation from a capitalist to a socialist world order, in the Soviet view. According to a leading article in the November 1975 issue of the official Soviet journal, *Communist of The Armed Forces:* "The militant alliance of the socialist countries and all anti-imperialist forces is the most important factor in international politics. The forces of peace now have sufficient power to prevent the outbreak of a new world war by their energetic, coordinated actions. . . . There is no doubt that all of the factors of the struggle for peace would not have played their part if the powerful armed forces of the socialist states and primarily of the Soviet Union had not existed." Quoted in *Soviet World Outlook,* Advanced International Studies Institute, February 13, 1976. It is clear that, in recent years, the Soviets believe that they have "closed the gap" between themselves and their chief adversary, the United States, in the development and deployment of modern strategic weapons systems. They do not say that they are "superior," but they do claim that they have achieved what is called "parity" or essential equivalence. In any case, their view is that the military might of the Soviet Union is the principal deterrent to the malevolent forces of the West unleashing a new world war. The theme of U.S. war preparation was repeated again by Soviet Defense Minister Dimitri Ustinov during the February 1981 opening of the 26th Congress of the Communist Party of the USSR.

8.   For a comparison of Nazi and Soviet military preparations, see R. J. Rummel, "Preparing for War? The Third Reich Versus The Soviet Union Today," *International Security Review,* Volume IV, Number 3 (Fall 1979), pp. 207–30.

9.   According to General David C. Jones, Chairman of the Joint Chiefs of Staff, "A very serious weapon system concern is the growing vulnerability of our land-based ICBM force, the key contributor to our time-urgent hard target kill capability." *United States Military Posture, Fiscal Year 1982,* p. IV. The increasing vulnerability of the U.S. land-based ICBM force to a potential Soviet "first strike" has been the animus for current congressional debate on the deployment of the MX missile system and has stimulated further debate on the revival of an ABM system or even a space-based anti-missile laser defense.

10.   Dr. Igor Glagolev, a high level Soviet defector who prepared papers for the Soviet SALT I negotiating team and who served as a consultant to the Soviet General Staff revealed that in his discussions with the Soviet military authorities problems concerning the potential employment of the new Backfire were cast in terms of potential attacks on the American homeland rather than employment of the bomber as an intermediate range aircraft.

11.   The newest addition to the large Soviet undersea fleet is the Typhoon class submarine, a deep diving model that can carry as many as twenty submarine launched ballistic missiles. The intercontinental mission of the Soviet submarine force is carried out with a complement of 950 submarine launched ballistic missile launchers. Soviet "Yankee" class subs normally patrol the Atlantic and the West coast of the United States, and the striking force of that fleet has been strengthened with the deployment of the so-called Delta class of submarines; the Delta class subs are capable of carrying the SS-N-18, an SLBM with multiple warheads. According to General Jones, "All Delta class submarine missiles can strike targets in the U.S. from Soviet waters." *United States Military Posture, Fiscal Year 1982,* p. 100.

12.   "The Marxist-Leninist proposition on the class nature of politics, the continuation of which is war, is crucial to any understanding of the essence of war. This, in fact, constitutes the fundamental difference between the Marxist-Leninist view on war and the doctrines of the bourgeois ideologists who try hard to conceal

the links between the politics which lead to war and the interests of definite classes." Byely, et al., *Marxism-Leninism on War and The Army,* p. 18.

13.   "The military ideologists of imperialism cannot but take into account the fact that the outcome of a world nuclear war unleashed by the imperialists would inevitably lead to the death of capitalism as a system." Marshal V.D. Sokolovsky, ed., *Military Strategy: Soviet Doctrine and Concepts* (New York: Frederick Praeger, 1963), p. 169. An excellent synopsis of recent Soviet military doctrine, particularly the war-fighting, war-winning emphasis, can be found in William Van Cleave's essay "Soviet Doctrine and Strategy: A Developing American View" in Lawrence L. Whetten, ed., *The Future of Soviet Military Power* (New York: Crane, Russak and Company, 1976), pp. 41–71.

14.   "In the new war, if it should be allowed to happen, victory will be with the countries of the world socialist system, which are defending progressive, ascending tendencies in social development, have at their command all the latest kinds of weapons, and enjoy the support of the working people of all countries. The balance of forces between the two systems, the logic of history, its objective laws, prescribing that the new in social development is invincible—all this predicts such an outcome." Byely, *Marxism-Leninism on War and The Army,* p. 46.

15.   There are strong disagreements as to the efficacy of the Soviet civil defense effort. All agree, however, that it is an ongoing concern in the overall Soviet military effort. According to former Secretary of Defense Harold Brown, "There are approximately 100,000 people engaged in the Soviet civil defense effort full-time. Counting all civilian units and formations supposedly available, the total number of people in the program would be upwards of 16 million." Secretary of Defense Harold Brown, *Annual Report, Fiscal Year 1981,* Department of Defense, January 29, 1980, p. 77.

16.   In his annual report on the American military posture, General David C. Jones stressed the gravity of the resource problem as part of the overall military and strategic difficulties confronting the United States and its allies: "The countries of the Gulf littoral, many strife prone and politically unstable, supply about 65 percent of total world imports and hold about 55 percent of projected world oil reserves. . . . The Soviet Union must import only six minerals critical to its defense industry, and only two of these are brought in for as much as 50 percent of requirements. In contrast, the United States relies on foreign sources to supply in excess of its need for some 32 minerals essential for our military and industrial base. Particularly important mineral imports (for example, diamonds, cobalt, platinum, chromium, and manganese) come from southern Africa, where the Soviet Union and its surrogates have established substantial influence, and where U.S. access, given the inherent instabilities of the region, is by no means assured." *United States Military Posture, Fiscal Year 1982,* pp. 2–3.